NOVEMBER 22, 1963

NOVEMBER 22, 1963

Reflections on the Life, Assassination, and Legacy of John F. Kennedy

Dean R. Owen
Foreword by White House Correspondent
Helen Thomas

Skyhorse Publishing

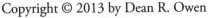
Skyhorse Publishing books may be purchased in bulk at special discounts for sales promotion, corporate gifts, fund-raising, or educational purposes. Special editions can also be created to specifications. For details, contact the Special Sales Department, Skyhorse Publishing, 307 West 36th Street, 11th Floor, New York, NY 10018 or info@skyhorsepublishing.com.

Skyhorse® and Skyhorse Publishing® are registered trademarks of Skyhorse Publishing, Inc.®, a Delaware corporation.

Visit our website at www.skyhorsepublishing.com.

10 9 8 7 6 5 4 3 2 1

Library of Congress Cataloging-in-Publication Data is available on file.

ISBN: 978-1-62636-034-1

Printed in the United States of America

To my other and more important legacy: my wife of thirty years, Janet B. Owen; our older daughter and son-in-law, Whitney, and Josh Hammar; our younger daughter, Embry Wood Owen; and my parents, Edward and Elvira Owen, who taught me life's most important lesson, reflected in Luke: 6:31.

TABLE OF CONTENTS

Section Two
Civil Rights Leaders   65

Section Three
Children of Kennedy Advisors and Others   87

Section Six
Journalists and Commentators   169

SECTION SEVEN
Political Figures   241

SECTION EIGHT
Those with Humorous, Poignant, Quirky, and
Tragic Encounters and Connections   269

✐ FOREWORD

IT is hard to believe fifty years have passed since John Fitzgerald Kennedy, the most inspired and inspiring of any president I covered, was assassinated in Dallas.

For journalists, his election three years earlier ushered in a new era of excitement and anticipation, marked by the memorable reference in his inaugural address: "Let the word go forth from this time and place, to friend and foe alike, that the torch has been passed to a new generation of Americans." At age forty-three, he was the youngest president ever elected. (Theodore Roosevelt ascended to the presidency at age forty-two after William McKinley's assassination.) Kennedy was the first president born in the twentieth century. He had an abundance of charm, elegance, wit, and humor. Other presidents enjoyed some of those qualities, but John Kennedy had them all, and he used them effectively.

For example, responding to allegations of nepotism with the appointment of his brother Robert as attorney general, the President, speaking at Washington's Gridiron Dinner six weeks after taking office, remarked: "Bobby has just received his law degree and we thought he should have some experience before he goes into private practice." Or at the conclusion of a state visit to France accompanied by his wife, he quipped, "I am the man who accompanied Jacqueline Kennedy to Paris and I have enjoyed it."

When Dean Owen contacted me in March of 2011, he already had been working on this book for four months. In *November 22, 1963* he has compiled a series of reflections from people that reveal diverse perspectives and engaging anecdotes. Many people in this book are well known: Kennedy family members, civil rights leaders, journalists, and people who served in JFK's administration. Others are unknown to the general public, but provide interesting and poignant stories, some never before told: a second-year pediatric resident who saved John Kennedy Jr.'s life when he was born not breathing; children of Walter Cronkite and Edward R. Murrow, as well as those of Kennedy's advisors, such as Robert McNamara, Dean Acheson, and Arthur Schlesinger Jr.; the surgeon who tried desperately for thirty hours to save the life of the Kennedys' second son, Patrick; and one of, if not the only, person who knew both John Kennedy and Lee Harvey Oswald.

I believe people from all walks of life, including those for whom John Kennedy's life and legacy comprise a footnote in a history book, will find in *November 22, 1963* compelling commentaries about an engaging leader whose presidency remains one of the most studied in our nation's history.

Like anyone old enough to remember that tragic day, the events of November 22, 1963 and the following weekend are etched indelibly in my mind. The day before I watched the president and Jackie walk across the South Lawn of the White House and board the presidential helicopter. He was holding his son's hand. All three flew to Andrews Air Force Base; John Jr. loved helicopters and airplanes and the president probably wanted to indulge him. The little boy, who would turn three the following Monday, the day his dad was buried, was driven back to the White House later that morning.

The next day, I was having lunch with Fran Lewine of the Associated Press and Pierrette Spiegler, a member of Mrs. Kennedy's staff. I was preparing to leave Saturday for Detroit to visit my family. Suddenly, we heard on a transistor radio that Kennedy had been shot. All of us bolted out of the restaurant, hailed cabs, and went to our offices.

My boss, Julius Frandsen, saw me and said, "You're on vacation."

I said, "No, I'm not."

Later I was told, "OK, go to Andrews Air Force Base. You're going to Dallas."

A plane was standing by to take journalists to Dallas, and en route to the air base in a cab, I heard the official announcement: The president was dead.

I was stunned. And I did not want to believe it. I soon learned Lyndon Johnson had taken the oath of office and that he, Jackie, and John Kennedy's body were returning to Washington on Air Force One.

Upon their arrival at Andrews, I was struck by the fact Jackie still was wearing the bloodstained suit. That took a lot of bravery on her part.

Over the next three days, I covered every event at the White House involving the funeral. I stood on the steps of St. Matthew's Cathedral when Jackie and the family entered. It is unusual and uncharacteristic for reporters to cry while they are working; we're not supposed to show emotion. But I was dictating to UPI with tears running from my eyes.

John Kennedy understood his time was short, that he had a rendezvous with death. The deaths of a sister and brother during World War II, as well as the horrors of war he experienced in the South Pacific, may have given him a sense of melancholy and foreboding.

He also had an infectious sense of hope and optimism for the future. The sky was not the limit. He believed in setting goals and taking steps to achieve them. John Kennedy instilled in young people the belief that public service was honorable and could be the capstones of their careers. He also wanted to demonstrate the American promise of excellence to other countries and so created the Peace Corps. He had his eyes on the stars and challenged the nation to send a man to the moon and bring him back to earth safely before the end of the 1960s, an historic achievement he did not live to witness.

One of his campaign themes in 1960 was "A time for greatness." That greatness he envisioned is reflected in the remarks he would have delivered at a luncheon that fateful day in Dallas:

"Finally, it should be clear by now that a nation can be no stronger abroad than she is at home. Only an America which practices what it preaches about equal rights and social justice will be respected by those whose choice affects our future. Only an America which has fully educated its citizens is fully capable of tackling the complex problems and perceiving the hidden dangers of the world in which we live. And only an America which is growing and prospering

XVI ✒ NOVEMBER 22, 1963

economically can sustain the worldwide defenses of freedom, while demonstrating to all concerned the opportunities of our system and society."

As I have said so often, "Thank you, Mr. President."

Helen Thomas
Washington, D.C.
February, 2013

✑∞ PREFACE

MAJOR, sudden, and tragic events create unforgettable images, mental snapshots that enable people, decades later, to recall where they were when they heard the news: the September 11 attacks; the deaths of John Lennon and Diana, princess of Wales; Pearl Harbor.

For me and millions of others age fifty-five and over, it was the assassination of President John F. Kennedy. November 22, 1963 will forever be known for the shock and horror when the charismatic leader of the free world was killed with a gunshot to the head in Dealey Plaza in Dallas.

I was seven years old in Mrs. Gurley's second grade class in Burbank School in Hayward, California. The older sister of a friend stopped by the classroom and told me the president had been shot. Like many of those whose reflections are in this book, I greeted the news with disbelief: "Oh, yeah, sure."

Later that afternoon and over the next three days, I was riveted to the television and read everything in the local newspapers about the details of Kennedy's assassination. Fifty years later, I can still hear the solemn funeral dirges and muffled drumbeats of the funeral procession from the White House to the Capitol. Then, Sunday morning, I watched Jack Ruby shoot the accused assassin, Lee Harvey Oswald, live on television.

As Tom Brokaw remarks in section six of this book, "The television set was, if you will, the centrifuge for the country. Everybody drew from it in some fashion." For me, that weekend was the catalyst for my fascination with journalism and how the news media shape public opinion.

In December of 2010, I turned fifty-five, wondering about my legacy, and I realized everyone has two legacies—a personal one and a professional one. The former is solid, as reflected in this book's dedication. For the latter, I decided to go back to that weekend in 1963, made a list of more than one hundred people I wanted to interview, and started making phone calls and writing letters.

My pitch was simple: Each person was offered the opportunity to review and edit a transcript of the interview, and I would not ask any questions about assassination conspiracy theories or John Kennedy's sex life. More than enough words have been written about both topics. After nearly two and a half years of early mornings, late nights, and long weekends, *November 22, 1963* is presented for your interest and enjoyment. I intentionally omitted any summation or analysis of the contributors' reflections, and prefer to allow readers to draw their own conclusions about the life, assassination, and legacy of America's 35th president.

Dean R. Owen
Seattle, Washington
March, 2013

✒ ACKNOWLEDGEMENTS

CREATING *November 22, 1963* has been a labor of love, but could not have been accomplished without those I interviewed, for whom I am deeply grateful, as well the encouragement of family and friends. Many thanks to all of you, including: Gardi Wilks, my literary agent Marilyn Allen, Roger Flessing, Tom Parks, Ken Churchill, Manen Clements, Debbie Durham, Jeff Peabody, Steve McFarland, my brothers Dennis and Don Owen, Jeff Wright, Jeff Warnke, John Leckie, M. Joseph Sloan, Eddy Rodriguez, my mother-in-law Shirley Biggerstaff, Kari Costanza, Mike McLeod, John Yeager, Paul Nordlund, Betsy Grabinski, Bill Wolfsthal and colleagues at Skyhorse Publishing, Doug Boyles, Bill Dotterwick, Hope Swecker, Rachel Cota Hochstetler, Brian Vasey, Katy Krippaehne, John Jensen, Dave Wittenberg, Margaret Larson, Char Haake, Steve Matthews, John Clum, and Laurie Austin at the John F. Kennedy Library.

November 22, 1963

SECTION ONE:

Members of the Kennedy Administration and White House Staff

Letitia Baldrige Hollensteiner
White House Social Secretary, expert on etiquette

"When the president has people sticking to him like parasites and not letting go, I managed to get in there and uproot both of them, and let him escape."

THE first time I met him was on a train going to Newport, Rhode Island for a weekend in the summer. He had been elected to the Senate, and he was already being talked about as a handsome young man. Very, very ambitious. Member of a large political family. I already had heard all the gossip about him. And he personified it all.

He was so good looking and had a great sense of humor. And he had been everywhere in the world. It was an enthusiastic first sighting (laughter).

We were both going to stay at Jackie's mother's house, Hammersmith Farm. I would have loved to have spoken with him more that weekend, but there were too many people at him—or after him. I could hardly get in a word.

When the president has people sticking to him like parasites and not letting go, I managed to get in there and uproot both of them, and let him escape. That's where I was needed and that's one of the things a social secretary does. She watches over the boss, the host, and never lets him out of her sight, and removes anything that's too abrasive, too forceful, too boring. There are so many reasons to get rid of people who are surrounding your president, or your ambassador, whoever it is. You must get rid of those people, and let the ambassador or the president do his job. You take all the criticism and let people hate you. But you're doing it for the boss.

Excerpt from *A Lady First: My Life in the Kennedy White House and the American Embassies of Paris and Rome,* by Letitia Baldrige © 2001 (Used with permission of author):

> *I had just sat down to lunch with* Town & Country *magazine editor-in-chief Henry Sell at the Mid-America Club atop the Prudential skyscraper. In the middle of our chicken crepes, a waiter brought us some more wine and said, 'I can't believe it. Someone has shot the president.'*

It was an extraordinary moment in my life. I couldn't believe it. In fact, I'm shaking my head right now as I'm saying this. It shouldn't have happened.

I called the White House and spoke with Clark Clifford. He said, "Get on a plane and come down here."

I arrived in Washington, went to the White House, and stayed there for the next seven or eight days. I was involved in a little bit of everything: protocols, greeting people, calming people down, getting information for people. It was a time none of us will ever forget.

Jackie was completely stunned. She was appreciative of my help later. But while it was going on, she was stunned. And she handled herself with beauty and grace. She knew it was the funeral of the century. Everything was planned. The words she used. It was all carefully thought out. It was a script on how to plan a state funeral. She would think, "This would mean so much to the children"—some particular phrase. She was incredible.

You just adored the man! He would not dwell on anything that was sad or gloomy. He was funny about anything that he could be funny about, and he taught us all how to do that. He would say, "Don't dwell on that, that sad stuff. Start talking about what happened at the such and such."

He taught us public relations in many ways. He knew about public relations and he knew how to use it, how to control it. He was a real teacher. He was so naturally aware of the world. I've never known anyone like that. That was one of his major talents that most people don't think about, because they're so into the one talent or skill being discussed at the moment. But people should look at him with a wide lens. He had a wonderful team of people around him, but he would not have had them if he had not been an extraordinary person. The team devotes loyalty to its leader and grows more loyal when they see it in the leader.

I was in contact with Jackie every once in a while after she left the White House. It was always in conjunction with some meeting. She worked very hard. She always had something on her plate. She would call me and ask me, and I would come spend a few days working with her on the event or activity. She was always grateful.

The main part of his legacy is to reach out to the young—ages eight to eighty. He would have something to say to each group. To motivate them, to make them feel they have a real place in the government, in our country, and in future aspirations of this country. He was always thinking of the future, and how one issue or event would affect another.

ᘒ Joseph A. Califano Jr.
Senior official in the Pentagon, Carter administration cabinet member

"(Robert Kennedy) whispered to me: 'This is where we'll bury the President.' I will never forget the words."

I first noticed John Kennedy watching the 1956 Democratic convention on television. I was twenty-seven years old and working in the Office of the Judge Advocate General in Washington. Adlai Stevenson had thrown open the nomination for vice president to the delegates and Kennedy mounted a strong—though ultimately unsuccessful—effort against Estes Kefauver, the Democratic senator from Tennessee.

At that time, Kennedy had little going for him besides the glamour and wealth of his family and his socially prominent wife, Jacqueline Bouvier. But he came astonishingly close and lost to Kefauver by fewer than two hundred votes. I was impressed watching him make a politically adept and gracious appeal to the delegates to unanimously nominate his rival.

Fast-forward three and a half years. I woke up on February 20, 1960 ready to enjoy a long weekend for the George Washington birthday holiday. I had recently purchased James MacGregor Burns's campaign biography, *John F. Kennedy: A Political Profile,* after seeing so many news stories about John Kennedy's campaign for the presidency—the first Catholic to seek the presidency since Al Smith in 1928. I spent most of the weekend reading that book.

I identified with Kennedy as a strong anti-Communist Catholic, a cold warrior committed to defeating the atheistic Soviet Union—a true struggle of good against evil. He also expressed concern for the poor and underprivileged, which was in line with the commitment to social justice that the Jesuits at Holy Cross and Brooklyn Prep had instilled in me. Burns wrote that Kennedy believed it was essential to "track down the best talent" to lead the United States in this "revolutionary time." As a former editor of the *Harvard Law Review*, I believed I swam in that talent pool.

A month later, I contacted John Stillman, a college friend of JFK who was chair of a New York area chapter of the Democratic Party, and enclosed my resume, indicating I was "quite anxious to do anything that will further Senator Kennedy's candidacy." He wrote back and we later had lunch in Manhattan. I came away inspired. And three days later, I received a letter stating:

> *"I am very glad to know that you are in contact with our mutual friend John Stillman and you may be sure that I am most appreciative of your interest and support. I hope you will keep in close touch with John, as he will be aware of our plans in New York."*

It was signed "Jack Kennedy." And I immediately felt part of the campaign.

Four days before the election in November, I saw John Kennedy for the first time—standing in the rain at a rally in Manhattan. He was on stage with Lyndon Johnson and Johnson's wife and two daughters. The rain intensified our excitement as it drenched our clothes (and Kennedy's and Johnson's). He gave an ardent and amusing campaign speech: "You have seen these elephants in the circus. They have their heads of ivory, thick skins, no vision, long memory, and when they move around the ring in the circus, they grab the tail of the elephant in front of them. Well, Dick (Nixon) grabbed that tail in 1952 and 1956, but in 1960 he is running, not the president."

Five months later, I took my first steps as a member of Kennedy's "New Frontier." My position? Special assistant to Cyrus Vance, the

Defense Department's General Counsel. Over the next two and a half years, I served as Special Assistant to the Secretary of the Army and later General Counsel of the Army.

One of my proudest moments, indeed, one of the greatest moments of Kennedy's presidency, was his televised address to the nation on civil rights in June of 1963. He made an impressive argument: "We are confronted with a moral issue. It is as old as Scriptures and as clear as the American Constitution. The heart of the question is whether all Americans will be afforded equal rights and equal opportunities, whether we are going to treat our fellow Americans as we want to be treated."

That statement came out of a meeting in the White House at which there was a discussion among several of his advisors, then-Vice President Johnson, and JFK regarding their concern about the politics of the whole civil rights movement, because of the damage it was doing among white voters, including white Democrats. In the course of that meeting, there was a wonderful exchange in which one of Kennedy's political advisors raised all these issues and Lyndon Johnson said, "Wait a minute. This is a moral issue; this is not a political issue." There was silence for a minute. Everyone looked at Kennedy and the president said, "Lyndon's right."

On November 22, 1963, I was in West Virginia inspecting a dam built by the U.S. Corps of Engineers. When I heard the tragic news out of Dallas, I flew immediately back to Washington and hurried into Vance's office and promptly informed him I was leaving the administration. He suggested I reconsider and, in the meantime, I had a new and urgent project: locate the burial place for John F. Kennedy.

The next day, I met a devastated, zombie-like Robert F. Kennedy at Arlington National Cemetery. In the pouring rain, we walked the perimeter of a 3.2-acre parcel of land above the Memorial Bridge and below the Lee-Custis Mansion. He whispered to me: "This is where we'll bury the President." I will never forget the words.

John Kennedy inspired me to enter public service. From ringing doorbells in the 1960 campaign to my work today in association with the National Center on Addiction and Substance Abuse at Columbia University, I have felt this calling. By playing a role in the struggle against substance abuse, I believe I am fulfilling his admonition, "To those whom much is given, much is expected."

Kennedy's legacy is one of courage, hope, and determination. He was courageous during the Cuban Missile Crisis, standing up not only to Soviet Premier Nikita Khrushchev, but also to the American generals anxious to launch attacks on Cuba. He inspired hope in millions of young Americans that our nation and the world could flourish by their service to the less fortunate, both here and abroad. And he was determined to expand our exploration of space and land a man on the moon.

Those profound words in his inaugural address, "Ask not what your country can do for you. Ask what you can do for your country," are still a clarion call a half century later.

✌ Mortimer M. Caplin
Commissioner of the Internal Revenue Service, founder of Caplin & Drysdale

"He was like a caged lion—walking up and down the room, smoking the small cigarillos he enjoyed so much."

I first met John F. Kennedy in 1958 at the University of Virginia where I was teaching at the law school. JFK was the honored speaker at Memorial Gymnasium celebrating the first "Law Day" set by President Dwight Eisenhower to mark United States' commitment to the rule of law. John S. Battle, former Governor of Virginia, introduced him as, "The next president of the United States!" You could hear the crowd gasp. A Virginia audience. And here, the son of a high Episcopalian minister was presenting a Roman Catholic as the next president of the United States.

We had a small gathering that evening at the home of William C. Battle, who had served in the Navy with JFK during World War II. Bill was the son of the former governor and one of his law partners. It was a great party—hardly more than a dozen guests. Jackie was there, too. She was lovely.

I taught two of JFK's brothers at UVA law, Robert and Edward, and also spent part of my time as counsel to the Battle firm. JFK knew I was teaching and asked about my recent testimony on tax reform before the House Ways and Means Committee. He asked that I send him a copy, which I was very happy to do.

As a professor at a state university, I found it prudent to publicly keep out of the 1960 political campaign, although I did write a brief piece in support of JFK in the *Charlottesville Daily Progress*. Sure enough, JFK won the election and in early December I received a telephone call from his principal aide, Ted Sorensen, asking me to serve on the President's Task Force on Taxation. The group met over a period of roughly a month, putting together a report on reforming our tax laws and stimulating our economy. On January 9, 1961, we delivered the report to the president-elect at Arthur Schlesinger's home in Cambridge.

The president-elect soon joined us. He was something to see: The pressures and strains of a close campaign had stretched him beyond belief. He just oozed confidence. Now, back from a brief vacation with his father in Florida, he was all tanned and lean. He was like a caged lion—walking up and down the room, smoking the small cigarillos he enjoyed so much. We summarized our report and discussed his reactions and suggestions. He was well aware of our key issues and had already considered them with outside economists and others. We had a lively meeting.

After we finished, JFK took me aside for a moment and said, "Now, I want to talk to you. You'll be hearing from me or from Bobby in a week or so." That's all I wanted to know. While it certainly was on my mind, this was the first meaningful signal I'd had that a presidential appointment might indeed take place.

I'd previously spoken by telephone with Robert Kennedy. He asked me to fly up and visit with him in Washington at the Democratic National Committee headquarters where he was quarterbacking appointments for posts in the new administration. I thought my meeting with Bob would be rather simple—his former professor, brother Ted's professor, Bill Battle's law partner—what could be better! And yet, while Bob was very cordial, he was also very business-like. We went through the interview in some detail and he then asked me to write him a letter on my views on tax administration in general and what I thought it would be like to head the IRS. I later wrote the letter, and it ultimately became my proxy statement and commitment on what I'd emphasize and how I'd run the IRS. It was sent to him December 5, 1960.

Not much later, I received a telephone call from a local IRS revenue agent who said he was coming to my office to audit my tax returns. While the agent was still there, we were interrupted by a telephone call from the White House. It was the president's assistant press secretary, Andy Hatcher, who said, "I'm going to announce this afternoon that you're the president's nominee for commissioner of the IRS."

After the phone call from the White House, I immediately went to Washington and waited for the formal nomination and hearings. Matters moved far more quickly in those days, and the IRS commissioner was given a good deal more attention. In fact, my nomination was referred to the committee on January 30, confirmed by the committee on February 1, and confirmed by the Senate itself on February 6. My official certificate of appointment had President Kennedy's signature on it the following day, February 7, 1961. Very hard to believe!

My first meeting with all my regional commissioners and district directors at the IRS was set for May 1, 1961. In making arrangements in March, someone in my office suggested, "Wouldn't it be great if the president could come?"

I hadn't fully taken into account the magnitude of what was said. But I did call Kenny O'Donnell, the de facto chief of staff at the White House. I told him how important this would be to the IRS and to me. Kenny immediately replied, "Are you kidding? Come on, there are no votes at the IRS!"

I called Bob Kennedy after that and raised the same question. He said he didn't know but would see. A week or so later, we were talking about something else and at the close he said, "Oh, incidentally, Jack will be over."

That was the last time I heard him say, "Jack." It was all so new. After that, it was always, "the president."

The president did come over on May 1, 1961. It is the only time in history—to this very day—that any president has ever visited the IRS. The president's visit had me walking on water with the whole organization.

President Kennedy was very supportive of the IRS, but totally hands off. All the way. There were very few times he called for any special treatment. On one occasion very early in the administration, he called to talk about some IRS related matter and then asked, "Have you found a house yet, commissioner?" I had been out house-hunting. You could see the smile on his face.

During the Bay of Pigs crisis, I did hear from JFK through Ted Sorensen. The message was for a tax exemption ruling for a private group seeking release of the Cuban prisoners captured on the beach. Supported by the White House, certain prominent citizens—Eleanor Roosevelt, Walter Reuther, Milton Eisenhower—organized "Tractors for Freedom" to raise funds to finance exchanges of farm machinery for the prisoners. Castro had agreed to the exchange, but it was important to assure tax deductions for donors. At the same time, an uproar took place in Congress criticizing what some said was equivalent to the U.S. government paying ransom directly.

I was very hesitant about the phone call. I didn't want to issue the ruling unless we had time to study the law. But fortunately, our lawyers saved the day when they uncovered, among other things, an old English statute, the Statute of Elizabeth I, which clearly treated payment of ransom as a charitable act. A favorable IRS ruling was quickly issued.

Later, the agreement with Fidel Castro was changed making food and medicine, not tractors, the swap. It was much easier for the public to accept; but we did have a number of valuation battles with donor companies seeking to increase tax deductions.

On November 22, 1963, in the middle of an IRS business meeting with my top people, we were suddenly interrupted by the head of our inspection service, Mike Acree. Mike rushed in and whispered in my ear that he'd just heard the president had been shot. In a minute or so it was announced on the general news. Then other people started coming into the office saying, "We just heard it over the radio." The room was hushed. The meeting had just begun; I looked around and said right away, "We have to call this off. We better go home." The room cleared immediately.

Next day, we—all the Cabinet officers and presidential appointees—were invited to the White House to view the casket. I later went downstairs to get my automobile and saw, standing against the wall waiting for his car, President Lyndon Johnson. He saw me, immediately stepped forward and put those big hands of his on my shoulders saying, "Mortimer, I need you, Mortimer. I need you." He was trying to get as many Kennedy people as he could to stay in the administration with him.

John F. Kennedy was an inspiration to all of us. He was a vibrant man with extraordinary intelligence and vitality. When he came to office after President Eisenhower, there was an unbelievable excitement throughout the country.

His inaugural address stressed the importance of public service, the theme he enlarged upon later at Vanderbilt University when he urged all, particularly the student body, "to act, to enter the lists of public service." I had former students writing and calling—and young people throughout the country—who wanted to be a part of this, this special period in U.S. history. I put JFK very high on the list of our presidents.

JFK was a devoted student of Thomas Jefferson, who in writing to an old friend said, "There is a debt of service due from every man to his country, proportioned to the bounties which nature and fortune have measured to him."

Jefferson wrote this in 1796.

Some 165 years later, in his inaugural address, JFK underscored this same call to service with the message, "And so, my fellow Americans, ask not what your country can do for you. Ask what you can do for your country."

It was a privilege for me to serve, and I look back on this time as the best years of my life.

✧ Charles U. Daly
White House congressional liaison, writer

"I feel fortunate to have been associated with this person who really did have vision. He was not perfect. From the waist down he had the same habits of his father. So what?"

I went to the Columbia Graduate School of Journalism and was awarded an American Political Science Association fellowship under which I spent eight months working with congressmen—three in the House and three in the Senate. I chose Stewart Udall because he was from the West. In California, I had become interested in conservation. He (Udall) had a very open office. He was one of Kennedy's early supporters, so he suggested I take the other half of my fellowship with Kennedy.

I had not been active in politics at all. By instinct, I was an FDR-Stevenson Democrat. I didn't think much of old Joe Kennedy, due to his record as weak on Hitler, and I didn't know a whole lot about his kids. But I thought, "This could be interesting." So I went over to JFK's office, where I was welcomed due to Udall's good boost.

During my fellowship with Kennedy, the best relationship I had was with Ted Sorensen. I had combined my fellowship with work for the Democratic Study Group which provided campaign information for House members more liberal than their national party. It became hectic. I could sense too many campaign stooges only focusing on positions in what they hoped would be a new administration. I decided to opt out.

(A few years later) I was in the shower one day in our home in Menlo Park, California when my wife said, "The White House is on the phone." It was Larry O'Brien, Kennedy's special assistant for congressional relations. He said many of the northern and western liberal members of Congress were being overlooked. He asked if I would come back to help out. We agreed I would call back ASAP.

I (traveled to Washington) and went down to the Executive Office Building. They had no record of me! A guard called to a sentry at the northwest gate of the White House who said I was expected there. I went over and was ushered in and met Larry and his staff. He showed me my office. I was amazed: a big corner office on the second floor of the West Wing. "That's yours." It was huge.

John Kennedy's crew was very compartmentalized. Staff in the West Wing apparatus had little contact with staff in the East Wing. The exception was Arthur Schlesinger Jr. I think Kennedy figured him to be what he was—a most able historian who worshipped at the Kennedy altar. Members of Congress had little direct contact with the president, so it was up to me to make my charges feel close to him.

A good example of Kennedy's personal touch involves Dick Donahue, who was a vital member of O'Brien's staff. There was a congressman from Toledo, Ohio, Lud Ashley, whose dad had busted his hip during celebrations just before the inauguration.(The congressman's father) Old Meredith, who enjoyed a drink as much as the rest of us, ended up in Bethesda Naval Hospital. The night before the inauguration, at a party put on by Joe Kennedy, Congressman Ashley ran into Dick, whom he had never met before. Dick, as irreverent then as he is now, said, "I'm sorry your father got drunk and broke his ass." Lud responded, "Well, fuck you, pal." A great start to a new president's key staff man to start a relationship with an important member of Congress!

On the morning of the inauguration, Meredith Ashley was in in his bed of pain at the hospital. A Marine sergeant, his uniform still wet from the blizzard outside, handed him a big brown envelope. "I've been ordered to deliver this to you." Inside was an advance copy of the inaugural address. At the top, John Kennedy had written: "Dear

Mr. Ashley, I am sorry to hear from Dick Donahue of your unfortunate accident. Hope you will enjoy reading parts of this address I'm going to give later on today."

Later, when I introduced myself to Congressman Ashley as the new presidential assistant responsible for White House relations, he told me the story, adding, "You've got an easy job with me." Lud and I became very close and remained so until the day he died.

November 22, 1963, started as a slow day. It was a Friday and most of the Congress usually worked Tuesday through Thursday. I was sitting at round table in the White House mess, at the members-only table, that most exclusive of restaurants operated by the Navy in the West Wing's basement.

Around 1:30, (Presidential Assistant Jack) McNally came in and just said very quietly, "The president's been shot."

"How bad?" I asked.

"I don't know," he replied.

I darted up to my office and called (my wife) Mary.

She said, "They've killed him."

I responded, "No they haven't. I've been shot and I'm not dead."

I went down to the press office. No one was there except for (Special Counsel to the President) Lee White. (Assistant Press Secretary Malcolm) Killduf was in Dallas. I read the first AP bulletin, which said, "President Kennedy was shot today as his motorcade left downtown Dallas."

Then came the second bulletin. He was dead.

The president was going to be taken to Andrews Air Force Base. I thought about going there, but decided I didn't want to go out there—or anywhere. So I sat down on my old brown leather sofa for a while, watching television as the president, inside a box, was being lowered on a forklift and then into an ambulance headed for Bethesda and an autopsy.

Around midnight, I walked out on the little patio behind the president's office. It was a beautiful night. Henry Wilson (White House Liaison with the House of Representatives) came by, followed by Evelyn Lincoln, the President's secretary, hugging herself.

Around four o'clock someone from the northwest gate of the White House called. "The president's being brought in." I went down. There were floodlights focused on the road and the shadowy mass of a crowd beyond. I went to the East Wing. The windows were covered with black drapes. I left. Sometime later I wandered back. The casket was atop an elevated black catafalque. Now there was an honor guard and priests. Fortunately, the lid was closed. (During the Korean War) I had seen heads shattered by bullets, so I tried not to envision the mess under that lid. Then I thought of Mrs. Kennedy in that car, her husband's brains on her outfit. That was tough.

On Saturday morning, the mail arrived. Most of it was sent before the assassination. But there was one letter—I don't know how it arrived so fast, perhaps hand-delivered—sent by a congressman from California. I read it then threw it down on the sofa. About that time, a guard at the northwest gate called, "Mr. Daly, Jimmy Breslin's out here. He says he's your pal and he won't go away. Do you want me to run him off?" Breslin was working for the *New York Herald Tribune* at that time; I had known him for a long while. I said, "Have him come up."

Now Breslin is in my office the day after the assassination, saying, "Well, I just want you to know that right now the whole world feels just the way you do."

I said, "Oh yeah? Take a look at this letter." And I handed him the letter from the congressman.

Jimmy said, "Geez. Now I've seen it all."

I said, "You can't do anything with it."

He said, "That guy crawls."

On Sunday, (Press Secretary Pierre) Salinger came in and handed me a copy of the *Herald Tribune* and said, "I don't know where Breslin got this goddamn letter."

The column read:

> *On Saturday, almost an entire 24 hours after the murder of the President of the United States, a member of Congress who represents one of the great centers of culture and decency for which California is so famous, sat at his desk on Capitol Hill, dictated a letter to President Lyndon Johnson.*

Dear Mr. President:

Just to say that I and, I hope, all Members of the Congress believe it is our duty to support you and stand
behind you at this time. I would also like to say that
in 1960, at the Democratic National Convention in
Los Angeles, I voted for you against John F. Kennedy.

I tried to call Jimmy's house. He knew I was going to scream at
him. So Rosemary (his wife) told me he was in the shower. When I
finally reached him, he said, essentially, "That freaking congressman is
as dead as Kennedy." I hung up.

On Monday, we went to St. Matthew's Cathedral. I watched everyone hustling for aisle seats. I thought, "Are they praying for their own
survival or a promotion by LBJ, or are they praying for Jackie and the
country?" I still wonder.

God did not enter my mind during the service, and if he had, I
would have been pissed off at him for fucking up this whole deal.

We came out of the church and there were two long lines of limos.
Two or three single cars right behind the hearse then double rows of
cars farther back. First, of course, the singles carried Jackie, the Kennedy clan, then Johnson. The rest of us got into the other cars. One
row of VIPs was scheduled to follow the singles. The head cars of that
group included this midget Haile Selassie (Ethiopian emperor) with all
his medals, towered over by (French President Charles) De Gaulle. All
of a sudden, Jack McNally jumps in front of the VIP row, raises out a
mighty arm, and yells, "Hold it!" He directed all the staff cars to proceed. Then, and only then, he allowed the VIPs to move.

I think John Kennedy's legacy is that he inspired millions. I feel
fortunate to have been associated with this person who really did have
vision. He was not perfect. From the waist down he had the same
habits of his father. So what?

He really did make a difference in the world. I think that is where
legacy and inspiration meld. Another part of the legacy is Robert Kennedy. Ethel and company cannot get over the fact that Bobby was
never president. Again, so what? The fact is that much of his devotion

to civil rights, and it was devotion, came from watching his brother learn about civil rights.

Possibly the biggest part of John Kennedy's legacy was Ted Kennedy. He was a spoiled guy. You talk about nepotism with Bobby? Ted was handed a seat in the United States Senate. He got into the bottle of despair and couldn't get out. He left a girl to die at Chappaquiddick. Then he went on to become the most significant senator for shaping our present and, I hope, our future as a country. A woman who was at Chappaquiddick that night told me she said to Ted, not long before his death, "I am so proud of what you have become."

Overall, we are left a lasting legacy of this forever young president who, today, would be ninety-five years old.

❧ John Gunther Dean
Senior State
Department diplomat

"Kennedy was interested in moving the world forward."

AS you know, 1960 was the big year—when African nations gained independence. In 1962, Kennedy invited the President of Togo, Sylvanus Olympio, to come as an official guest of the United States. He was among the first African presidents to come to the White House. Olympio came away feeling that Kennedy was interested in helping the newly independent African nations. I had been, in 1960, the diplomatic adviser to Olympio in Togo. The meeting with Kennedy was very cordial. Kennedy was so nice.

He said, "Here's my friend John, who works with you." He had a way of doing things that put people at ease.

Kennedy was interested in moving the world forward. That was well understood by the newly independent African countries and also by the rest of the world. Eisenhower, of course, had been the commander of the U.S. and Allied forces during World War II, and he knew North Africa well. He showed an interest in North African affairs. Kennedy sought to establish relations with newly independent nations in sub-Saharan Africa.

In November 1963, I served as an advisor to the U.S. delegation to the United Nations General Assembly in New York. They needed French speakers, such as myself. I was assigned to the head of the American delegation, former governor Adlai Stevenson. When we heard about the assassination of President Kennedy, he called for a formal meeting of all the U.N. delegates. Stevenson told them what had happened. Nearly everyone, and there were hundreds of people, came forward to shake hands with Stevenson to express their dismay at the loss of Kennedy. It was interpreted in a very personal way, as if they all had lost a great friend. All the delegates were affected by Kennedy's tragic disappearance from the scene.

Even after Kennedy's death, many people around the world associated the Kennedy name with efforts to avoid war. You must remember the Kennedy-Khrushchev confrontation over Cuba. For many, that's when this association started.

I was definitely influenced by Kennedy and what he stood for. In 1961, he issued a personal decree that every U.S. ambassador to a foreign country was his personal representative to that country, and therefore, each ambassador became responsible for all the services in the embassy. Very often, the various services in each embassy—the military people, the State Department people, the antidrug people, the intelligence people, the political people—were at odds with each other. They would send messages, and sometimes complaints, to the president. Kennedy's order made each ambassador the coordinator of all U.S. policies and interests, thereby enabling the embassy personnel to speak with one voice. This was a major contribution. I later found out how important this was when I served as ambassador. Unfortunately, this practice has been abandoned for the last thirty years.

The great legacy of the Kennedys is giving people hope. Hope is what religion is based on.

❧ Clint Hill
U.S. Secret Service agent

"My objective was to get up on the back of the car and form a shield for President and Mrs. Kennedy to prevent any more damage from being done. Any agent would have done the same thing. I happened to be one. . . . I did have that opportunity, but it was too late."

KENNEDY called each and every one of us agents by our first names. Johnson, when I first met him, was not too pleased to meet me, because I had been with the Kennedy detail. Jerry Ford was extremely friendly. His youngest son and my oldest son were high school classmates. He lived not far from where I was living in Alexandria, Virginia.

One of those situations where I learned of balancing my obligations and loyalty to Mrs. Kennedy involved an obnoxious UPI photographer, Roddy Mims, who once breached security at National Airport to take photos of her. As the agent responsible for the first lady's protection, I grabbed him, took his camera, and took all his film. I turned him over to the police because of his activities.

When I got to the White House, I was advised that the president wanted to see me. So I went in to the Oval Office and there was the president and Pierre Salinger, his press secretary. I explained to them what happened. The president looked at me and said "Unfortunately, you're going to be the scapegoat in this situation. We can't afford to have the press angry at us for what happened at National Airport and so you are going to get the blame. And we're going to return the film."

When things like this happened, I had to weigh the risk of being chastised by the president himself. Eventually, the first lady gave me more and more responsibility for many things.

When we traveled—she often traveled alone overseas, or with Lee, her sister—she no longer brought staff, except for a personal assistant. I became social secretary, press secretary, personal shopper. Whatever was necessary. I was trying to establish an environment in which she could function and do those things she wanted to do. And do them safely and with as much privacy as possible. It was difficult, but that's what I tried to do.

Neither he nor Mrs. Kennedy ever carried cash. If she did, I was not aware of it. We'd go places and the children were along and if she wanted them to have ice cream or something, I would buy and later submit a personal expense request to the president's secretary, Mrs. Lincoln, and I'd be reimbursed. I'd buy Mrs. Kennedy magazines, newspapers, whatever was necessary.

I remember when she was giving birth to John Jr. at Georgetown Hospital. After the baby was born, she was in her room and asked for the agent to come in. She wanted to borrow twenty dollars because she needed to tip her hair dresser. The agent didn't have any money. So he got the money from me. He gave it to her, and I got it back from Evelyn Lincoln.

Privacy for Mrs. Kennedy was difficult. She was well recognized, respected, and loved by people. They always wanted to be near her or associated with her in some way. That made it difficult.

After leaving in 1964, yes, she called occasionally with questions about the children, recommendations about travel. In 1966, she sent me a Christmas gift, a book the president had written, and she inscribed it to me. That inscription is on the back of my book, *Mrs. Kennedy and Me*.

The last time I spoke with her was in 1968 at Robert Kennedy's funeral. It was very brief because, at that time, I was the agent in charge of presidential protection. I was there with President Johnson. It wasn't conducive to having any kind of conversation. I just expressed my sympathy and deep condolences.

On November 22, when I first heard the gunshots in Dealey Plaza, there was no hesitation at all. It's a reaction. And you immediately react. You do what we are taught to do and that's provide cover and hope we can evacuate before any damage is done.

In this case, the damage was already done by the time I got to them. In Dallas, my objective was to get up on the back of the car and form a shield for President and Mrs. Kennedy to prevent any more damage from being done. Any agent would have done the same thing. I happened to be one. The only one to be in a position to do anything because of the way it developed that day.

None of the other agents had a chance. I did have that opportunity, but it was too late.

I wedged myself up on top of the back seat of the presidential limousine as high as possible to form a shield.

President Kennedy has a mixed legacy. His speech at the inauguration—"Ask not what your country can do for you. Ask what you can do for your country"—that resonates still today. Some people go into public service and try to serve their country. He will always be known for establishing the Peace Corps and going into space and landing a man on the moon. That was his long term goal and it was accomplished. There were some bad moments like the Bay of Pigs and some good moments, such as when he prevented the nuclear holocaust with the Soviet Union during the Cuban Missile Crisis.

✃ Harold Hill
White House communications officer

*"My boss responded, 'What are you going to do?
The president wants it.'"*

I saw John Kennedy in passing a few times in Washington while I was still working with President Eisenhower. The first time I really met John Kennedy was in February of 1961, shortly after his inauguration. Within short notice he knew me by name. My job and the others' meant we put mikes in front of the president all the time. When you're face-to-face with him, you get acquainted pretty quickly.

He was very direct. If he asked you something, he wanted an answer. I saw him angry or unhappy only once—when somebody's stupidity got him behind schedule. It was OK for him to get behind on his own, but not if it involved someone else's mistake.

The mission of our office was to record all public utterances of the president—no matter where or when—even though they might be social or political in nature, such as toasts at state dinners and the responding toasts. In Berlin, when he did the famous "Ich bin ein Berliner" speech, I was in the plaza setting up for his address to the crowd. Following the speech there was to be a luncheon. I had plenty of time to handle both, I thought.

All of a sudden a Secret Service agent came over to me and said, "The president wants to see you. Now."

So I left my position in the adjacent room and walked up the president. He leaned over to me and said, "Harold, they do the toasts here before we eat the meal, not afterward. Did you know that?"

I replied, "No, Mr. President," and did what I needed to do to get the recording.

During the speech in the plaza, I've never seen anything so well organized. They had runways five to six feet wide every thirty to forty feet. It was humid and the crowd was so large and crammed that when someone fainted from the heat, the person would be handed overhead by other people to one of the openings for first aid.

One of my fondest memories of President Kennedy involved his secretary, Evelyn Lincoln. She always kept bags and bags of PT 109 tie clips in her desk to give as gifts. When we traveled with the president, I always had a pocketful of them. They would help open doors. One day, I was at her desk and she said, "Here, you deserve this." She handed me a white bound copy of the president's inaugural address. There were about a thousand of them made. All of a sudden the president walked out of his office and she said, "Here, sign this for Harold." So he stopped, and I watched as he inscribed it for me and handed it to me.

He was a voracious reader. One day, we were recording his voice for a film celebrating the Chinese Year of the Tiger. So he came down and asked me, "This is for the thing for China, right? What am I supposed to say?"

Just then, a guy came in with the script—three or four pages, double-spaced. I watched him glance at each page for just a moment. He never looked at the script again and we did the recording. I later absconded with the script and read it while playing the tape. Except for a few "ums" and "ahhs," it was verbatim. One reading.

In October of 1962, I was with the President Kennedy in Chicago. He was supposed to fly to Seattle to close the World's Fair. Air Force One stayed on the runway for a long time in Chicago. I couldn't figure out why. Finally, the plane took off, and they announced to the press that the president had a high temperature and was going back to D.C., rather than Seattle. Three days later, on Monday night, JFK made a nationally televised speech about "Cuber"—the "Cuber missiles."

I flew on a red-eye that night, got to the White House, and was told the president is going to speak with the prime minister of England, Harold Macmillan. They were going to use a secure line with a scrambling device on both ends in the Situation Room, and they want it recorded.

I said, "Ohhhhh no. It's against the law to record a call on a scrambling device."

I knew what the law was. Recording a call like that, you are subject to five years in prison and a fifty thousand dollar fine.

My boss responded, "What are you going to do? The president wants it."

I replied, "I'm not doing it unless the president himself tells me he's authorizing the recording."

So JFK came down to the Situation Room and the duty officer was standing tall and straight; so was my boss, Colonel McNally.

The president said, "Hi Harold. Are we all set to go?"

The duty officer responded, "Yes and no."

The president was quite taken aback. "What do you mean, 'Yes and no'?"

The officer replied, "There's some question about using recording devices on cryptographic equipment."

The president turned to me. "You can do it, can't you Harold?"

"Yes sir."

"Then let's do it."

I took that as a direct order. So I recorded their conversation, and they got into the nitty-gritty. Which platoon was going to hit which beach and what time. It was a long and elaborate phone call.

On Friday, November 22, another member of the communications staff and I were sitting in a rental car outside the hotel in Austin waiting for the third member of our crew. We were about to drive out to Bergstrom Air Force Base and prepare phone lines. At that time, the president always had to be within two minutes of a secure phone, and the LBJ ranch then was on a phone system with twenty-three other people run by a man with a hand-cranked phone, so we were working with the local phone company to set up a secure line.

It was just after lunch, and a couple of people walked by and said, "Did you hear? The president's been shot."

"Oh sure," I replied.

We didn't believe it. We had heard similar things before, and of course, they were always hoaxes. Within a minute or two, two businessmen in suits came out of the hotel, and I overheard them talking to each other about the president being shot in Dallas.

I said, "Turn on the radio," and we heard the news. Indeed, he had been shot.

I thought, "That's awful. But as hard as this is, we now have to serve the new man."

I ran into the hotel, up to the White House communications center, a special room set up with a secure line and a secure teletype. I sent a message on the teletype to our office in Dallas: "What's the story?"

A moment later I received the reply: "JFK dead. LBJ to be sworn in. More later."

So I went to my room, turned on the TV, and watched Walter Cronkite deliver the news of the president's death. A little while later, I got a call from Colonel McNally. He said, "You're the most experienced person I've got. We need you to help put in a communications system at the ranch."

I drove out to the ranch to begin the plans for laying cable—telephone lines—underground for several miles. Then I got a call from the White House. "Mrs. Kennedy is asking for you. When can you get to a phone?" I drove back to Austin—about an hour. It was now Saturday. I spoke to Tish Baldrige, the White House social secretary who worked with Mrs. Kennedy.

Tish asked, "Can you get back to town overnight? Mrs. Kennedy is asking for you to record the entire funeral."

So I flew from Austin to Dallas and then to Washington, and upon landing, the pilot came on the sound system and said, "Will Mr. Harold Hill identify himself?" I was the first one off the plane, and a White House car was waiting for me. It was Sunday the 24, between two and three in the afternoon. We had only six people in the office, and we arranged to have police escorts to enable having an open mike at the Capitol, at St. Matthew's Cathedral, and then at the Arlington National Cemetery.

Tish came to see me two weeks later and gave me an invitation to and program for President Kennedy's service at St. Matthew's, with a handwritten thank you note from Mrs. Kennedy. To me, John F. Kennedy was a young, vital newcomer who led us out of the desert. He was the first really vibrant president we had had for some time, probably since Theodore Roosevelt.

❧ Lem Johns
U.S. Secret Service agent

"I got off and walked right by President Kennedy's car. I saw the bouquet of flowers and blood on the upholstery. My first thought was, 'This is serious.' There was a clear indication someone had been hit."

DURING the inauguration of President Kennedy, I was given the assignment of protecting family members. I was up at the top of the stairs at the Capitol for the inauguration. I met President Kennedy briefly that day.

I got to see President Kennedy more regularly when I came back to the White House with the security detail for Vice President Johnson. I saw him as a very energetic young man, concerned about this country. He was very competent, and I thought he would carry out his plans, but he did not have enough time.

During the Cuban Missile Crisis, we expanded security for the vice president to twenty-four-seven. There were three shifts. I observed President Kennedy coming to the meetings from the mansion. I knew it was extremely serious. He seemed very concerned, very worried. It occupied him totally. And as the tension mounted, it showed on his face.

On November 21, 1963, I accompanied Vice President and Mrs. Johnson via helicopter from the LBJ Ranch to San Antonio and met Rufus Youngblood, the senior agent in charge of the vice presidential detail. In a few minutes, the Vice President and Mrs. Johnson met and joined the President and Mrs. Kennedy on their arrival.

We visited the Space Center in Houston, Texas, and then went on to Fort Worth. We arrived after dinner and stayed at the Texas Hotel. The next morning, the president spoke at a rally across the street, then at the chamber of commerce breakfast in the hotel. We then departed for the airport and flew to Love Field in Dallas.

We got the Vice President and Mrs. Johnson into Love Field first. They greeted the Kennedys upon their arrival. The President and Mrs. Kennedy worked the lines of people by the fence, and then got into the cars for the motorcade. The president's limousine was an open convertible, although it had a clear bubble top in two pieces. It was kept in the trunk of the car. Immediately behind the president's car was a Secret Service car, then a Lincoln convertible that contained the Vice President and Mrs. Johnson and Senator Ralph Yarborough. Behind the vice president's car, I was in a four-door sedan with two other agents. All three of us were assigned to LBJ. We had gone through downtown Dallas at what I call a parade speed, and as the cars slowed down, the agents were running behind the car with the president.

I was sitting on the right side in the rear of the car with the window down, and was watching the right side. As we started down the incline on Elm Street, I heard the shots. I saw people on the grassy knoll hitting the ground. I started opening the door and jumping out to run to the vice president's car, which had slowed. Because of the way the door of my car was hinged, I had to jump backward. By the time I got out to start running forward, my car was speeding up. They left me standing in the street. Behind me were two convertibles with photographers, and the second one contained one of the photographers assigned to the White House. He saw me and said, "Hey. That's Lem! Wait, pick him up." I jumped in the back of their car, and we went underneath the overpass.

We pulled up to the Trade Mart. There was a police officer with a three-wheeled motorcycle. I identified myself and asked, "Where have they taken President Kennedy?"

He responded, "Right up the street to Parkland Hospital."

I said, "Would you mind taking me up there?"

He said, "No," and I jumped onto the padded seat behind his seat.

The officer took me to the emergency entrance. I got off and walked right by President Kennedy's car. I saw the bouquet of flowers and blood on the upholstery. My first thought was, "This is serious. There was a clear indication someone had been hit."

I walked into the hospital. I ran into an agent and asked, "Where have they taken the vice president?" He said they had separated him from Mrs. Kennedy and the others in the group. I did not see Mrs. Kennedy. I went into a room where the vice president was waiting.

So the vice president and his staff talked. "Do we keep Air Force One at Love Field or send it to the air force base in Fort Worth?"

They decided they would keep it at Love Field, close the airport, and place a security contingent there. Then it became, "How do we get Vice President Johnson to the airport?" I was asked to find an exit we could leave from without going through the press area. I went looking for a hospital administrator. We got the police cars lined up and they left the hospital. There were no photos of Vice President Johnson leaving Parkland.

I saw the "bag man" in civilian clothes—the guy who carries the briefcase with all the military codes. He was walking in the hallway. I told him to come with us. Then I saw (LBJ aide) Jack Valenti and pulled him into the car to go with us to Love Field. We got to the airport and went aboard the plane.

The vice president had called Bobby Kennedy and the president's mother, Rose Kennedy. The big question was whether he gets sworn in as president on the plane, or whether we wait until we're in Washington.

Mrs. Kennedy and the president's casket arrived. Some of the seats in the rear of the plan were removed to make room for the casket and to give Mrs. Kennedy some privacy.

(United States District Court) Judge Sarah Hughes arrived. The mood was very solemn. When they got ready for the ceremony, the vice president asked someone to request Mrs. Kennedy to witness the swearing-in. She came forward, still in the same dress. Her leg was covered with blood. The Vice President and Mrs. Johnson greeted her warmly. After the swearing in, the judge got off the plane and we took off for Washington.

Over the next few days, I stayed on duty for the funeral events. We had two groups of agents. It did create some uncertainty. The guys on the Kennedy detail, of course, were very upset. The loss they felt was so great. Rufus later became the agent-in-charge for President Johnson, and I became the assistant agent-in-charge.

John Kennedy's legacy is extremely good. I'm not really aware of all the bills or programs, but just as a representative of the country, he did a good job. One of the most telling things was when he went to West Berlin and made the famous remark, "Ich ben ein Berliner." It was a city and a country divided. That was quite good.

✎ Nicholas deB. Katzenbach

Deputy Attorney General, Attorney General in the Johnson administration

"President Kennedy asked, 'Where's the vice president?' Someone said, 'I don't think he was invited.' And the president replied, 'Go get him. We need him.'"

I first met John Kennedy a few days after he took office as president. He had a reception for all the new appointees for the government. I remember the receiving line with him and Jackie. And he said to me, "Mr. Katzenbach. You're going to be dealing with Bobby and the Justice Department. I'm so glad."

And I looked around at this enormously crowded room and thought, "How did he know my name?"

He certainly had done a lot of homework; although he likely received my name on a card from the aide who was introducing the guests, he knew I would be in the Justice Department. It was very flattering.

So my first impression of him was one of awe (laughter).

My more substantive impressions of him came later in meetings with him, as things went along, and how he reacted to problems and people. The first meeting that I recall having with him, which I describe in the book, had to do with the Federal Power Commission.

Kennedy wanted to appoint Joseph Swindler as head, and the existing head, Jerome Kuykendall, did not want to resign. There was a U.S. Supreme Court opinion on the independence of the commissions that said you couldn't fire people because they were of a different political persuasion.

My assistant Harold Reis said, "I think that's wrong. I think the president probably could fire the chairman as chairman, but not from the commission." Later, I went over to the White House on the issue to talk with Ralph Dungan, who was handling appointments for the president. I knew that Bobby was in with the president, and so I got in touch with Bobby and asked if I could come in to join him on that matter. So he said, "Come on in."

So I came into the Oval Office. The president was there. And Ralph came in the other door. He said, "I agree with Nick. He (chair of the commission) either ought to take this, or we litigate it."

So, the president took one look at it and said, "I agree with Nick, too." That was very nice. The first time he called me by my first name. So my first two meetings with him were very nice. I came to admire his judgment (laughter).

President Kennedy had all of the attributes one can reasonably attribute to a Harvard graduate. He was personable, well-mannered. He was intelligent and he was articulate. And he got along very well with people. He had all of the social graces that you have with that kind of an education and money as well.

But he had something more, which I think he acquired in World War II. The thing that always interested me about his naval career and his service as the captain of PT 109 was not the mission or the dangers, but the responsibility he felt for his crew. He risked his own life to save his crew. That was an attribute I admire greatly. He demonstrated loyalty to people, and he had responsibilities from his position, and he had to meet those responsibilities.

He took that sense of responsibility into the presidency.

I have no doubt that President Kennedy and his brother Bobby, despite not knowing much about civil rights, did not approve of the second class citizenship that was evident and the very nearly caste system that existed in the South at that time. I think the problem was not whether you wanted it or liked it; the problem was what could be done about it.

So in that sense, the moral problem was, "What are my obligations? My obligation is to make it better. But how in the name of God do I do that?" And that was the most difficult problem we faced during the Kennedy presidency.

That was true of both the integration of the University of Alabama and the release of the Cuban prisoners. Allow me to explain.

President Kennedy felt that he had made a bad mistake on the Bay of Pigs, which he had. All these Cuban prisoners were being held, and I think he felt a strong obligation for them. As long as they were there and being held hostage, he had a moral responsibility for them.

Both incidents, I think, reflected his position, essentially, "I have a position of authority and I have a responsibility for these issues, and therefore, I have a moral obligation to do something."

And the seed that grew into that moral obligation was planted in the Solomon Islands with PT 109, as well as earlier, during his time in England when his father was ambassador to the Court of St. James. He saw Hitler rising to power. He saw that morality and politics are not necessarily different.

In regard to the introduction of civil rights legislation, which the president did right after the integration of the University of Alabama, he and Bobby and (Assistant Attorney General for Civil Rights) Burke Marshall were probably the only people who were really for it in the White House. Nobody, maybe not even those three, thought it was possible. And my guess is that Bobby was urging it, but I don't think Bobby thought he was going to succeed.

I think the squabble between Bobby and Johnson, which President Kennedy did not share—but a lot of his staff did—was harmful not simply to Johnson, but also to Kennedy. And one of the ways it was harmful was to civil rights. I say that not because I think Johnson should have or could have done anything particularly outside of what he did in his role on the Federal Employment Commission regarding government contracts for minorities. He did not have much to do during the Kennedy presidency, which was a mistake.

I can remember on one occasion, it was a meeting on legislative tactics on the first civil rights bill that we had drafted. All the interested people were there. But no Lyndon Johnson. And President Kennedy asked, "Where's the vice president?" And someone said, "I don't think he was invited." And the president replied, "Go get him. We need him."

It was sad. And I'm sure Johnson knew what had happened. He came to the meeting and pointed out a section on fair employment was essential for the bill, and I think he was right.

Excerpt from *Some of it was Fun—Working with RFK and LBJ* by Nicholas deB. Katzenbach © 2008 (Used with the author's permission):

> *On November 22, I went to lunch at a restaurant near the department with Joe Dolan (colleague from the Department of Justice Anti-Trust Division). We had just been seated when we heard the radio behind the cashier's desk announce that the president had been shot in Dallas. We jumped up and ran back to the department, where we went to the attorney general's office. His secretary, Angie Novello, was there. Bobby was at Hickory Hill. He had had a meeting of his organized crime task force that morning and had taken Bob Morgenthau, the U.S. attorney for the Southern District of New York, home for lunch. Angie told us that it looked as though it might be fatal and that the president had been rushed to the hospital. The FBI was keeping her and Bobby informed.*
>
> *It is impossible to describe the feelings all of us in the department had. It seemed as if all the lights had gone out, all senses down. I went to my office and after a few minutes called Bobby, feeling I should, but having no idea what to say. He answered the phone.*
> *"Hoover just called me," he said. "The president is dead. I think Hoover enjoyed giving me the news."*
> *I don't know what I said. There was nothing adequate to say. I turned on the TV and just sat. People started to come into my office. Mostly we were just silent. The phone rang. It was Bobby.*

"They want to swear him in right away, in Texas. That's not necessary, is it?"

He could not bear the swearing in. In some mythical sense, I think he wanted President Kennedy to return to Washington on Air Force One as if he were still president. I think, too, that swearing in JFK's successor in Texas was an offensive idea to him.

"No," I said. "Not necessary."

"They want to know who can swear in the president. Does it have to be the chief justice?"

"No," I replied. "Anyone who can administer an oath—a federal judge, for example."

He rang off. I was, frankly, appalled that Johnson's people were seeking legal advice from Bobby at this time. I could understand, however, and even sympathize for a prompt swearing in as a demonstration to the world that the government was intact and functioning.

A few minutes later the phone rang again. It was (LBJ aide) Jack Valenti, calling from Air Force One.

"We want to swear Vice President Johnson in as president. The attorney general said you would have a copy of the oath."

I got up and found a copy of the Constitution and read him the oath…

Those days between the assassination and President Kennedy's funeral are something of a blur in my memory. I do remember a group of us going to the White House to pay our last respects to our fallen leader, a meeting arranged by Bobby to include an unusually large number of career attorneys. I can remember watching the procession to the Capitol from the department as it passed directly below us; the funeral with its foreign dignitaries and Bobby in close attendance on Jackie; and finally Bobby returning to the department the day after the funeral and trying his best to pretend things were normal. He looked like the ghost of his former self, and his efforts to tell humorous stories about events at the funeral were brave, but flat.

I view this period as eight years of Kennedy and Johnson, since I served both presidents. Those eight years are remembered for both—some of the successes on foreign policy going to Kennedy and other successes on domestic issues going to Johnson. Kennedy handled the economy much better than Johnson, as well as foreign affairs. I may have a bias because I served in both. And maybe I'm protecting myself (laughter).

Newton N. Minow
Chairman of the
Federal Communications
Commission

"Mr. President, I think you'll be pleased to know that Jackie's program had a higher rating than your press conferences."

I first met John Kennedy in 1954 or 1955. I was a friend of his sister and brother-in-law, Eunice and Sargent Shriver, and John Kennedy came to Chicago to give a speech. We (my wife and I) were invited by the Shrivers to accompany them to the speech, and then later there was a small reception in the hotel. I had followed his career before, and I was very taken with his intelligence, his charm, and his wit; I liked him immensely.

I had decided prior to the 1960 campaign that I hoped Adlai Stevenson would not run again and I urged him to support John Kennedy. But when he (Governor Stevenson) didn't do that, I stayed supporting Adlai Stevenson all the way until Kennedy was nominated at the Democratic convention in Los Angeles. Then after that, we all supported Kennedy.

The day after the 1960 election, Sargent Shriver called me and said President-elect Kennedy asked him to be a recruiter and talent scout for the new administration. And he asked me if I was interested in joining the new administration in Washington. I said, no, I couldn't because I had a young family and had little financial resources. But he asked me if I would help him in the recruiting process for others, and I said, "Of course." I worked with Sarge over the next few months helping him— interviewing people, recommending people. Someone in that process knew how interested I was in television. They were looking for a new chairman of the FCC (Federal Communications Commission). They talked to Bob Kennedy and to Sarge and they both thought I would be good for that. So when they asked me to be chairman of the FCC, I couldn't resist, even though it was financially a disaster. It was the only job in the administration that I would undertake because I felt so strongly that I could accomplish something there.

I had no interview with President-elect Kennedy. He knew me. I had seen him a number of times over the years, but he did not discuss the job with me.

President Kennedy would call me occasionally, sometimes on a serious subject, sometimes not. He once called wanting to know what the ratings were when Jackie's tour of the White House was on television.

It was on CBS and I called Frank Stanton, then the president of CBS, and he said, "We don't get those ratings for another couple of weeks."

I said, "I've got to have it today."

He later called me back with what were called the "overnight ratings."

I called the president back and said, "Mr. President, I think you'll be pleased to know that Jackie's program had a higher rating than your press conferences."

I would see him occasionally. The most interesting experience was when he invited me to accompany him in early May of 1961, when he was to speak to the National Association of Broadcasters. He asked me to meet him at the White House. So I was waiting outside the Oval Office and he came out. He had with him Alan Shepard, the astronaut who had just come back from his space flight, Mrs. Shepard, and the vice president.

The president said to me, "What do you think about taking the Shepards to the National Association of Broadcasters?"

I said, "That would be perfect. Very exciting."

So he said, "Just wait here a minute" and he went back into his office.

He came out a moment later and said, "We're all going to go together. Come with me. I'm going to change my shirt and I want to talk to you."

So he took me up to the living quarters. He said, "What do you think I should talk about to the broadcasters?"

And I said, "I think you ought to say that in our country, when we have a thing like a space shot, we open it up to the press and radio and television, so that all Americans could see and share the experience. Whereas in the Soviet Union, everything was done behind closed doors because it is a closed society. You ought to contrast the difference between our system, an open society, and a closed society."

The president didn't say anything. He didn't say, "That's good," or "That's bad."

He finished changing his shirt and we went down and got in the car. The president and the Shepards got in the back seat. Lyndon Johnson, the vice president, and I got in the jump seats and drove to what was then the Wardman Park Hotel. It is now the Sheraton. The president got up and gave a perfect speech about the differences between an open society and a closed society, and in an open society why we have the broadcasters there. He had no notes; it was all extemporaneous.

I left Washington in the summer of 1963 and went home to Chicago. On November 22, I was working in my new job at the Encyclopedia Britannica and was having lunch in the cafeteria, when my assistant came to get me and said, "The news is on the radio and television. The president's been shot." So I immediately went to my office, heard what I could, and went home to be with my wife and children. And then we went to the funeral; we were invited to participate. It was so sad and so shocking. All of us were numb; literally speechless.

Looking back, I felt that there was a five-year period in which four people died: Jack Kennedy, Martin Luther King Jr., Pope John the 23rd, and Robert Kennedy. In that terrible five-year period, the loss of those four great leaders moved all the institutions they had led backwards. The United States went backwards. The civil rights movement went backwards. And the Catholic Church went backwards. That Pope had convened Vatican II. The church was moving into the contemporary world.

Television news came of age that weekend in November of 1963. The fact that they (the networks) cancelled everything else. They cancelled all the commercials. They covered everything live, including the murder of Lee Harvey Oswald. It (the news coverage) held the country together in a way that was extremely valuable and important. When television is live, it is especially important because it enables every viewer to feel that he or she is there.

John Kennedy, particularly during the Cuban Missile Crisis in which I had a small role, saved our country from what could have been the end, with destruction from a nuclear exchange. I think he ushered in a whole generation of younger people who believed, as he did, that politics could be an honorable profession. He stimulated interest in public affairs and politics.

Unfortunately for all of us, his life was too short. But I think his legacy will endure forever.

Nelson C. Pierce
White House usher

"I wondered what I would say to the first lady. As she came around the corner . . . she was still in her pink suit with bloodstains and I knew immediately. Our eyes met."

PRESIDENT Kennedy was a wonderful man. When he smiled, you smiled. You couldn't help it. And he smiled quite often. For a luncheon, he had the guests in the Red Room, and when he came over from the office, I announced him to the group in the Red Room. I was shaking like a leaf, because that was my first time doing it. It was a real thrill.

One evening, I had a message for Maud Shaw, the children's governess, and I took it to the family dining room. The president and first lady were out of the city. And I gave the note to Miss Shaw. And Caroline said, "Mr. Pierce, I have a terrible time doing somersaults, my legs either go to the right, or they go to the left."

So I said, "Caroline, concentrate, now think hard about making your feet go straight over your head." And she did a couple, much improved, and I complimented her on them, but she said, "Mr. Pierce, do somersaults with me." Miss Shaw came to my rescue, and I did not have to do somersaults on the dining room floor.

One day, Mrs. Kennedy was having trouble with her stereo in the West Sitting Hall—that was their living room. And I had to escort the signal corps man upstairs to work on it. And while we were there, little John-John came over and said, "Read a story."

He brought a book over to me, and I sat on the edge of the couch thinking he would be standing in front of the couch and leaning in, so I just sat on the edge. And he jumped up and sat back and then jumped down from the couch and pushed me in the chest and said, "Sit back, sit back."

So I sat back and put my arm around him and read the story to him, and as soon as the story was over, he got down, put the book back, and went on his way.

Mrs. Kennedy, every once in a while, would call down to whoever was on duty and say, "I need some help; could you come up and help me, please?" So I went up and she said, "Mr. Pierce, I would like to move the sofa from here to over there and move that chair somewhere else." And I asked, "Do you want me to get the doorman to come up to help?" And she said, "No. I'll pick up one end and you pick up the other." It was a quite light sofa. So we moved it. And she didn't like it in that spot, so we moved it again.

She was wonderful to work for—but you always knew your place. And you never went out of that place.

The night before the president left for Texas, they had a reception, with many members of the judiciary, including members of the Supreme Court. And the president had invited all of the ushers' wives to come, so Mr. (J. B.) West (head usher) arranged for us to have dinner served in our dressing room down in the basement, and then we all went up and he (Mr. West) escorted all the (ushers' wives) into the judicial reception.

After a while, they all came back into the office. And when we heard that the president was coming, they all stood in our doorway. The president came around the corner to the elevator, and started in the elevator, and then backed up, and with a big, broad smile on his face said, "Oh, you girls checkin' up to make sure your husbands are working tonight?"

And that big smile is what stayed with my wife months after that.

On November 22, 1963, I was working on an off-set press for a customer across the street on Fifteenth Street. It was just a little over a block to the East Gate of the White House. When I got to the gate, the police officer said, "Pierce, hurry and get to the office. The boss has just been shot." And that started the day.

I took the call from Texas that the president's death was official. So I called the engineers and had them lower the flag at half-staff at the White House. And I called the General Services Administration

Control Center which notified all the embassies and all the ships at sea. Right after they lowered the flag to half-staff, there was a TV cameraman on the north grounds and he panned up to the flag, and that really shook me up because I knew I was the one who gave the order to put it down. And for all thirty days after the assassination, the flags were at half-staff. It got to me emotionally.

And within ten minutes after Air Force One left Texas, Mrs. Kennedy's Secretary, Mary Gallagher, got on the phone and we got a radio patch from Air Force One that Mrs. Kennedy wanted the funeral as much like Lincoln's as possible. And so the curator's office and the U.S. Library of Congress did a remarkable research job in a very short period of time to find out the details of the Lincoln funeral.

I was the "day man." I relayed messages to the carpenter's shop, to the other shops that were involved, telling them what we needed, how soon we needed it. Basically, when the president's body arrived at Andrews and went to Bethesda Naval Hospital, they said the casket probably would arrive at the White House around ten o'clock (that evening). But that didn't happen. They called back and said it would be longer. And it was. It was about 4:20 am when he arrived at the White House.

The First Lady and Bobby Kennedy came in together and went to the East Room to open the casket. I was still in the office.

When I heard they were coming down the hall, my doormen were busy with other members of the party. I locked the elevator and I wondered what I would say to the first lady. As she came around the corner, and of course, she was still in her pink suit with bloodstains and I knew immediately. Our eyes met. And we had a rapport and I knew that I didn't need to say a thing. She realized how I felt. We were all silent. I took them up to the second floor, the living quarters on the second floor.

That first night, we didn't get any sleep at all. It was the second night that I slept in the chair, Saturday night. Taking care of whatever needed to be done that I was asked to do.

President Kennedy was a wonderful person. The first time I announced him, he turned to me and mouthed the words, "Thank you." That made me feel better, but I got back in the office and my knees were still shaking.

I'm asked time after time after time, "Who was your favorite?" I didn't have a favorite. I worked for the President of the United States, regardless of party affiliation. It was thrilling to work for six presidents. That's how I describe it: You have six friends. You like them all equally.

❧ Sue Vogelsinger
White House press aide

*"One of the stewards came through and said,
'We've got to pack up and get ready to move.
Somebody's been shot.'"*

I was hired in the fall of 1958, the year I graduated from college, and his entire staff was in Massachusetts, with the exception of Ralph Dungan, who was his counsel on the Senate Labor Committee. Ralph had hired me. So nobody was there when I was hired. I did not meet anybody until after they returned from the November election, an election Kennedy won by a huge vote.

The senator did not come back to the office for a while. I did not meet John Kennedy until early the following year, or maybe briefly in late December of 1958. I was struck by his good looks and vitality, but I had no particularly outstanding impression at that stage of the game.

What was "exhilarating" about Kennedy? It was partially his youth. He was a presence. He seemed to emanate intelligence, humor, curiosity. Extremely out of the ordinary.

My first assignment was to work on what we called, "political cards." The cards were designed to keep track of people the senator had met, to collect information on potential volunteers, potential contributors, and potential voters who would support him. Needless to say, that was a fairly boring operation. This was before the campaign started; even before he announced, actually. I was quickly bored with typing names on index cards and decided I was going to leave. Senator Kennedy heard about it for some reason.

He took an interest and called me in and asked, "Why are you leaving?"

I really hardly knew him at this point. I said, "Well, quite honestly, I don't like what I'm doing. I'm bored."

He said, "Give me a little bit of time. I'll see what I can do about it."

Indeed, a couple days later, I found myself working on the legislative staff, which means I was doing a bit more stimulating work than typing cards. He also started asking me to take dictation—that was exciting. He was so fast. It was a challenge to be able to do that.

Everybody was working on the campaign one way or the other. There weren't that many of us. It wasn't too long before he did announce, and I was asked at one point, whether I wanted to work with Ted Sorensen or Pierre Salinger.

I said, being twenty-three years old, "Which one will involve the most travel?"

The answer was, "Pierre probably."

So I said, "OK, that's what I want to do."

I did both. I did Senate work, and then I would be involved in the campaign. I was in West Virginia for the West Virginia primary. Then I'd come back and work on legislative stuff some more. Then, I became campaign staff.

Senator Kennedy had won the Wisconsin primary just prior to West Virginia. Wisconsin had a fairly large Catholic population. He needed to win in a state that didn't have many Catholics. West Virginia did not, of course. So it was vital for him to win there. West Virginia was also real Hubert Humphrey country. He was beloved there.

The Kennedy campaign did a number of interesting things. They brought in FDR Jr. Of course, his father had been beloved in West Virginia. He campaigned with Kennedy and on his own. The Kennedy organization was a good one. They worked hard. They went to every door they could get to. They did a fabulous job.

Bob Kennedy, of course, was there. My roommate, a very good friend, had also been sent to West Virginia to work on the campaign. We did not have a big staff at the headquarters in Charleston. We all would go out at night and have a drink and dinner. And if Bob was around, he would go with us.

He said one night to Susan and me, "You aren't Catholic, are you?" And neither one of us were.

He said, "How about if you come down the street with me tomorrow on your way to some non-Catholic church, wearing your Kennedy buttons?"

He was only half-kidding. It was a good idea. So we did.

After the primary, I went back to Washington. The labor bill was still being debated. I joined the presidential campaign around Labor Day. I was in Hyannis on election night. There were only three of us setting up in there. I was working with the press. My job was helping set up for media to be able to cover election night. The morning after the election, I was told I would be going to Palm Beach. That's where the president-elect was going. He needed some staff down there. So I pleaded with the pilot of the plane to stop in Washington, so I could get some warm weather clothes.

It's interesting, the differences between then and now. The fact was, if reporters asked and we could tell them something, we did. If we said, "We can't tell you," we didn't. If we said, "We'll find out," we might have to come back and say, "We can't tell you." Reporters trusted that you were not lying. And we never were. It was really a very good relationship.

The night before the inauguration, I went to the Mayflower Hotel to give President Truman a copy of Kennedy's inaugural address. He had only one Secret Service agent. I was able to just take the elevator up to his floor and go knock on the door. He greeted me wearing slippers and invited me in to meet Bess.

I was on the trip to Berlin and Ireland in 1963. Berlin was fascinating and a little frightening. I was with the crowd out in the square. It was an incredibly huge crowd, people pressing from all directions. Happily so, but it was a little frightening.

On November 22, we, of course, were working with the press. But part of my job, always, was getting press copy—press releases and schedules—ready, so the media had the speech and the schedule and knew what was going on, as well as getting the speech copy ready for the president. In Dallas, that's what I was doing. Chris Camp, another member of the White House Press Office, and I were on Air Force One in the president's cabin working on the president's speech copy for the next stop.

One of the stewards came through and said, "We've got to pack up and get ready to move. Somebody's been shot."

So we started putting everything together to leave. We still did not know who had been shot or what had happened. There was a small television set on the plane. We turned it on and found out what had happened. Shortly thereafter, we found out he had died.

"Shocked" is the only word you can use, but it doesn't even come close to saying what you were feeling.

We took our things and went to the back-up plane. We were not there when Johnson was sworn in. At that point, we did not know where the president's body would be taken. But we figured Air Force One would be needed for Johnson and his staff. The back-up plane held off-duty Secret Service agents and members of the Texas delegation. There were some Texans who were not unhappy with what was going on. I still remember it. At one point the Secret Service agents, hearing the same thing, came and sat with us, so we weren't too close to the Texans.

Back in Washington, we were frantically busy for days on end. The role of the White House Press Office was to make it possible, as best we could, for the press to cover the funeral. Journalists came from all over the world, and the logistics involved to help them cover the funeral were extremely complicated.

It's astonishing that John Kennedy still generates the interest that he does. Part of it was him, of course, young, handsome, funny, smart, romantic, an attractive and exciting young family. Part of it, too, was that he followed eight years of Eisenhower, who was much older with a much older staff and a much older wife. So that, consciously or unconsciously, was the impact of a lot of the press stories. The feeling of excitement with Kennedy permeated everything.

✎ Lee C. White
Special Counsel to the President

"After I was hired, I told my then-boss where I was going. He commented about John Kennedy, 'He's just a dilettante. He'll never amount to anything.'"

THE first time I met John Kennedy was in his office, May or June of 1953. I had come up from Tennessee from my job with the Tennessee Valley Authority to interview with him.

Excerpt from Oral history for the John F. Kennedy Library, volume 1, page 2, recorded May 25th, 1964 (copyright retained by Mr. White; used with his permission):

> *He was a little bit disorganized in the sense that his suit was rumpled and I recall he was not wearing any trousers. Mrs. Lincoln (Evelyn Lincoln, Kennedy's secretary) was trying to get some ink out of his trousers that he had spilled. He was going someplace or another and he just looked a mess. But he took Sorensen (Ted Sorensen, JFK's assistant) and me to lunch in the Capitol in the senators' dining room. Ted told me later this was fairly unusual. He didn't frequently have lunch with staff members.*

I went home thinking, "Nice to meet that young senator." He was a lively guy, though at that time I had not realized his physical condition. He was spry and zippy.

Later, after I was hired, I told my then-boss at the Tennessee Valley Authority where I was going. He commented about John Kennedy, "He's just a dilettante. He'll never amount to anything."

Working for John Kennedy, you learned how to juggle. You do what you have to do and you get stretched a bit. As a boss, there were two qualities I admired about him. First, he expected staff to perform miracles, and the staff we had were pretty good, especially the indomitable Ted Sorensen. He was not easy, but he was fair, and he never asked or expected us to do anything that was impossible or degrading. On that front, he gets a good grade.

When I left him as a senator, it was to go to the staff of the U.S. Senate Small Business Committee. It really was because I wanted to earn more money. It was funny. I was leaving at a time when everyone wanted to join his staff. But he didn't think I was nuts. He encouraged me and when I told him I was not going outside to make a fortune, but rather to work as a top dog for Republican Senator John Cooper from Kentucky, Kennedy said, "Oh, that's different. When you want to get rid of the stigma (of working for a Republican), you come back to work for me." And that's how it worked out.

John Kennedy did not go peacefully over that little hump of turning forty. I remember the event even today. Sometimes we joke or make gags about turning forty, but he was not joking. I don't quite know why, but I know damn well that he was not happy. I was not aware, as others were, about his medical and physical problems. He might have thought, "Wow, I've been going uphill and now I'm going downhill." But it was a rude awakening, especially for a hot dog like he was.

After his election to the presidency, I contacted Gloria Sitrin, Sorensen's assistant, and later Ted contacted me. About a week later, the word came back, "You can go down and get your identification." I was in. It was either the last week of November, or the first week of December of 1961.

Excerpt from Oral history for the John F. Kennedy Library, volume 7, pages 382-384, recorded May 11, 1970 (copyright retained by Mr. White; used with his permission):

On the day of the assassination, I was having lunch in the White House mess when Jack McNally came in—about one-forty in the afternoon—and said that the president had been shot. My first instinct was that it was some sort of bizarre sense of humor . . . but all of a sudden, it was evident to me that nobody could have joked at that and his face made it clear.

So I quickly left and went upstairs to Pierre Salinger's office where the only (news wire service) ticker was located. . . . The tickers had the story. . . . Then, in a matter of just minutes, that room began to fill up with reporters. By default, I became the acting press secretary at the White House, although obviously (Malcolm) Kilduff, who was with the president, was the acting press secretary. So for those couple of hours, I had the responsibility—self-designated—to kind of work with these reporters and keep in touch with what was going on with Sorensen.

What is John Kennedy's legacy? He and his wife Jackie created tremendous interest in the presidency. Some of us had an old saying: "Franklin Roosevelt demonstrated that a man with a physical handicap could be president. Harry Truman demonstrated that a man with a mental handicap could be president, and Eisenhower demonstrated we didn't need a president."

So, here comes this young, good-looking whippersnapper, who was charming with a God-given smile that was irresistible. And suddenly, he's in the Oval Office. Boy, did that make a difference.

It really was the passing of the torch to a new generation.

✑ Harris Wofford
Special Assistant to the President on Civil Rights, Associate Director of the Peace Corps, Peace Corps director in Ethiopia, U.S. senator

"The Bay of Pigs was a huge disappointment to the president. He was angered at himself and those who had planned it. So he asked his brother Robert from then on to keep a special eye on the CIA . . ."

(JOHN Kennedy) came across to me with a personality that would be able to win the election of 1960. I thought, and do think, that Kennedy had more of what we call charisma than anyone since Roosevelt and before Obama. A combination of seriousness and humor, I thought was appealing; a sort of political gaiety, like Roosevelt, "The Happy Warrior."

Beyond that, Kennedy represented what the world, as I knew it, had hoped for America. That we were young, optimistic, can-do, and full of energy and idealism.

(B)y the time he left for Dallas, he had lived up to what he had promised in the campaign to try to do. Now I think that the revisionist writers about Kennedy, or at least the first wave of them that still ripples, view him as making low-level political judgment that would get him in trouble if he moved too fast (on civil rights and other issues). That is what I would call a low way of stating why Kennedy was very careful and, some would say, slow in acting. I would say there are maybe three key factors in measuring what he did.

First, he, his father, his family, his "Irish Mafia," as we jokingly called the staff and some of his closest gang, they very well knew the prejudice among whites in the North, epitomized by South Boston and what was also already evident in terms of the reaction of the whites to school integration in Boston, and their own Irish Catholic Americans. These were not the priests and the bishops and the serious devoted Catholics like Sargent Shriver, but the plain, American Roman Catholics who shared in their own way their own form of discrimination or prejudice racially.

They (JFK, his family, and the "Irish Mafia") genuinely, from the time they started paying attention to civil rights, worried that it was going to be counter-productive and that the backlash of moving too fast would set civil rights and the country back—not just that they might lose an election. Most of the time they could not really tell whether action would win more votes from African Americans or lose more votes from prejudiced people. And they weren't just thinking only of the South, but very much they were thinking of the North.

The second thing that is a factor in measuring Kennedy is his overwhelming personal interest, that from the time he was doing anything public, it was international affairs. He wrote the book *Why England Slept*. He was forever interested in the world and for me, the chief appeal of Kennedy, aside from his charisma, was the fact that for him the world was the big question. And that was my own view—the biggest question of all was the world.

I came back from India thinking that civil rights was the great stain on the American soul and for us in our relations with the world. Beyond the reason of living up to ideals of the Declaration of Independence, it was crucial for our leadership in the world that we remove that stain, And John Kennedy not only thought that racial discrimination and prejudice were irrational and were problems that ought to be solved, but I think his biggest impetus in trying to get them solved was his sense of America and the world.

Now remember, those I call the revisionists, they like to say that there wasn't a message on the inaugural address about civil rights which had been such a vital part of the campaign. The inaugural address had no domestic issue at all—civil rights, or the economy—aside from the call to service, "ask not." No issue of domestic importance was pointed out, though Louis Martin (publisher, civil rights leader) and I got in those two words, "'at home' and around the world."

Now, the last thing that occurs to me. Beyond charisma. Beyond any particular issue, Kennedy's great promise that was beginning to be fulfilled (at the time of the assassination) was his political skill. He was forever trying to see what would really work. He was genuinely balancing his best judgment on that—the way Lincoln did on when to sign the Emancipation Proclamation and how far-reaching that proclamation should be. In his first year, Lincoln was denounced by most of the abolitionist leaders for not signing it, and when he finally did, he was denounced for applying it initially only to the states in rebellion.

The main disappointment for me with Kennedy was the delay in signing the executive order (ending housing discrimination). Not because I thought that was an earth-changing action—it was always necessarily limited in terms of how much it would end discrimination in federally assisted housing. It was frustrating that twice it was about to be signed and postponed. It came about because a few words he picked up from me: "One stroke of a pen and you can do it." I was completely underestimating the ability of Congress and the political forces to make it dangerous to stroke that pen.

In retrospect, if he had done it right away, it would have caused less trouble than all the delay. It was not the main issue that people had in the civil rights movement. The issue going forward was what the platform promised and what he had espoused during the campaign: how to go forward with the most far-reaching Democratic platform—any party's platform—on civil rights. He was weighing whether the promise to do it in the first session of the first Congress was a wise thing to do. I happened to agree with him once we faced the fact that his margin of victory was one hundred thousand-plus (votes), and that his majority in Congress, in both houses, was dependent on Southern segregation-committed people. I think if he had gone forth with the civil rights legislation, it would have had a catastrophic effect. It would have fizzled out, and/or been viewed as a major defeat. It would have reduced his capital.

I would add that (President Lyndon) Johnson was able to get both civil rights acts—the first and then the Voting Rights passed in the name of fulfilling Kennedy's promise. Public opinion was stirred in part on Kennedy's support for civil rights and the platform.

The Bay of Pigs was a huge disappointment to the president. He was angered at himself and those who had planned it. So he asked his brother Robert from then on to keep a special eye on the CIA, and Robert got increasingly important to Kennedy on foreign policy. Robert had come from being an arch cold warrior, starting with his own first passion which was (his opposition to) organized crime and the Communist infiltration of some labor unions. Robert Kennedy, by the time of the Cuban Missile Crisis, was profoundly shaken, as was (President) Kennedy, by the responsibility of dealing with nuclear war.

The first proposition of the inaugural address was "man holds in his mortal hands the power to abolish all forms of human poverty and all forms of human life." Having that button to push and knowing the Russians had theirs was the great sobering thing.

I believe that because John Kennedy was so rational and so cool and increasingly concerned about the violence of war, he would have been able to do what Johnson emotionally and irrationally could not do: Find a way to get out of Vietnam. He was on the way to resolving that. Remember, Kennedy's other great speech was the peace speech at American University—the same week that he gave the civil rights speech. The civil rights and the peace speeches and the inaugural address are his greatest words.

In November of 1963, I was the director of the Peace Corps in Ethiopia. I'm sure by cable I was communicating with my boss and friend Sargent Shriver. I think he said that, "If you can find a way to get here (for the president's funeral), we'd love to have you."

I gave up the thought of getting there (to Washington). Then, suddenly my administrative officer came and interrupted my wife and me playing tennis to tell me that the (Ethiopian) Emperor Haile Selassie was going to the funeral. His big jet was landing in Addis Ababa to pick up some members of his party or his family or whoever. My administrative officer Ed Corboy said he was given the understanding that they would be quite happy if I could get there in time to join the plane.

(My wife) Clare said, "You certainly can't do that, they said the plane is about to land and would only be there a short time." And I was in shorts and tennis shoes. I looked at my administrative assistant. Ed was about the same size and he had been dressed for church—it was a Sunday morning. Clare said, "You can't do it."

We said, "If you drive the Land Rover, we can change." So on the way I changed into Ed's business suit. We got there and Ed knew all the airport people. They said, "We're waiting, hoping you'll make it. They're just about to leave so you can drive onto the field." And they opened the gates. And as we sped along toward the plane, it zoomed forward.

Where does Kennedy fit in the whole list (of presidential rankings)? Because he was killed after one thousand days, rationally, he can't be at the top with Lincoln or the greatest presidents. But he left an image of the kind of America that, at our best, we like to think of ourselves as—that which the world has yearned for and believed in. That has to do with hope, optimism, can-do spirit. That image became more deeply etched in political memory because of Robert Kennedy's transformation, or change, or growth or transfiguration—that's a romantic way of putting it. The two of them together was a high point in American politics and the promise.

What if we had had thirty more years of John Kennedy, Robert Kennedy, and Martin Luther King? Who knows? No one knows. I like to think of those three figures as a whole.

SECTION TWO:

Civil Rights
Leaders

✧ Julian Bond
Founding member of the Student Non-Violent Coordinating Committee, chairman of the National Association for Advancement of Colored People, professor

"Kennedy watched the pictures of young people being fire-hosed in the streets of Birmingham, and he told onlookers, 'This makes me sick.'. . .For him to feel that way and to say that, means he was moved by it, and it shifted him."

(ON November 22, 1963) I was having lunch and somebody came into the restaurant and said, "The president's been shot." My first reaction was, because they did not say, "The president's been killed," I thought, "Gee, what a terrible thing. But he's not dead."

We continued with our meal. I was having lunch with a journalist, and she did not get up and say, "I've got to go and take care of this." It did not seem that pressing to me.

I went back, after lunch, to the office of the Student Non-Violent Coordinating Committee and talked to some other people. And I think, by then, we knew that he was dead.

We were a civil rights organization. We had been contending with President Kennedy. He had not done most of the things we had wanted him to do. He seemed disinterested in civil rights. He was not our favorite politician.

And when we found out he was dead, we knew that meant Lyndon Johnson would be president. We began to call people we knew in Texas who could tell us something about him—progressives, liberals in Texas, who could tell us what kind of person he was, what kind of president he might be.

They were not encouraging. They thought he would be a step backward. If Kennedy had been, pretty much, a do-nothing president, Johnson would be worse. And we discussed it. We were the kind of people who talked all the time.

Like everybody else, I was glued to the TV. What's going on? What are people doing? What are they talking about? All those iconic scenes that everybody else was drawn to, they drew me, too. Television brought this catastrophic news event into our homes in ways we never thought it would. I never imagined it would.

When he ran for office, we were inspired by him. But after he took office, it became fairly clear to us, at least we thought so, that he would not be the flaming liberal we had hoped he would be. Instead, he was cautious. He said early on that he saw no changes coming in the filibuster rule. That was just an awful thing for him to say from our point of view.

So we thought it was just going to be business as usual. And we were not enamored of him. We were of mixed emotions. On one hand, he and his wife were such attractive figures. Everybody was drawn to them. On the other hand, good looks alone wouldn't do it. It was deeds we were interested in, and there did not seem to be any good deeds forthcoming.

As time went on, in the months—not the years, but the months—before he was killed, he had begun to shift direction a bit. And you could see him becoming a different person. He introduced a civil rights bill, which became the civil rights bill the next year—the Civil Rights Act of 1964. And that was a wonderful act, but could not have been done without Lyndon Johnson. If Kennedy had lived, it would not have been the bill that Johnson put through Congress. It would not have been as strong.

It seemed that he (Kennedy) was coming our way, though not as quickly as we wanted him to. Of course, we were young and impatient, angry and so on. When he was killed, you thought something good could happen here. But it's not going to happen now because this guy's been killed. And Lyndon Johnson is going to take his place and God knows who he'll be.

Kennedy watched the pictures of young people being fire-hosed in the streets of Birmingham, and he told onlookers, "This makes me sick." And it must have had that effect on most people who saw it. But for him to feel that way and to say that, means he was moved by it, and it shifted him.

I think both John and Robert Kennedy were naïve about civil rights. They knew almost no black people and had few associations with them. This was alien territory to them. And so the Birmingham movement was an eye-opener for John F. Kennedy. And it was an eye-opener for Robert Kennedy, too.

✧ Dolores Huerta
Labor leader, advocate for rights of workers, immigrants, and women, co-founder of the National Farm Workers Association

"One of my friends used to call John Kennedy 'our first Mexican president.' He stood for economic rights, as well as civil rights."

I had the chance to meet John Kennedy and his brother, Ted, and turned it down. I was leading a non-partisan voter registration drive in San Diego in 1960 when he was running for the presidency. Being very innocent—running the non-partisan Community Service Organization—I felt I could not do anything partisan. I sent some of my volunteers.

Later, I did see him because he had a parade in San Diego. But it was just a fleeting glimpse.

I also met Robert Kennedy for the first time in San Diego. It was also during the campaign of 1960, during the voter registration drive. *TIME* magazine had published an article saying that a group of Latinos who were political and who called themselves "Kennedy Clubs" had organized the voter registration drive. We had asked some of these people to help us with the drive in San Diego, but they told us they were too busy to walk the streets with us. But then, they took credit for our work, saying they had registered all these people.

Robert Kennedy was going to be speaking at the Hotel Del Coronado in San Diego. With the *TIME* magazine in hand, I went to see him. He saw me walking up the aisle, and he saw my copy of the magazine, and before I could even speak, he stopped me and said, "Oh, I know it was your C.S.O. (Community Service Organization) that did the voter registration. We'll correct that." And he did. He wrote a letter to *TIME* magazine, giving credit to our organization.

By 1963, Cesar Chavez and I had started the United Farm Workers Union. I was living in Stockton, California. On November 22, I was driving my young daughters to school. I had the radio on in my car, and the news came on that the president had been shot. And then they announced that two Latinos were seen in the grassy knoll (in Dallas's Dealey Plaza) and that these were the people believed to have fired the shots. Being a Latina, I just felt horrible about it.

I was devastated.

The first instinct I had—and many other people had—was to go to church immediately. I remember the churches were packed with people. They were absolutely full. We prayed for him and our country.

I was influenced by the 1960 debates (between Kennedy and then-Vice President Richard Nixon). And, being from California, Nixon was not a favorite of ours.

The very, very famous statement he (Kennedy) made in his inaugural address, "Ask not what your country can do for you. Ask what you can do for your country," I still believe that now, especially with young people. We live in an age when some people believe that they are so entitled. Being a community organizer, this is basically what we say to people: "Think about what you can do to help others."

One of my friends used to call John Kennedy "our first Mexican president." He stood for economic rights, as well as civil rights. When the steel workers went on strike, and the steel companies were refusing to settle, he made them (company owners) bring the books in. He said, "I want to see your books." I always thought that the reason he could do that was because he was one of their peers. He could say to them, "I want to see your books."

Comparing that with what President Obama had to go through when he was trying to get Congress to approve the health care bill—everything that the (health care companies) put him through, he did not have that peer authenticity that Kennedy or (President Franklin)

Roosevelt had with the wealthy, when he (FDR) got the New Deal legislation passed. It was much harder for President Obama.

John Kennedy had that kind of authority and he wasn't afraid to use it.

✧ John Lewis

Chairman of the Student Nonviolent Coordinating Committee, Freedom Rider, author, member of United States House of Representatives

"After the March on Washington . . .the moment we walked into the door of the Oval Office, he greeted us saying, 'You did a good job.' He was beaming like a proud father . . .When he got to Dr. King, he said, 'And you have a dream.' That was my last time seeing President Kennedy alive."

THAT day we met with President Kennedy (in June 1963) was my first opportunity to meet him, to literally be in his presence (two months before the March on Washington). I had heard him speak from a distance during the campaign in 1960, but this was my first time standing in the same space with him. I was so moved, honored, and blessed to be in his presence. I admired President Kennedy. The man gave me a great sense of hope and optimism, like he gave the entire country. As a candidate for president, his demeanor and style inspired young people during the sixties.

I did not have much to say during that meeting, not speaking up. I was the youngest person in the r dolph, who was considerably older, was the dean dean of the group. He was our spokesperson. J in his baritone voice, as I recall, and said, "M masses are restless." And he went on to describe what was happening in America and to say that we were going to march on Washington.

When President Kennedy heard that, you could tell from his body language that he was not pleased. He began rocking a little more vigorously in his rocking chair. He responded briskly and said something like, "Mr. Randolph, if you bring all those people to Washington, won't there be violence and chaos and disorder?"

And Mr. Randolph responded and said, "This will be a peaceful, orderly, non-violent protest." The others said a few other words, and before we got up to leave, the President said, "We have problems, man-made problems that must be solved by men and women of goodwill."

John Kennedy listened. He listened very well. He listened intently. I just felt that my presence, being a young guy, that I didn't have to say much of anything. After the meeting, we went out to the lawn of the White House to talk with the press and said, "We had a productive and meaningful meeting with the President of the United States."

Even before we met with President Kennedy that first time, he had made, in my estimation, one of the most meaningful speeches that any president had ever made at that time on the question of civil rights. I think that was the speech he gave on June 11 when he said that the question of civil rights and the question of race are moral issues. That confirmed in my own mind, his heart, my sense of his commitment.

Along the way, I think that he became reluctant to take action because he was concerned about the next election, about holding on to some of the Southern states. And he didn't want to do anything that would make it difficult or impossible to get some of his nominees through, especially in the judiciary. Senator (James) Eastland was the chairman of the Judiciary (Committee), and he (Kennedy) was very concerned about that. He had to be very cautious.

After the March on Washington (August 28, 1963), we met with President Kennedy again. He had invited each of the speakers to the White House. The moment we walked into the door of the Oval Office, he greeted us saying, "You did a good job." He was beaming like a proud father. He was glad that everything had gone off so well. ... said to each one of us, "You did a good job, you did a good job."

And when he got to Dr. King, he said, "And you have a dream." That was my last time seeing President Kennedy alive.

(On November 22, 1963) I was in Nashville, getting into a car on my way to Detroit, and I was going to make a stop in Urbana at the University of Illinois at Champaign-Urbana to recruit students for the movement. Then I was planning to go on to Detroit to speak at a union event. When we heard the president had been shot, we cancelled the meeting in Illinois and we drove straight to Detroit. That meeting turned into a memorial service for President Kennedy.

It was just a very sad time. I had had family members pass, my great-grandfather, great-grandmother, other relatives, but never someone so prominent whom I had met, someone whom I admired and identified with. I felt that President Kennedy, even during his campaign, and then in his election, he created such a sense of hope and optimism. I've said that when President Kennedy was assassinated, and I've said the same thing about Dr. King and Bobby, something died in us. I know something died in me. I think something died in America.

Those of us who lived through that period can never, ever forget it. I sometimes wonder what would our country be like, what would our world be like, if President Kennedy had lived.

The place for him (in my heart) is still real, still strong and deep. His personality, his voice, his sense that we as a nation can do almost anything. That drive, energy, the commitment, the dedication. The idea that we can go places as a nation and as a world community that we have never gone before. It is still there.

Sometimes when I'm working in politics, I often think, "What would President Kennedy do? What would President Kennedy say?" The same can be applied to Dr. King and Bobby Kennedy. I think these three men helped influence and mold my life. I'm eternally grateful that somehow, some way, they impacted me.

During the weekend leading up to the funeral service for President Kennedy, we were holding a meeting in Washington at Howard University, and I proposed at the Student Nonviolent Coordinating Committee (SNCC) conference that we go out to the John F. Kennedy grave and pay tribute to him. But my fellow members of the SNCC staff did not want to be part of that. For many reasons, they vetoed the idea. Much later, I had the opportunity to go (to the gravesite). From time to time, I go out and (pause). . . .

There are ups and downs in life and in a nation's history, but you can never lose hope. I think that's what the lives of Dr. King and Robert Kennedy and President Kennedy say to us. These three young men inspired us to hold on and keep the faith, to be hopeful, be optimistic about the future.

President John F. Kennedy's commitment, his dedication, his inspiration, his leadership continue to inspire people today. Many young people and many people not so young, many my age, people younger, people older still say, "I got involved in public service, I got involved working for a non-profit, got involved with the Peace Corps because of President Kennedy."

And several members of Congress say, "It was John F. Kennedy who inspired me to do something with my life." People became teachers, they became lawyers and doctors. When I went to Africa for the first time in 1964, young Africans in West Africa, Central and East Africa, were talking about President Kennedy. And still, all these years after his death, he is a great source of inspiration. All over America and around the world.

✒ Roger Wilkins
Assistant to the Administrator of the United States Agency for International Development, Assistant Attorney General in Johnson administration, Pulitzer Prize–winning journalist, professor

"He said, 'Keep up the good work. We're lucky to have you.' I floated for a week. He was really interested in what this young, Negro man was doing and how it felt to be working in his administration. . . . It was no b.s."

I knocked on doors for John Kennedy in 1960. We said, "We're from the Democratic youth group and we'd like you to vote for Kennedy." We handed people pamphlets. Sometimes, we got the door slammed on us. But I would say more than 50 percent of the time people were decent. I was twenty-eight years old.

I met John Kennedy after he was elected president. It was in the basement parking garage of the State Department. My boss, the USAID Administrator, was driven to and from the office in a limousine, so he allowed me to use his parking spot. As you may know, Kennedy did many of his press conferences in a theater in the State Department building, and one day, I came driving in and there were four or five cars lined up, including the presidential limousine. I got out of my car and the Secret Service agents looked at me, then all of a sudden, there he was. He was smiling and we walked toward each other.

I said, "Hello, my name is Roger Wilkins."

He remarked, "Oh yes, Mr. Wilkins, very nice to meet you."

And I thought to myself, "He's heard of me? He knows me?"

I was three degrees from peeing in my pants.

He asked me, "Well, how do you like it here at USAID?"

I responded, "I'm very pleased to be here."

The President went on. "What are you working on?" he asked.

I told him I was trying to fashion programs for Africa and also trying to make some sense out of the war in Vietnam.

"What else do you do?" Kennedy asked me.

"Whatever the administrator wants," I responded. "I deal with the inspector general. In fact, I meet with him every two weeks."

The President said, "You're doing good work."

At this point, I'm giddy.

Then, it clicked: He asked if I was related to Roy Wilkins, and I said, "Yes, he's my uncle."

"Oh," the President responded, "He's a fine man. We rely on him a lot."

He said, "Keep up the good work. We're lucky to have you." And then he got into his car.

I floated for a week. There was no question John Kennedy was a nice and polite man, as well as a good politician. He was really interested in what this young, Negro man was doing and how it felt to be working in his administration. I think we chatted for five to ten minutes. It was no b.s. I had heard from my uncle that Kennedy was like that, very engaging.

On November 22, 1963, there was an enormous explosion in my life and in my spirit. I was in Puerto Rico looking at possible locations for a police training center as part of USAID's work in Central America. We recognized that if you do not have good police, you cannot have an enriched economy. We were staying in the San Juan Hilton and I walked into the lobby. It was very quiet. It was weird. People looked shell-shocked. People were moving quietly. There was a kind of eerie silence.

I said to myself, "Something's wrong." I asked a busboy, and he looked at us and said, "Kennedy el morte," and he made a fist and bounced it on the side of his head.

I thought, "What?! The President of the United States killed? No way. It didn't happen!"

We soon learned it indeed had happened and we cut our trip short and flew back to Washington.

John Kennedy helped us believe in ourselves, that we, as Americans, could do big things. He lifted our spirits and made us proud of ourselves. His youth, his attractiveness, his elegance of phrase. And, of course, Jackie. He was Mr. Cool. His self-effacing humor, as demonstrated by his comment when he visited France, "I am the man who escorted Jacqueline Kennedy to Paris and I enjoyed it."

(Senator) Pat Moynihan said it right: "We may smile again, but we will never be young again."

❧ Andrew Young
Executive Director of the Southern Christian Leadership Conference, mayor of Atlanta, U.S. Ambassador to the United Nations during Carter administration

"His legacy really is hope in the American people. He put the burden of responsibility to maintain this vision on the people."

(IN 1960) there was almost no attention paid to the black vote, and the fact that he showed up in a black community in Chicago—I think the name of the place was Park Meadows. I had an aunt who was living there. It was a middle class high-rise on the south side. They had a rally there in the parking lot. We weren't used to seeing presidential candidates come into the heart of a black community that way. He stood on a truck and addressed the crowd directly.

He had a very interesting speaking style. You felt like he was talking to you. And he wasn't making promises. He was, by and large, reaffirming his faith in the country and his faith in us as a people. And I think part of what inspired me—and this was before he asked, "Ask not what your country can do for you. Ask what you can do for your country." That message was: "We've got to pull together to straighten this world out, and we can do it."

I knew Hubert Humphrey. And I liked Hubert Humphrey. I was always a Hubert Humphrey fan. It was like Obama and Hilary (in

2008). I knew Hillary (Clinton) much better than I knew Obama. And I was a supporter of Hillary. I didn't give up on Hillary as quickly as I gave up on Humphrey. I just felt that Kennedy was a younger clarion voice that the country would respond to.

(On November 22, 1963) we were working with the citizenship education program, where we brought local leaders from across the South together, to train them in non-violence and citizenship education. To organize their neighbors to pass literacy tests and to get the right to vote. We had about fifty people at Penn Community Center in South Carolina. And these were poor black people for the most part from Mississippi, Louisiana, Alabama, South Carolina, and Georgia. And they were all very religious.

Not only did we cry, but immediately we ended the conference, and the whole thing turned into a prayer meeting. People got down on their knees and prayed for the life of the president.

Dr. Martin Luther King Jr. saw President Kennedy's death as his own death. At the time he said, "If they can't protect the president, there's nothing we can do. When they're ready for you, you're gone. And you don't have anything to say about when you go or how you go. You're gonna die. We're all gonna die. That's the one universal for all mankind. And we have no choice about when or how. The only choice we have is 'What is it that we are willing to die for?'"

(I was inspired by John Kennedy) in his willingness to insist that America be a global leader and I think that's what is required now. He was leading the nation and the world politically and in the area of atomic weapons and outer space. But what's needed now is someone who can create an economy that works well for everybody. And the strength that he brought to the office was that he was not an ideologue. He was a visionary.

His legacy really is hope in the American people. He built on the early constitutional vision and the government of the people, by the people, for the people of Lincoln. He put the burden of responsibility to maintain this vision on the people. The term usually used is "American exceptionalism." I think what John Kennedy was saying is, "We have to own up to the privileges and blessings that God has allowed this nation to develop."

And I would say that my version of his legacy would be that "to whom much has been given, of them much will be required." That was true of his brothers, Robert and Ted. They believed not only in the exceptionalism of the nation, but of their family and of the people. Those who are blessed must choose to serve others.

SECTION THREE:

Children of Kennedy Advisors and Others

✒ David Acheson
Attorney, scholar, son of former Secretary of State Dean Acheson

"I think Jack was a first rate public figure, that is, he knew how to handle himself in public. He was not, I think, a distinguished public servant. I was always a little disappointed in Jack because I thought he did not come up to the glamour he inspired."

I first met Jack Kennedy in late September of 1960. I and a couple of others, because of our experience in previous campaigns, had been asked to go to New York City and run the five borough area for his campaign. The first time Jack came through, we were billeted at the old Biltmore Hotel—that was the location of both the statewide and local Democratic headquarters. Mike Prendergast was the state chairman. Carmine DeSapio was the New York chairman, so we brought Jack into the hotel for a meeting with them.

He looked at me and asked, "Do you mind if I ask you a question?"

I said, "Of course not."

He said, "What am I doing in this crummy hotel?"

We explained why we were there. He was used to the Carlyle. The Biltmore was a few notches below his standards.

Then he asked, "So, what are we up to?"

"The first thing on your calendar tomorrow is to meet the cardinal," I said. "And the problem you have, of course, is that the Southern Baptists don't like you being a Catholic. And if you offend the cardinal, your Catholic supporters will take it amiss. So the question is, 'Do you kiss his ring when you are introduced to him, or do you just shake his hand?'"

Jack, without any hesitation, said, "Most of my Catholic friends and supporters think I'm not a very good Catholic, so I don't have much to fear from them. I have more to fear from the Southerners. So I think it's pretty obvious. I'll just shake his hand."

I said, "Well, that's our recommendation."

He said, "OK, what's next on the agenda?"

So we organized his moves for the next couple of days and then he left town. He came back several more times and the last time was the debate with Nixon. We took him over to the studio. But we were not permitted to be visible. We were very confident that he was doing well in the campaign. He was almost idolized by the press. Everything in his nature seemed to be in contrast with President Eisenhower.

And he was quite the opposite of Nixon in his manner, appearance, and personality—all of that was helping him immensely. Nixon regarded reporters as a risk and wanted to minimize his risk by not talking to them any more than he had to. Jack, like FDR, saw them as a medium, a medium that was perfectly prepared to cooperate.

We didn't see a lot of him during the campaign. We organized his moves in New York, communicated them to his campaign staff, and they would take off and handle it. We were not very visible and we did not want to be.

After he was elected, I only saw him socially once or twice.

I was taken with his personality. The thing that worried me was whether he was just a glib, attractive, superficial phenomenon. And close to the time he was assassinated, I began to realize that he was not really happy about being a leader in the civil rights campaign, because that threatened his position in the South.

On the other hand, Bobby Kennedy was attorney general when I became U.S. Attorney for the District of Columbia. I reported to Bobby, and I became convinced that Bobby, in spite of his reputation as being ruthless and cynical, really wasn't. He made some bad alliances early in his life through the political connections of his father.

Bobby was really interested in public service, including promoting civil rights. I completely changed my opinion about Bobby. We were never intimate friends, but we got to the point where, since I had a place on Cape Cod, we would fly up together and talk about various issues. Toward the end of his tenure as attorney general, some were pushing him to be LBJ's running mate in 1964. We would joke about this on the plane. When Johnson announced that no one in his Cabinet—or sub-Cabinet—would be considered to be his running mate, this was obviously a transparent formula for dismissing Bobby.

Jack seemed always preoccupied by his image, by the publicity about him. He was very sensitive to that. I got the impression he was a little too self-obsessed. And a little too cynical. He was worried about the civil rights movement because he did not want to alienate the South. He was worried about national security issues and worried about risking war with the Soviets over Berlin. All those things were worth worrying about, of course. I felt he was sort of paralyzed by the size of those problems and the difficulty of those decisions. I don't think he handled foreign affairs very well. He was risk-averse, and he was inexperienced. He did not have people around who were very good. Dean Rusk, who had worked for my father, was very hesitant, very timid, very poor at clear communication about what he thought the president should do.

On November 22, I had been working in my office and walked up half a block to a sandwich shop to get a quick lunch, and when I came back, my secretary said, "Oh, Mr. Acheson, have you heard the awful news?"

And I hadn't. There was no television in the place where I was having my sandwich. But everyone in the office had heard it by then. It was, of course, a very, very sad day.

I think Jack was a first rate public figure, that is, he knew how to handle himself in public. He was not, I think, a distinguished public servant. I was always a little disappointed in Jack because I thought he did not come up to the glamour he inspired. He had a potential that was greater than what he realized.

Jack had a breezy manner. His mind was quick; his responses were quick. He had a sardonic sense of humor. He liked ironies and gallows humor. I was attracted to him immediately for those reasons. My father enjoyed him as a person, but was more skeptical.

✑ Fernando Chavez
Attorney, son of Cesar Chavez, co-founder of the National Farm Workers Association

"(L)ook at that time period, in the homes of Latinos, you would see calendars, posters, and photographs of President Kennedy. And you would see images of the Virgin Mary. That's the stature, that's the reverence with which he was perceived in Latino homes."

I saw and heard him at a rally in Los Angeles in 1960. I was probably eleven years old. We were living then in East Los Angeles, and my dad was running the Community Service Organization. For its time, it was quite a militant organization, advocating things that were just not kosher: trying to register people, especially Hispanics, to vote; and forming what were called "Viva Kennedy" clubs.

It may have been the first time there was an organized, concerted effort on the part of Latinos to form a campaign for a presidential candidate. A lot of it had to do with the fact John Kennedy inspired a sense of hope and aspiration in people like my dad and Dolores Huerta, who were young, idealistic, and who were looking for a better way, not just for their children, but for their community as well.

During the campaign, my dad was doing the "get out the vote." One day, he recruited about thirty kids to distribute leaflets. It was a Saturday and it was raining like hell—a miserable day. We made our own leaflets on an old mimeograph machine. We made thousands and thousands of flyers, and we kids were distributing the flyers to homes in Los Angeles. It was all day. We each were to be paid five dollars.

At the end of the day, someone from the Kennedy campaign gave a speech. It may have been a family member. My dad then asked everybody to come up onto the stage. He gave each one of the kids five dollars and then the campaign representative shook the hand of each kid. My name was called last. I had earmarked my five dollars and planned to spend it on something special. I walked onto the stage, and as I am about to get my five dollars, my dad turns to the audience and says, "And Fernando is going to donate his five dollars to the campaign!"

Keep in mind, I am eleven years old. I don't know anything about the political process. But I'm determined to buy something very special with this money. And, all of a sudden, I have it taken from me. I wanted to die. My dad never thought how impactful that would be. When we got home, I told my mother and she could not believe it. She wound up giving me the five dollars.

My dad said, "I'm sorry. I didn't mean it. I just wanted people to know how much we believe in this and how important this campaign is. How important this candidate (John Kennedy) is. How his election will make life better for us." He started giving me the political speech.

So I was baptized very early.

In 1962, we moved from Los Angeles to Delano, California. At that time, my father was starting to attract some national notoriety for his work creating the National Farm Workers Association. There were not a lot of Hispanics who were particularly prominent. That's when he was offered a job with the Kennedy administration running the Peace Corps in Latin America.

There are maybe a half dozen events that are imprinted and etched in my memory. This is one of them. My father had this habit—with important decisions—to gather our family for a family meeting, a discussion, and a vote. I don't know if this was to get us to endorse a decision he already had made, or in this case, to accept the fact that we were taking a vow of poverty. We were a family of ten living in a two-bedroom home. We all sat down at the dinner table and he said, "Listen, I have been given this offer. It's a good offer. It's more money than I've ever made."

Whatever the salary was—twenty or thirty thousand dollars a year—in the 1960s, that was pretty significant money.

He went on, "We won't have to live in a small house. We'll have a big house with plenty of bedrooms. We'll probably have a maid, who will cook. We'll have people who will clean the house. And people to help your mom."

He went on and on about all the positive things. All these things are impressionable for children who don't have anything. Who are struggling and just trying to get by day-to-day.

Then he says, "But I won't be able to help farm workers." And he had a tear in his eye. For me and the older children it was very impactful.

He said, "OK, let's vote."

He cut up pieces of paper and wrote on them, "Yes to go," and "No to stay and help farm workers."

We all voted and put our pieces of paper in a little plastic bowl. He mixed them up. He pulled out the first piece and read it: "No to stay and help farm workers." All but one were the same, "Stay and help farm workers." One of the votes said, "I want to go and have a big house." It was my little brother, who afterward, said, "I want to go. I'm tired of eating potatoes all the time!"

I don't tell that story very often. As I got older, I came to realize how important, how committed he was to what he was doing. He had a lifelong commitment, a commitment beyond the human norm. For people committed to causes, it is beyond just a commitment, it is your essence. It is who you are.

On November 22, 1963, I was fourteen years old and in middle school in Delano. President Kennedy's assassination was announced over the loudspeaker. My dad was devastated. I remember watching the (funeral) procession on our little black and white television with my father and my mother. And seeing my dad's tears coming down from his eyes. He said, "This was a special person. He was going to make a difference for the country."

Kennedy's election triggered a sense of idealism, of hope, or antici-pation. The Kennedy aura was elevated and grew out of the 1960s. A lot of the legislation that impacted minorities came afterward, from the Lyndon Johnson administration. But if you look at that time period, in the homes of Latinos, you would see calendars, posters, and photographs of President Kennedy. And you would see images of the Virgin Mary. That's the stature, that's the reverence with which he was perceived in Latino homes.

✑ Nancy, Kate, and Walter Jr. ("Chip") Cronkite
Children of Walter Cronkite, former CBS News anchor

"Once Dad told me he thought his breaking down on air was unprofessional, but apparently he didn't say this to anyone else and it may have just been a passing thought."

Nancy Cronkite

ON November 22, 1963, I was on the bus after school—the Brearley School in New York—and the flags were at half-mast. The rumor spread on the bus that the president had been killed. I got off the bus and went to my friend's house on East Seventy-Eighth Street. Her mother answered the door, and I pushed past her.

She was a friend of my mother and quite pretentious; she looked shocked and astonished. I said, "I have to watch TV right now." She must have thought I was quite mad, but she soon realized the catastrophe that had happened.

I probably turned on CBS to watch my father, but I truly cannot remember. When I first heard the news, I don't believe I thought of my father necessarily. It's hard for me to watch the news footage of my father announcing the president's death. I feel nostalgia when I see those images of him.

Growing up, the conversation at our dinner table was always about world affairs and politics. I've kind of rebelled against that. I don't follow politics in any great depth.

How would I describe John Kennedy's legacy? I was twelve years old when he was elected. He was a charming man, the first handsome president I ever saw, the kind a girl could have a crush on. I can't imagine anyone having a crush on Mr. Johnson or Mr. Nixon. Presidents Clinton and Obama also are charming; they were so gracious to come to my dad's memorial service.

Of course, one of Kennedy's most important legacies is the Peace Corps.

Kate Cronkite

I was thirteen years old on November 22 and was on the bus after school with a friend on the way to Woolworth's to buy cheap makeup. It was announced on the bus that the President had been killed and we thought it was a joke. I remember saying, "Yeah, sure—Lincoln!" It was announced again in the store and we headed home. Like other people, I watched Dad on TV the rest of the day. It was comforting to have Dad to watch.

Once Dad told me he thought his breaking down on air was unprofessional, but apparently he didn't say this to anyone else and it may have just been a passing thought.

What is John Kennedy's legacy? To me, he was the first youthful president who seemed to look to an optimistic and exciting future, with a vision of how great a nation we could be, revolutionary in its inclusion of social justice and science in that vision. That was the impression of a teenager who previously hadn't paid much attention to politics.

There was a lovely book I still remember called *That Special Grace* by Benjamin Bradlee. It summarized the John Kennedy that I like to think of.

Walter Jr. ("Chip") Cronkite

Today, watching my father's announcement of President Kennedy's death, I think of my father, not necessarily President Kennedy. I feel a bit emotional when I see him emotional. We're not used to seeing our fathers get emotional.

I've also watched with some emotion the interview my father did with President Kennedy in September of 1963, the one that inaugurated the thirty-minute news broadcast for CBS. And during the 1960 campaign, my father called John Kennedy on his political sportsmanship after Kennedy wanted to re-shoot some portions of an interview.

My dad generally never discussed the assassination coverage at the dinner table. Rather, he often talked about minutiae from that evening's broadcast, not necessarily the big policy issues or stories of the day.

Kennedy's legacy, at least one aspect of it, is a celebrity legacy. How that affects the president and his own self-image can become a trap. You sometimes do what you think is expected of you because you want to look good.

And, of course, one wonders whether he would have pulled us out of Vietnam. Going back, a few years after the end of World War II, we got engaged in Vietnam. Kennedy was just a middle layer in that whole process.

✑ Casey Murrow
Educator, son of Edward R. Murrow, journalist, director of United States Information Agency

"It was a brave step to give that speech during the campaign in relation to the Catholic Church. It also was a great message for people of my age at the time—that we need to separate religion and politics."

I met John Kennedy for the first time when my father was sworn in as the Director of the United States Information Agency. I was sixteen years old and, for a kid that age, just going to the White House was exciting. I was, of course, excited that President Kennedy had been elected. He was interested in everyone around him, including me. He didn't focus on me to any great degree, but he was welcoming of someone of my age and not just looking to the "more important" people who were there.

In addition to my parents, the president, and me—those in the photograph—there were others there. It may be that Dean Rusk, the Secretary of State, was there. And I'm sure other White House staff members were there. I was very proud of my father. Of course, I didn't fully understand the job he was taking.

On November 22, 1963, I was a senior at school at Milton Academy outside of Boston. I was dumbfounded, like all my other classmates, when we heard the news. It was private school with children of many

Republicans. They weren't all Kennedy supporters, but they were all shocked. They were all stunned. I went downstairs in my dormitory into a room with a television.

My father also was stunned and overcome. Because he was recuperating from cancer surgery, he couldn't do much for the administration. He was in the hospital; he wasn't at his post. He was quite upset that he could not be part of the USIA effort in reporting the story.

My parents later told me that Washington felt so subdued. A lot of people had questions on how the Johnson administration would function, especially in the first few days. No one really knew and my dad was somewhat out of the loop. My father's reflections would have been completely different if he had been able to participate.

Yes, I was influenced by John Kennedy, especially in his call to public service. Within two years of the president's death, I was in college at Yale and volunteering for a program tutoring inner-city kids in New Haven. I have worked in or with public schools ever since. In retrospect, I was very influenced by John Kennedy, but I'm not sure at the time I realized it.

One of his legacies was the focus on the separation of church and state. It was a brave step to give that speech during the campaign in relation to the Catholic Church. It also was a great message for people of my age at the time—that we need to separate religion and politics. I have often wished that part of his legacy could have been to see a way through the quagmire of Vietnam that Johnson was unable to avoid.

He (Kennedy) was one of the most influential figures of the middle of the twentieth century. He touched the lives of so many—even those who did not agree with him. He reached out to a variety of constituencies and pursued what, at the time, seemed like forward looking progressive ideas in so many realms.

He really was the first young, energetic president since Teddy Roosevelt.

❧ Craig McNamara
Organic farmer, son of Robert McNamara, Secretary of Defense

"Dad, if you felt our strategic involvement in Vietnam was wrong, why could you not have spoken out on that earlier?' He believed it was his role to serve those presidents and not to be a public voice against foreign policy. His concept of service was different than mine, as was his concept of allegiance."

I have several fond memories of meeting both President Kennedy and Mrs. Kennedy on many occasions. One of the earliest memories is when Mrs. Kennedy invited several of us to the screening of the film *PT 109*. I recall sitting in the White House private screening room. It was warm, relaxed, and very kid-friendly. All of Bobby and Ethel's children were there and the adults were happy. I remember sitting on the floor watching the film.

Our family's friendship with Bobby and Ethel Kennedy's family was very strong. Kathleen, Joe, and Bobby Jr. were all my friends so we spent a lot of time together. The screening in 1963 included the Shrivers and other Kennedy family members.

I also remember some other occasions: flying off from the South Lawn in a helicopter with the President and Mrs. Kennedy, and my mom and dad going to Camp David. I knew at certain times in my life, some things were very unique, very special. But I had no understanding of just how unique and special this particular event was. The fact is that this would happen only twice in my life and it would be a memory I would have forever. Landing at Camp David, I remember the natural beauty of the forests and the rustic cabins. President Kennedy was in his rocking chair in his cabin, sitting around the fireplace; this, too, left a lasting impression. I also recall there were no other kids there at that particular time, so I was encouraged to head off to the bowling alley. "Go try some bowling," said one of the Secret Service agents.

I have many memories of my father's work with President Kennedy: the allegiance, the pride, the call to service that my dad felt to this remarkable human being. Jackie wrote to my dad throughout the sixties, seventies, and eighties. The letters demonstrated a deep respect and friendship between the president and my father, and among my father, Jackie, and my mother. The letters were very supportive and complimentary, thanking him repeatedly over these decades for his service to the president and the country. Jacqueline Kennedy was one of my father's closest confidants after my mother's death.

And even years later, when I asked him, "Dad, if you felt our strategic involvement in Vietnam was wrong, why could you not have spoken out on that earlier? And why did you wait so many years to reveal these beliefs after you were Secretary of Defense?"

He responded that he was appointed by two presidents as a cabinet member and believed it was his role to serve those presidents and not to be a public voice against foreign policy. His concept of service was different than mine, as was his concept of allegiance.

My father would come home from the Pentagon, sometimes at eight or nine o'clock in the evening, and he would rest his hand on the Cuban Missile Crisis calendar that President Kennedy gave him. This is a silver calendar mounted on black walnut with the month of October of 1962. The thirteen days of the crisis are embossed. Dad kept it on the coffee table in the living room. He would put his three middle fingers on the indented dates of the calendar, similar to reading braille, and remember those fateful days. I didn't understand it at the time, but I could see him so deeply moved. He lived with that memory for the rest of his life.

The letters from Jackie to him at that time are incredible. One of them, dated October 25, 1962, reads in part:

Dear Bob,

> *You must be very tired. I cannot find the right words to say all the things I feel. I am so proud of you and so grateful you are here. That sounds so pompous and sentimental. Please know, this is not said as Jack's wife, but just as a plain person…*

She went on to say that she felt the whole world might be coming to an end.

On November 22, 1963, I was a student at Sidwell Friends School in Washington. I received the news of the assassination over the school PA system; the principal requested that I come to the office during his announcement to the student body. I remember walking out, and my mom was in our blue Ford Galaxy with our dog, picking me up at three o'clock that afternoon. I was absolutely crushed. Driving home, I was wondering how this could have happened; then I think I just fell into my bed sobbing, with my dog as my companion, for the next several hours.

That night, Mom and Dad and I drove that same Galaxy out to Bethesda Naval Hospital where the president's body had been driven. I was waiting in the car while Dad was in with Mrs. Kennedy. These are very profound memories. I have photographs of that evening that are rather haunting, to say the least.

Dad was very involved in selecting the president's gravesite. Along with Bobby, he chose one of the most strategic and beautiful locations overlooking the Lincoln Memorial and the Washington Monument.

After the assassination, when Mrs. Kennedy moved out of the White House and into her home in Georgetown, I went over multiple times after school to play with Caroline and John. I would have been thirteen and I cherished these times with them. Mrs. Kennedy sent me some of John-John's drawings and his little notes to me. As tragic as it may sound, they were all of airplanes and helicopters, and him flying. From age three.

The early sixties were a magnificent time in our collective history. I'm not certain that had the president lived, his vision of Camelot, the New Frontier, and the goals of his Cabinet members would have been fulfilled. He was taken away from us in such a violent and critical fashion. This vision is frozen in time. But nothing really freezes in time; everything effects change. And I think life for that presidency would have changed significantly. I can't predict. It's like predicting where we would have been in the seventies, eighties, and nineties if we had not struggled so desperately in Vietnam. How would our lives have changed today if we had not invaded Iraq?

These are issues one cannot fathom.

My own personal feeling is that Camelot would have changed and that the realities of Vietnam and civil rights would have significantly altered his presidency. But he was successful in bringing together a remarkable group of people.

There was a tremendous amount of humor and goodwill. For these young Cabinet members and their families, can you imagine what it was like to be in that era? There was tremendous hopefulness coming out of the fifties. We had a president and first lady who demonstrated grace and had an appreciation for culture, worldliness, and justice. It must have been pretty damn exciting.

✎ David Rusk

Urban policy expert, scholar, son of Dean Rusk, Secretary of State

"I began to wander around the family quarters all alone. I blundered into the Lincoln Bedroom and there, on the Lincoln night-table next to the Lincoln Bed, was a hardcover copy of Ian Fleming's Thunderball. *"*

I saw President Kennedy twice. The first time was from afar. He came to the campus of the University of California at Berkeley in March, 1962 to speak in Memorial Stadium for Cal's Charter Day. There were fifty thousand to sixty thousand people there.

The second time was up close. It was October 22, 1963. The night before, my dad called me and said, "Tomorrow is the one-year anniversary of the height of the Cuban Missile Crisis, and the President has invited all the members of the ExCom to meet with him. He wants to give each of us a memento. Why don't you come by the house tomorrow morning, and we'll drive down together and I'll introduce you to the president?"

So I went with my dad to the White House. President Kennedy did indeed have all the members of the ExCom there and I got to meet all of them. Kennedy gave each an engraved calendar of the month of October, 1962, with all the crucial days outlined, and with October 22 having a double outline.

The group had initially convened on the second floor of the White House in the family quarters. My first impression of President Kennedy was that he was standing very straight, almost as if he was suspended from a coat hanger. He must have had his back brace on.

He was quite cordial. He asked me, "Have you ever seen the family quarters?"

I said, "No."

He said, "Well, while you're up here, why don't you have a look around?"

So when shortly thereafter all the ExCom members went downstairs, either to the Cabinet Room or the Oval Office, I began to wander around the family quarters all alone. I blundered into the Lincoln Bedroom and there, on the Lincoln night-table next to the Lincoln Bed, was a hardcover copy of Ian Fleming's *Thunderball*. You may not be aware, but it was President Kennedy who helped launch the James Bond mania in the United States when it became known in 1962 that he was a great fan of the James Bond novels. Just after I stepped out of the Lincoln Bedroom, a White House usher caught up with me. I'm quite sure that *he* did not want strangers running around the family quarters so he gave me a hurried and perfunctory tour and I was on my way.

A month later to the day, President Kennedy was assassinated.

(On November 22, 1963) there was no school as the D.C. public schools were holding training sessions for teachers. As a local Urban League staffer, I was asked to speak on the civil rights movement to a group of teachers at an elementary school on North Capitol Street, a few blocks from the Urban League offices. The classroom where the session was being conducted must have been next to the school's office, and at one point, I heard a loud gasp through the wall. A few moments later, a secretary came in, clearly shaken. I was the panelist sitting closest to the door, and she handed me a note saying that President Kennedy had been shot and killed in Dallas. At that moment, her principal was speaking. I waited until she finished and then I got up and made the announcement.

It was like a thunderbolt. Most of the teachers in the room were black women and they were stricken, tears running down their faces. But we finished the workshop because the world's work must go on.

After leaving the school, I walked down New York Avenue toward the White House. People on the street were grey. I took a bus home to (my wife) Delcia. Watching the TV news, we talked. We commiserated. And I have a photo taken that weekend, lying on a sofa with my eyes shut and with my week-old son Gregory lying on my chest. Having this new life at a time of a sudden and tragic loss of such an inspiring figure gave me great comfort.

My mom and dad that day were on an airplane over the Pacific heading for Japan with other members of the president's administration. They turned the plane back to Washington and I spoke with my dad on Saturday. I saw him the next day, Sunday, when I rode with him in a State Department car to the Treasury Department next to the White House. Treasury Secretary C. Douglas Dillon had set aside a corner office in the building for Cabinet members and their families to view the procession transferring the President's coffin from the White House down Pennsylvania Avenue to the Capitol for public viewing.

On the drive to the Treasury Department, my dad remarked that, "What really worries me is that I hope they've got tight security around Lee Harvey Oswald." No sooner had we arrived in the garage of the Treasury Department then a security man opened the door to the car and said, "Well, they got Oswald." That was the first we had heard that Jack Ruby had shot Oswald, which had just happened on national TV. My dad really wanted to get to the bottom of the assassination, and of course, Oswald's murder helped generate an industry of conspiracy theories that, for some people, haven't ended yet.

I would characterize John F. Kennedy's legacy by the title of Robert Dallek's book, *An Unfinished Life*. I was an admirer of Kennedy, but I was savvy enough not to be starry-eyed. In the summer of 1963, I volunteered through the Urban League (which subsequently offered me a staff job) to help organize the great civil rights March on Washington for Jobs and Freedom. I remember full well that the march was launched, in part, to motivate President Kennedy and his brother Robert, the attorney general, to do more about civil rights. Ultimately, the president embraced the event, hosting some of the civil rights leaders at the White House afterwards.

President Kennedy faced great difficulty moving his proposal on civil rights through Congress because of the alliance between southern

Democrats and conservative Republicans. My dad said that President Kennedy approached civil rights issues in a cool, dispassionate manner as contrasted with Lyndon Johnson, who felt racial injustice in every bone in his body.

∽ Steven Schlesinger
United Nations expert, scholar, son of Arthur Schlesinger Jr., Special Assistant to the President

"On Vietnam, which is the one issue where there's the ambiguity that hangs like a black cloud over Kennedy's presidency . . . I think he was desperately looking for an exit."

MY father taught at Harvard from 1946 up until the time he joined the Kennedy Administration in 1961. He used to give a lawn party at the end of the college year, following the university's commencement ceremony. He would always have an afternoon reception for people who got honorary degrees, or who were guests at Harvard. Then-Senator Kennedy and Jackie Kennedy came occasionally to those parties, and I think that was the first time I ever met them. Even though, then, he was not yet president and did not have a national reputation, he and his wife were still a rather glamorous couple. I don't recall necessarily talking to either one of them.

The first encounter I had with him that was of any real value was when then-President-elect Kennedy came to my father's house in December of 1960 to use my father's house as a meeting place to talk to a number of different people—professors at MIT and at Harvard—to ask if they would join his administration. He came with a police escort and stopped in front of our house which was on Irving Street in Cambridge. I recall a lot of photographers and Secret Service agents around our house. When he came into our home, he sat in our living room.

The door was closed when he was interviewing people. At one point, my father opened the door and brought me into the living room and Kennedy got up and shook my hand. And that was my first real encounter with him as president-elect and also as somebody who recognized me as an individual, as opposed to just being one of the children in the backyard during the time my father is giving commencement parties.

The second time—and the one time I had a really vivid encounter with him—was when my father was in the White House as a Special Assistant to the President. We (my father and I) were wandering down one of the outside porticos leading to the Rose Garden and we bumped into the president. He was then on crutches because his back was acting up. But he was in an ebullient mood. He was swinging his legs back and forth while leaning on the crutches. He must have just returned from Palm Beach because he had a tan. He honestly looked like a Roman god in my young eyes. He was such an attractive-looking guy anyway, but that tan and the vitality that exuded from his persona were overwhelming. It was almost like he was an immortal figure, in the classic sense of the word.

He and my father were talking about Latin America. He (the President) was kind of half-looking at me and saying, "Should we intervene? Should we send down the troops?" I was amazed that he was even talking to me about what I expect were national security secrets, although I couldn't tell if he was joking, or whether he was actually serious.

He asked me what I was doing, and I told him at that time I was working for Senator Paul Douglas from Illinois as an intern. It was the summer of 1962. And he (the president) said, "If you can help us on the Hill, we'd be delighted." And I thought, "He's asking me to help him? I'm just this lowly intern." But I was also kind of flattered that he said that to me.

At one point, I thought, I'd love to ask him the question that was raised by (author Leo) Tolstoy in *War and Peace*, which is whether one person can make any difference in history or whether history consumes everything, and people who are in power actually are instead driven by the dictates of history, and not able to have any impact themselves. But I could never summon up my courage to ask that question, and the moment passed.

My father was standing there, and I did not want to appear to be taking advantage of my father's presence and be some idiot son trying to horn in.

That was the last time I saw President Kennedy.

On November 22, 1963, I was a senior at Harvard and I was in Leverett House (a student residence) when somebody told me the news. And like many others, I thought, "Oh, they're just joking. They can't be serious." When I realized they were serious, I called my home—the rest of the family were living in Washington—and said, "I want to come home." My father wanted all of his family to be surrounding him when he was going through this ordeal. We obviously wanted to be there, too. Two sisters and a brother of mine were all there.

I cannot remember if I flew that day or the next day. Everything was in an uproar. Nobody really knew what had happened and why. Of course, I remember the television flickering in the background. And then, of course, (Lee Harvey) Oswald was killed by Jack Ruby. Everything seemed haywire. The world seemed to be imploding. Everything that was certain was no longer certain, and in the midst of this, my father was directly involved, and as he portrays in his book *A Thousand Days*, in greeting the plane when it came back from Dallas. Later, Bobby (Kennedy, the attorney general) asked him to look at JFK's body to see whether the casket should be open or shut. My father saw Kennedy's disfigured face and said, "No, it should be shut." He was not the only person asked to look at the body. It was eventually shut.

My father and I talked about JFK and his presidency a lot. I was an intern for the Democratic delegation from Massachusetts in 1960 in Los Angeles when JFK was nominated. I had been privy to a lot of conversations my father was having with key people. He tended to bring me in on a lot of this stuff. We (my father and I) had been talking about Kennedy for a number of years before the assassination. I adored Kennedy. He was such a charismatic figure that it was very difficult to go through those years and not be absolutely smitten by the guy.

I think if Kennedy had lived, he would have fulfilled the agenda which he had campaigned on in 1960 and advanced as president— including civil rights legislation, Medicare, the war on poverty, environmental protection, help for the arts, arms control treaties—all of the things for which LBJ later gets credit for in history. And he would have not have prolonged and enlarged the U.S. involvement in the Vietnam War. In many ways, because he was only there for about one thousand days, he has remained more of a romantic figure than a substantive figure. He got a bum deal. A lot of the policies that Lyndon Johnson accomplished in his term actually began in the Kennedy years.

On Vietnam, which is the one issue where there's the ambiguity that hangs like a black cloud over Kennedy's presidency, it is my belief that he would not have gone down the path Johnson did, which was to make it an American war and pour in three hundred thousand or four hundred thousand troops. I think he (Kennedy) was desperately looking for an exit. And even though he did increase troop levels in a small way, I think he was buying time in order to get a negotiated peace. So I don't think Vietnam would have been the albatross for him that it became for Johnson.

We certainly remember Kennedy for the Peace Corps. We remember him for initiating the race to put a man on the moon, which happened as he predicted, by the end of that decade of the 1960s.

The Cuban Missile Crisis is another memorable moment in the Kennedy presidency because it was the closest the world has ever come to a nuclear showdown. JFK handled the showdown in a way that got us out of the crisis, and we won the confrontation with Khrushchev—there was brilliance in the way he managed it. Everybody who looks at how each day went by during the thirteen days of that crisis remarks on how adeptly he was able to come to the right conclusion and produce a settlement that favored what the U.S. wanted. Observers looking back at the Cuban Missile Crisis are reminded of the brilliance of the Kennedy presidency.

I am a specialist on the United Nations. JFK was very much a proponent of the United Nations. He was the only president in his inaugural address who ever mentioned the UN. No other president has ever done that—before or since. I think he would have made the United Nations very much part of American security policy, which, from my point of view, is a very important thing.

One of the reasons people still have this memory of Kennedy, despite the shortness of his time in office, is the feeling that he was this charismatic, inspirational figure. And he still remains that today. When there are public measurements taken of presidencies in the Twentieth

Century, he's always up near the top. The only person, I think, who obscures him today is Ronald Reagan, even though I think Reagan was a below average president—except for his working out with (Soviet leader Mikhail) Gorbachev some sort of nuclear settlement. Reagan was able to glamorize the presidency the way Kennedy had. He gave it the same upbeat, exciting profile that Kennedy achieved. My own thinking is that the Reagan aura will fade over the years because he really didn't accomplish very much. Whereas, at least with Kennedy, you can point to specific things he did or that he initiated that soon came into fruition.

Kennedy is still an inspirational figure. Even with Vietnam, which, unfairly in my view, has become a blemish on his record. And his sexual escapades which have periodically become a matter of headlines. But all that is brushed aside when you look his overall presidency and—from that point of view—he certainly inspired me.

✒ Jim Swindal
Physicist, son of James Swindal, pilot of Air Force One

"(Flying back from Dallas) was 'the most awful mission I've ever been on . . .'"

MY father was in the right place at the right time. Just before he was assigned to be the pilot of Air Force One, he was the commander of the Special Missions Group at National Airport. He flew many important government officials and Washington dignitaries around the country and around the world. He also had an outstanding career as a pilot in the Air Force, starting with World War II. He also had a perfect safety record. All the important dignitaries liked him.

I remember my father saying he had been invited to have lunch with the president and Jackie in the cabin of Air Force One while they were on a trip. But he turned the president down. He's probably one of the few people to turn down the opportunity to have lunch with the president. He did it because he had been talking to a press person on the plane and he told the reporter, "If you guys found out that something bad had happened while I wasn't in the cockpit, you'd have a real good time at my expense."

My father thought very highly of the president and the Kennedy family. Kennedy loved Air Force One, as did my father. Actually, my father went to Seattle to pick up the plane when the Air Force bought it from Boeing. My father respected JFK, and JFK respected my father and the whole crew of Air Force One.

He visited my father from time to time in the cockpit, and Jackie frequently would sit in the cockpit on the console between the pilot's and copilot's seats. She would talk to the crew, look out the window, and watch them fly the airplane.

On November 22, 1963, I was walking down the hall at my office at United Aircraft Corporation, which later became United Technologies—I was an engineer there—and it was announced on the public address system. At the time, we only heard that he had been shot. I did not hear that he had been killed until later in the afternoon. I was twenty-six and living in Westport, Connecticut.

I knew my father was in Dallas. I frequently went home to my parents' house on weekends, and I talked to my father a good bit on the phone. He would tell me about trips he was taking with the president, unless of course they were secret. My father saluted the president's coffin as it was brought onto the plane at Love Field in Dallas. He was quoted in *The New York Times* as saying, "I didn't belong to the Lyndon Johnson team. My president was in that box."

While they were still in Dallas, nobody knew what was going on. As far as they knew, the president's murder could have been the beginning of something much more serious—possibly an effort by the Soviets to disrupt the U.S. government. So when they took off, they few as high as they could go safely and as fast as they could go. He said he pushed the throttle to the max.

The next time I spoke with my father, he told me it was "the most awful mission I've ever been on" even compared to those missions in World War II in the China-Burma Theater.

Three days later, my father flew Air Force One over the gravesite during the funeral. He flew very low and dipped the wings of the aircraft left and right in tribute. There were a lot of tears evident.

SECTION FOUR:

Celebrities

✑ Vincent Bugliosi
Attorney, author

"(T)here is little comparison between the nation's response to Kennedy's death and its response to the World Trade Center catastrophe on September 11, 2001 . . . The World Trade Center victims were known only to their loved ones. But the dazzling first couple of JFK and Jackie, and their two children, Caroline and John-John, were perceived by many as the closest to royalty this nation has ever seen."

ON November 22, 1963, I was twenty-nine years old and in law school at UCLA. I was between classes and walking past the front desk of the law school office. One of the assistants said to me (and I'm paraphrasing), "Mr. Bugliosi, the president has just been shot in Dallas, Texas."

I happened to be president of my senior class at the time, and I took it upon myself to go to the two classes that were in session. I told the professors what had happened and asked if I could address the classes. I announced to both classes that President Kennedy had been shot in Dallas, and that I did not have any additional information at the moment. The professors immediately excused the classes as well as the rest of their classes for the day.

Although there was the inevitable, immediate chatter around campus, one thing I remember is that there was a sense of numbness and there was mostly stunned silence. There was no loud chattering, as one might expect with a cataclysmic event.

Over the weekend, the main recollection I have is that there was absolutely nothing on television except that which pertained to the assassination. I had never seen anything like this before—or since. And there was no advertising.

The most indelible image from that weekend is TV showing throughout the night the silent, slow, endless progression of everyday Americans walking past the president's coffin in the Capitol rotunda. I've been told that there was some symphonic music playing, but I don't recall it. I don't recall any sound at all. The silent progression sticks in my mind.

Television made the tragedy so much more real and palpable, much more than just reading about it. Or listening to the radio. Television kept the extremely penetrating shock of the tragedy alive longer. If the horror started to recede in one's mind, it was not allowed to do so. Television kept covering it. It kept the feeling of sorrow alive. It was the biggest thing television had ever covered. You felt the horror. You could see the tears in people's eyes. For the first time in the history of the medium, television was used to give America a new dimension to grieve.

Kennedy's popularity, next to that of Lincoln, remains above all other presidents from most polls I've seen. Also, whenever one speaks of a presidential candidate, in terms of hope or inspiration or idolization, JFK, invariably, is the ideal. He is the model used for comparison. People often say, "He reminds one of JFK . . . "

Excerpt from *Reclaiming History: The Assassination of President John F. Kennedy*, by Vincent Bugliosi, © 2007 (Used with author's permission):

> (T)here is little comparison between the nation's response to Kennedy's death and its response to the World Trade Center catastrophe on September 11, 2001, even though the response to the latter was enormous. Just two indications among many of the differences. On the day of Kennedy's assassination and for three consecutive days thereafter, all three national television networks suspended all their commercial shows and advertising.

And while only a relatively small number of books have been written about 9-11, far more books continue to be written to this very day, over forty years later, about Kennedy's assassination. How could one death cause greater personal anguish to more people than three thousand deaths? The World Trade Center victims were known only to their loved ones, entirely unknown to the rest of the country. But the dazzling First Couple of JFK and Jackie, and their two children, Caroline and John-John, were perceived by many as the closest to royalty this nation has ever seen. Nearly all Americans felt they knew JFK intimately, his charm and wit regularly lighting up the television screen at home. This is why polls showed that millions of Americans took his assassination like a "death in the family."

Perhaps the most impressive testament of what Kennedy possessed was the way his death was greeted by the tens of millions of people behind the Iron Curtain during the very height of the cold war. The masses behind the curtain were only fed Soviet propaganda, the level of censorship being virtually complete, isolating people from the outside world. Yet, when Kennedy died, the evidence is overwhelming that millions of Soviet citizens and those in the Soviet bloc satellite countries in Eastern Europe took his death almost as hard as we did in America, these adversary countries being immediately swept up in national mourning and tears. Under the prevailing censorship, how much could the people of these nations have possibly been exposed to Kennedy, the tiniest snippet of his person or his words reaching them during his three years in power? In addition to the youthful vigor and the indefinable charisma that he projected, my sense is that these masses, who heard so few of his words and could understand none of them, picked up in the sound of his voice and the inherent decency and sincerity in his always pleasant face and smile, that he was different, and it was these additional

critical components that enabled the essence of the man,
from just a glance, to pierce the curtain of iron that had
descended upon these countries and to touch the hearts
of its citizens.

Second only to Lincoln and rivaled only by Franklin Roosevelt, Kennedy rose above the national constraints of politics. Even with his own patrician pedigree, he tried to do what was right for the average American.

John Kennedy was the most charismatic, attractive, and inspirational president in our history. He was a genuine American war hero. He truly was the Camelot figure who rekindled the notion that public service was a noble calling.

During his presidency, idealism was in the air, and the nation's capital had never seen such an invasion of young people who wanted to change the world for the better. Also, no one before or since JFK instilled in Americans the sense of hope and promise for a better America. People spoke of JFK's "irresistible charm;" it was well known that he was not vindictive toward his political opponents, and unlike his brother Bobby, he had few, if any, bitter enemies. Except for segregationists and the militant right, as *Look* magazine said, "Even his political opponents liked and respected him." There can be no question that there was something very special about John F. Kennedy.

⌘ Rev. Billy Graham
Christian evangelist

"During our conversations I became aware that he was concerned about the moral and spiritual condition of the nation. He was especially concerned about the scars which might have been left by the intense religious issue during the presidential campaign."

EXCERPTS from "Hour of Decision" Sermon "Our Fleeting Lives," broadcast on November 24, 1963, by Billy Graham © 1963, used by permission, all rights reserved:

Many memories flooded in my mind and heart this week as I thought of President Kennedy. I first met him when he was a congressman. Then I got to know him better as a senator. Four days before he was inaugurated as president he invited me to Palm Beach, Florida, to spend the day with him. I had two meals with him, played fourteen holes of golf, and then he took me to a little party in the evening. That day he drove me around in his white Lincoln convertible.

During our conversations I became aware that he was concerned about the moral and spiritual condition of the nation. He was especially concerned about the scars which might have been left by the intense religious issue during the presidential campaign. He asked me a number of questions about the Bible. One of his questions was, "Where do you think history is going and what is the objective of history?" I told him that the Bible teaches that history would someday come to a dramatic conclusion with the second coming of Jesus Christ and the setting up of God's kingdom on earth.

He replied, "I'm interested in that."

(On November 22) I thought of the president's elderly father and mother who had received the news from a workman who heard it on the radio. I thought of the shock and emotions that must have run through Senator Ted Kennedy's mind and heart as he heard the news while presiding over the Senate. Attorney General Robert Kennedy was having lunch in Virginia when the news came to him. The president's younger sister learned of the assassination as she watched a television program from Dallas.

The immediate sense of personal loss is much greater for the American people than it was at the death of McKinley, Garfield, and even Lincoln because by means of television the president was almost a daily visitor in our homes. A modern American president becomes a family friend and a familiar figure. Thus the sense of loss on the part of the peoples of the world is very deep.

This weekend the radio and television networks are playing religious music. The entire nation is thinking more about death and eternity than at any time since the war. If ever there was a time when Christians have an opportunity to witness to the saving grace and power of Christ, it is at this hour.

Longfellow once said, "It is not till time, with reckless hand, has torn out half the leaves from the book of human life to light the fires of passion . . . that man begins to see that the leaves which remain are few in number."

President Kennedy never dreamed last Friday morning when he had his breakfast that by two o'clock he would be in eternity. We never know when our moment is coming. Certainly in this tragedy of the last few hours we should learn a lesson of the brevity of time and our need for preparation to meet God at any moment.

❧ Lee Iacocca
American industrialist

I met John Kennedy when he was a senator. Ford Motor Company had an apartment in Washington, and Kennedy had an apartment nearby. I frequently went to Washington for meetings and sometimes saw Senator Kennedy in the morning wearing his Chesterfield coat. We exchanged pleasantries, but nothing more than that.

On November 22, 1963, I was crossing the street outside the world headquarters for Ford in Dearborn, Michigan, and someone came running up to the corner screaming the news that President Kennedy had been shot. I was stunned. That weekend, I read, watched, and listened to everything that was available. The poignant family images made the biggest impression on the enormous impact of the loss of President Kennedy.

John Kennedy was a fascinating man who was great with the press. But he didn't live or was in office long enough to judge him fairly on any accomplishments. He personified charisma and spirit. Kennedy had a twinkle in his eye that left a lasting impression. He knew where he was headed.

❦ Jimmy Piersall
Major League Baseball player, author

"I was playing golf in Cape Cod. Just ahead of us on the course was Rose Kennedy playing alone . . . a Secret Service agent drove by us in a golf cart and said, "'The president's been shot and he's probably going to die.'"

EVELYN Lincoln, President Kennedy's secretary, was a big fan of mine and of the Red Sox, so she invited me to the White House in 1961. A few minutes after I arrived at her desk outside the Oval Office, I saw the president approaching, and it was evident he was quite upset. Somebody hadn't done something he had wanted. He said a hello and gave me a PT 109 bracelet and a pen and pencil set.

I have a photo of him and me taken on opening day one year in Washington. He was standing behind the dugout, and these Secret Service agents came over and asked whether I wanted to have my picture taken with him. I said I'd be happy to.

My impression was that he seemed to enjoy people he wanted to know. And that was me at the time. He always had a big smile. I think being a Catholic with that smile helped get him into the White House. The next time I saw him, we were in Cape Cod. He loved to drive around in a golf cart and take his children and nieces and nephews into town to get ice cream.

On November 22, 1963, I was playing golf with three doctors in Cape Cod. Just ahead of us on the course was Rose Kennedy playing alone. The doctors and I were walking up a fairway and a Secret Service agent drove by us in a golf cart and said, "The president's been shot and he's probably going to die." I was really, really shocked. Of course, we stopped playing. I had tears in my eyes. I felt we had lost a great man who had done a great job.

I went to Washington for the funeral. I knew the man and he treated me very nicely. The fact he got shot broke my heart. I watched as the funeral procession went by the White House. He was a big baseball fan. And being from Boston, he was always there—whether in Boston or Washington, or other cities, on opening day. And after a while, he used to bring his kids to the game.

What's his legacy? Because he was Catholic, many people did not respect him. But I did. He had a happy way about him. Most presidents are ornery, but he wasn't; he got along with pretty much everybody.

❦ Cliff Robertson
Actor

"I arrived at the White House two hours early. . . . All of a sudden the door opened behind me, and I heard the voice, 'Hi, Cliff.'"

THERE had been a lot of talk at that time. (Studios) were playing with the idea of a movie about Kennedy's experiences in the South Pacific in World War II, the subsequent crash (with the Japanese destroyer) and the heroic efforts to save some of his men. There was a lot of talk in Hollywood about who was going to play the part. The two who were suggested among others were Peter Fonda and Ed "Cookie" Burns, the fellow who had the hair. But I don't think he had as much as Kennedy.

I had no concept in my wildest imagination that I would be considered. You don't identify yourself with presidents. And I didn't know him. I had never met him, though I had met Patricia, his sister, and I knew some of the Kennedys socially.

No one was more surprised than I, and when I was told I would be receiving a proposed script for *PT 109,* I was filming another picture at Paramount. They brought me this very impressive folder with all this information about Kennedy and PT boats. I was told to go home and learn some of the scenes. And I said, "I'm working on this picture."

And they said, "This is all right. It's been arranged."

I was surprised. But in this business, there are always conjectures. Rumors are always rife. So I went to Warner Brothers and shot several scenes and they treated me very nicely. Then I went back to work on the picture I had been doing previously.

I got a phone call a few days later from a friend of mine in New York, and she said, "Guess what?"

She said, "Your name has been printed in the columns and also in *The New York Times*, and they say you're going to play it." So she was calling me to congratulate me.

(President Kennedy) had seen the different scenes that were shot for tests. (Press Secretary Pierre) Salinger told me that they were in the screening room. He (JFK) was a very busy man who wouldn't take a long time. He'd look at an actor's scenes and he'd comment one way or the other.

Salinger said, "As soon as you came on and you did your scene, he (JFK) said, 'That's it.'" So, he was in a hurry. And I think the president said to himself, "I'm so bored with these actors," and "I'm going to pick the next one, even if it's a girl."

So there were pictures of me and the president in the papers. I finished the picture at Paramount, and then I started reading up as much as I could about John Kennedy. I made a habit of absorbing even more about Kennedy, anything I could get, whether from people who knew him or information I had read. I had an impression of him, and needless to say, I tried to enhance that by seeing as much and reading as much as I could about him.

Like so many Americans, I was a big fan of his, and I felt that maybe this was kind of a dream I'm having. But I thought, "I'll ride it out." I was delighted. I did not feel I was the best person for the part, but I certainly was not going to turn it down. I had such high regard for the President.

I began to study more closely. He'd be on TV, and I would read anything I could about him, as I would with any role, particularly a biographical role. I was told that he didn't want me to try to do the accent. He indicated that any nightclub comic could do "Ask not" (in Bostonian accent). That would have been a distraction.

So, I received more information from Washington. And then I was told we were going to shoot it in Florida. And we shot some at Warner Brothers. They actually had a PT boat on the stage, in the water. So we shot all that stuff, when we were cut in half by the (Japanese) destroyer. We had the fire on the water. And I swam through that; it wasn't a big deal. You have all kinds of protection. But I did a little bit of my own stunts.

After we finished, I got a call from the White House asking me would I like to come back and meet the President. And I said, "You bet."

So I went to Washington and I arrived at the White House two hours early. I wasn't about to be late. (He) had an innate ability to make you feel very comfortable, and I did immediately, because of his graciousness and ease, regardless of having waited for two hours and nervously checking my watch every five minutes.

All of a sudden the door opened behind me, and I heard the voice, "Hi, Cliff."

It was just as casual as that. He knew people that I knew, so it wasn't like we were complete strangers, and he said very nice things. I was very impressed. He could not have been more generous. And more helpful. We exchanged letters after that, for the short time left in his life. He also gave me a present for my daughter, Stephanie, because we talked a lot about our two daughters who were the same age.

I admired the qualities of his character. Even though he was brought up, some might say, with a silver spoon, he had parents who were strict as far as scholarship, ambition, energy, and working for the country went. He was a public servant.

I know that, in his younger days, he flirted with the idea of going into journalism, and he was a damn good writer. Those, too, had been my interests. I once worked for about twenty minutes for a daily paper, and I had visions of becoming a journalist, sort of jaded and cynical.

PT 109 was a seminal film for me, because of the attention it received, as well as the respect that President Kennedy had garnered from the American public.

We have lived in such a turbulent time. I think about how some people, who were very prominent, faded away so quickly in history. With all the troubles we've had since Kennedy was killed, I think people respect him all the more. So often, people say, "Well, Kennedy would not have done that," or "That doesn't sound like Kennedy." He was truly presidential.

✑ Alex Trebek
Television personality

"However, even though I was the most junior announcer on staff, I saw this for the huge news story that it was . . ."

LIKE most foreigners, I knew him primarily from news stories and from his televised press conferences, and like most foreigners, I was captivated by his intelligence and his great sense of humor, especially when he was dealing with the reporters. He and Jacqueline were so very different from their predecessors in the White House. They were much younger and so brought an element of youth and vigor to the capital as well as a certain style and elegance that were unprecedented.

In those days, I was working as a staff announcer for the Canadian Broadcasting Corporation at its English language headquarters in Toronto and hosting my first television show, *Music Hop,* a sort of Canadian version of *American Bandstand.*

On November 22, 1963, I was on booth duty doing news, weather, sports, and station breaks for the national radio network when the news came in from Dallas. I was the one who read the UPI wire that confirmed the death of the president.

At that time, the CBC had a standing protocol that with the death of her majesty the queen, the prime minister, or another major world figure, our regular programming would cease, and we would start playing classical music that was to be interrupted by announcements every fifteen minutes or so. That's what we did.

However, even though I was the most junior announcer on staff, I saw this for the huge news story that it was, and one that was ongoing, so I went to see the news director on duty and made the case that the tragedy of the American president's assassination was far too important to cease all broadcasting, and that the CBC had a responsibility to our listeners to keep them informed as to what was happening. Fortunately he agreed, and for the rest of the day and into the weekend, we aired news feeds from all the American radio and TV networks.

Letitia Baldrige, Jacqueline Kennedy's Social Secretary, gives remarks at an event at the White House in 1963, just a few months before President Kennedy's assassination. Joining the festivities are Mrs. Kennedy and her two children, Caroline and John. President Kennedy, Baldrige said, did not "dwell on anything that was sad or gloomy. He was funny about anything that he could be funny about, and he taught us all how to do that." (Photo: © Robert Knudsen, White House Collection, John F. Kennedy Presidential Library)

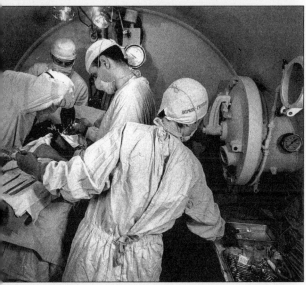

Dr. William F. Bernhard, left with his back to the camera, performs surgery in the hyperbaric chamber of the Industrial Medicine Department of the School of Public Health at Harvard. In 1963, Bernhard labored for thirty hours in the chamber to try to save the life of the Kennedys' second son Patrick. (Photo courtesy Dr. Bernhard)

President Kennedy and Senator Frank Carlson (Republican of Kansas) look on as the Rev. Billy Graham delivers remarks at the National Prayer Breakfast in February, 1963. It would be the last time Rev. Graham saw John Kennedy. (Photo courtesy the Billy Graham Evangelistic Association)

Civil rights activists Julian Bond, right with light-colored shirt, and Andrew Young, center in dark suit, holding hands with others in unity during the 1963 March on Washington. Bond remarks that "Kennedy watched the pictures of young people being fire-hosed in the streets of Birmingham, and he told onlookers, 'This makes me sick'—he was moved by it, and it shifted him." (Photo: © Francis Miller/Time Life Pictures/Getty Images)

Benjamin C. Bradlee, then a corre-spondent with Newsweek and later editor of *The Washington Post*, appears engrossed in conversation with John Kennedy, Jr. at the Kennedy estate near Middleburg, Virginia. The photo was taken less than two weeks before Bradlee's close friend, President John Kennedy, was assassinated. (Photo: © Cecil W. Stoughton, White House Collection, John F. Kennedy Presi-dential Library)

Future NBC Anchor Tom Brokaw sharpens his broadcasting skills as a student on KUSD radio at South Dakota University in 1960. He later covered President Kennedy's 1962 visit to Offutt Air Force Base near Omaha, Nebraska. Regarding the news cover-age of JFK's assassination and funeral, he remarked: "The television set was, if you will, the centrifuge for the coun-try. Everybody drew from it in some fashion." (Photo: © South Dakota Public Radio Collection, University of South Dakota Archives and Special Collections)

Charles U. Daly, a congressional liaison in Kennedy's White House, smiles alongside his boss. "He really did make a difference in the world. I think that is where legacy and inspiration meld." (Photo courtesy Mr. Daly)

Robert Dellwo, attorney and Spokane County Democratic Party chair, right, joins then-Senator John Kennedy at a downtown rally during the 1960 presidential campaign. "Bobby and Ted were 'doers,' and were expected to take care of their older, prominent brother. . . .'the boys,' as we called them, were always busy attending to details." (Photo: © Argenta Images)

Barry Goldwater Jr. photographs then-Senator John Kennedy at the U.S. Capitol. In 1963, Goldwater said his father, Senator Barry Goldwater, and Kennedy talked about running against each other (in 1964) and decided they would travel around the country together, stop at different cities, and debate each other. "It would have been very entertaining and would have set a high standard for future campaigns." (Photo courtesy Mr. Goldwater)

Then-Senator John Kennedy greets waitress Phyllis Elkins while meeting with Congressman Ken Hechler, right, and David Fox of the local Democratic Party during the 1960 primary in West Virginia. The brief encounter at Jim's Steak and Spaghetti House in Huntington is memorialized with a photo in the restaurant. (Photo courtesy Edward H. Dawson Jr., Editor and Publisher, *The Herald-Dispatch*, Huntington, West Virginia)

PRESIDENT
JOHN F. KENNEDY
SAT HEPE
1960

President-elect John Kennedy comments to United Press International White House correspondent Helen Thomas after visiting his wife and newborn son John Kennedy, Jr. at Georgetown Hospital in Washington, D.C. In her foreword, Thomas states that Kennedy was "the most inspired and inspiring of any president I covered." (Photo: ©Bettmann/ Corbis Images)

Senator John Kennedy, campaigning for the presidency in Portland, Oregon in May, 1960, addresses the opening ceremonies of the Riverside Little League. Mike Gefroh, who caught Kennedy's ceremonial first pitch, remarked that Kennedy made him more aware of politics and that, later that year as he watched on television the Democratic Convention in Los Angeles, "the suspense of the balloting was a terrific initiation into the political process." (Photo: © Argenta Images)

Dear Craig

Thank you for my letter and my helicopter and my card of the mountain —

I want to play with you if you come in my house

Craig I have time to draw you a picture

glider plane with no propeller

Not very good planes

Dead swordfish bitted by a shark

A drawing for and a letter to eleven-ye[ar-old] Craig McNamara, son of Defense Sec[retary] Robert McNamara, from John F. [Ken]nedy Jr., age three, less than a month [after] President Kennedy's assassination. The [letter] presumably dictated by the young bo[y and] written by his mother Jacqueline Ke[nnedy.] Mr. McNamara remarks: "I'm not [sure] that had the president lived, his visi[on of] Camelot, the New Frontier, and the g[oals of] his Cabinet members would have be[en ful]filled. He was taken away from us in [a] violent and critical fashion." (Images co[urtesy] Mr. McNamara)

John Kennedy, following his nomination for the presidency by the Democratic Party in 1960, greets his nephew Christopher Kennedy Lawford and his sister Sydney in Los Angeles. "(M)y uncle sat down and said he had just been nominated to be President of the United States, that it was going to be a very hard job, and that he wanted my help." (Photo: © Argenta Images)

John Lewis, then-chairman of the Student Non-violent Coordinating Committee, addresses thousands of civil rights supporters at the March on Washington, August 28, 1963. He and five other civil rights leaders, including the Rev. Dr. Martin Luther King, Jr., were congratulated later that day by President Kennedy in the Oval Office. (Photo: © Bettmann/Corbis)

Hearst reporter Marianne Means greets President Kennedy at a diplomatic dinner in Washington in 1962. Means first met then-Senator John Kennedy when she was a college student at the University of Nebraska and mentioned she wanted to be a journalist. "He said, 'Well, when you come to Washington, look me up.' Being naïve, I took him at his word." (Photo: © Bettmann/Corbis)

Fifteen-year-old Michael Medved, the future author, film critic, commentator, and syndicated radio show host, beams for the camera after the self-proclaimed "political geek" won an essay contest on American history. "I recently found my notebook from that period. It has a very carefully hand-lettered 'Kennedy for President' message on it. Of course, I spelled his name wrong—'Kenedy.'"(Photo: © Los Angeles Public Library Photo Collection)

Then-Minnesota Attorney General Walter Mondale meets with John Kennedy at the White House in 1963. Reflecting on JFK's assassination, Mondale remarks, "There still is a horrible sense of loss nearly fifty years later. We were robbed."(Photo: © Minnesota Historical Society)

Casey Murrow, left, observes his father, broadcast journalist Edward R. Murrow, and his mother Janet Murrow, joking with President Kennedy at the White House in March of 1961, on the day his father was sworn in as the director of the United States Information Agency. (Photo: © Cecil W. Stoughton, White House Collection, John F. Kennedy Presidential Library)

Al Neuharth, shown here in 1950 as the editor of the *Volante*, the student newspaper at the University of South Dakota in Vermillion, later founded *USA Today*, the Freedom Forum, and the Newseum, in Washington, D.C. He last saw John Kennedy at a speech in Miami, just a few days before the president's assassination. (Photo: © South Dakota Public Radio Collection, University of South Dakota Archives and Special Collections)

Father Oscar Huber walked three blocks from his parish to wave to President and Mrs. Kennedy as they drove through Dallas. Less than ninety minutes later, he administered the Last Rites of the Catholic Church to John Kennedy at Parkland Memorial Hospital. "During this most trying ordeal, the perfect composure maintained by Mrs. Kennedy was beyond comprehension. I will never forget the blank stare in her eyes and the signs of agony on her face." (Photo: © DeAndreis-Rosati Memorial Archives, DePaul University Archives, Chicago, Illinois, DePaul University)

Major League Baseball player Jimmy Piersall exchanges a baseball with then-Senator John Kennedy for a copy of Kennedy's book, *Profiles in Courage*. Kennedy's secretary, Evelyn Lincoln, was a fan of Piersall and later invited him to meet President Kennedy in the Oval Office. (Photo acquired through John F. Kennedy Library and Museum)

Future environmental lawyer and activist Robert F. Kennedy Jr. presents his uncle with a salamander in the Oval Office in 1961. He later writes, "(T)here had been a sense of foreboding even within our family as he and Aunt Jackie prepared for the trip (to Dallas)." (Photo: © Abbie Rowe, White House Collection, John F. Kennedy Presidential Library)

Actor Cliff Robertson meets with John Kennedy in the Oval Office shortly after completing the film *PT 109* about Kennedy's naval career. The movie, Robertson said, "was a seminal film for me, because of the attention it received, as well as the respect that President Kennedy had garnered from the American public." (Photo: © Cecil W. Stoughton, White House Collection; courtesy Mr. Robertson's daughter, Stephanie Saunders)

At a meeting during the Cuban Missile Crisis in October 1962, Secretary of State Dean Rusk looks on as President Kennedy examines a document in the White House Cabinet Room. Secretary of Defense Robert McNamara is seated to the right; Press Secretary Pierre Salinger stands at the rear. (Photo: © Cecil W. Stoughton, White House Collection, John F. Kennedy Presidential Library)

John Seigenthaler Sr. with Robert Kennedy. Seigenthaler first met John Kennedy when he covered the Senate for *The Tennessean* and later worked in the Department of Justice under Robert Kennedy. He was present when President-elect Kennedy convinced his younger brother to serve as attorney general, remarking, "So that's it, General. Let's grab our balls and go." (Photo courtesy Mr. Seigenthaler)

Ira Seiler, M.D., examines an infant as part of his pediatric practice. In 1960, as a second-year resident at Georgetown Hospital in Washington, D.C., Dr. Seiler saved the life of John Kennedy Jr. who was born not breathing. He later received a personal note of thanks from then-President-elect Kennedy, and three years later, upon learning of JFK's assassination, wrote a letter of condolence to Jacqueline Kennedy. (Photo courtesy Dr. Seiler)

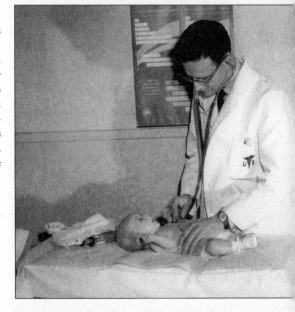

CBS News Producer Sanford ("Sandy") Socolow, left, works alongside Anchor Walter Cronkite. Socolow ended his planned vacation abruptly on November 22, 1963, to work four days with little sleep "looking for people to interview and feeding Cronkite and then later Charles Collingwood who spelled him." (Photo courtesy Mr. Socolow)

Al Spivak, reporter for United Press International, far left, joins President Kennedy and other journalists saying farewell to a visitor leaving by helicopter from the Kennedy compound in Hyannis Port, Massachusetts. "JFK felt that it was his job to protect the country and the world against Khrushchev. That was a great achievement. It kept the country out of a Third World War." (Photo courtesy Mr. Spivak)

President Kennedy greets Air Force One Pilot Colonel James B. Swindal and his wife, Emily, at a reception on the South Lawn of the White House. Swindal's son, James L. Swindal, said his father, who flew missions in the China-Burma-India Theater during World War II, referred to the flight back to Washington from Dallas on November 22, 1963 as "the most awful mission I've ever been on." (Photo courtesy Mr. Swindal)

NBC White House Correspondent Sander Vanocur, center, and other journalists corner John Kennedy at the 1960 Democratic National Convention the day after JFK secured the presidential nomination. The senator had just left a meeting with Senator Lyndon B. Johnson to discuss the vice presidential position on the ticket. (Photo: © Associated Press)

Mortimer Caplin, Commissioner of the Internal Revenue Service, second from right, comments to Kennedy aide, Kennedy O'Donnell, far right, after the president met with staff at the IRS offices. Kennedy, seen joking with Treasury C. Douglas Dillon, was the first and remains the only president to visit the IRS offices in Washington, D.C. (Photo: © Abbie Rowe, White House Collection, John F. Kennedy Presidential Library)

Assistant Attorney General Nicholas deB. Katzenbach, left, confers with Attorney General Robert F. Kennedy and Herbert J. Miller, another Department of Justice official. The artwork was a creation of Kennedy's son David. Katzenbach said he believed the issue of civil rights was "the most difficult problem we faced during the Kennedy presidency." (Photo: ©Bettmann/Corbis)

Bob Schieffer, who looks more like a detective than a reporter with the Fort Worth *Star-Telegram*, wore his "Dick Tracy hat" and trench coat while escorting Lee Harvey Oswald's mother Marguerite into the Dallas Police Department on the afternoon of November 22, 1963. After a few hours, an FBI agent called his bluff, moments before he was to question the accused assassin. "It would be the biggest story I almost got but didn't," he says. (Photo courtesy Mr. Schieffer)

Harris Wofford, associate director of the Peace Corps, chats with President Kennedy during an event with Peace Corps volunteers on the South Lawn of the White House in August of 1962. Wofford previously served as JFK's special assistant on civil rights and later represented Pennsylvania in the U.S. Senate. (Photo: © Rowland Scherman, Peace Corps/John F. Kennedy Presidential Library and Museum)

Fort Worth congressman Jim Wright, far left, the future Speaker of the House of Representatives, addresses a crowd outside the Texas Hotel, just prior to President Kennedy's remarks on the morning of November 22, 1963. Vice President Lyndon Johnson, who would take the presidential oath of office just a few hours later, and Texas Governor John Connally (waving) are to the left of Kennedy. (Photo: © Cecil W. Stoughton, White House Collection, John F. Kennedy Presidential Library)

SECTION FIVE:

Family and Friends

✧ Dr. Bob Arnot
Physician, journalist, author

"For all of us, it was the end of hope. It's one of the few moments that I remember—a particular time, a particular day."

HE was the only hero I ever had.

I first saw him while he was giving a speech at Boston College. He was running for president. I was twelve years old. I was mesmerized. I had never met anybody so electric, so charismatic. It was the most memorable event of my whole youth. I had that famous picture of JFK in his pinstriped suit right up above my bed, a three-by two-foot poster.

We lived, dreamed, and breathed John F. Kennedy. We knew members of the administration. I've been down to the Kennedy compound, playing tennis with Joe Kennedy (eldest son of Robert Kennedy). I was there the day Arnold Schwarzenegger first arrived and was down there for his wedding to Maria Shriver. It was spectacular.

My father had been a lifelong Republican. But he listened to one of the Kennedy-Nixon debates in 1960. He took his Nixon poster down and ripped it up and said, "I've had it. I'm voting for JFK." I think it was the only time he voted for a Democrat. We lived in the most Republican town in the world, Wellesley Hills, Massachusetts.

When he was president, there were a couple of occasions when I might have seen him from a distance. There was a motorcade in Boston where I saw him. Our best friends growing up were a family called Fulham. The father, Jack Fulham, was chairman of Kennedy's campaign organization in Massachusetts. One time, he was invited to a

White House dinner and sat with Marjorie Merriweather Post. He was dying to turn the china over to see where it was made, but of course, he didn't want to sitting next to the etiquette lady. But then she turns the plate over to look!

On November 22, 1963, I was in Mr. Leyden's chemistry class in the tenth grade. There was a TV set in the room and it was announced the president had been shot. And we all went home, and I learned later he died. I never cried so hard in my life. Not when my dog died. We just sat by the television for days afterward. For all of us, it was the end of hope. It's one of the few moments that I remember—a particular time, a particular day.

The most devastating image was when Air Force One came in at Andrews and the ambulance came by. We finally knew it was true.

My mother always told me, from the first minute I could understand language, "To whom much is given, much is expected." She said that all the time to all of us. It was an interesting message with no way to execute it. Then JFK came along with the Peace Corps.

JFK was pure inspiration. It wasn't necessarily inspiration just to join the Peace Corps or to do anything in particular. We all loved the Kennedy lifestyle. We spent summers down at Martha's Vineyard and Cape Cod. It was the same circle, all the same people, and so it could not be any closer to home.

And then to have a Texan come in, especially LBJ, after all that glamour. It was devastating. Not that I have anything against Texans.

Kennedy's legacy is inspiration and youth. Rather than anything specific, it was pure, intoxicating exhilaration and inspiration.

✑ Charles Bartlett
Journalist, introduced John Kennedy to Jacqueline Bouvier

"I talked to him the night before he left for Texas. Something nudged me to call him to say goodbye. I didn't normally do that."

I met him in 1946 in Palm Beach, Florida. It was just before he announced his plans to run for Congress. Jack Kennedy and I got along immediately because he had a very, very good sense of humor which came through quickly. We nursed a mutual interest in politics and we knew many of the same people. There was a lot of common ground.

He was very aware that he was being pulled into politics because his brother (Joseph Kennedy, Jr.) had been killed. Someone in the family had to take on public life. It was up to him. Jack was ready to leave journalism. He felt that as a journalist one could not do much to help the country. He had been writing during the war for Hearst, but he was ready to give up writing because he believed he could do more as an elected official. He was ready to go into politics.

I watched JFK's adjustment to the Washington scene. He was quickly immersed in the House because he was an instinctive politician with a good feel for the game. He had a quick mind, and his thinking went to the heart of a problem, avoiding the frills in a situation. He grabbed hard onto the issues he cared about and quickly matured as a legislator.

He told me he was going to run for president about four years before 1960. I was surprised, and I said, "Jack, you've never been around except to Palm Beach and Hyannis Port. You don't really know this country at all. Why not wait eight years?"

And he said, "We'll see. I'm going to get around."

And he did so intently that I felt by the time he was nominated that he was thoroughly immersed in the nation's political geography and its disparities.

I recall that in 1952 he was invited to address the Chattanooga Chamber of Commerce. This was his first exposure to a Southern audience. He did well, riding on the wave of his considerable charm.

When Jack came back to Washington from Boston in 1953 (after being elected to the Senate), it was clear he wanted to find a wife. He knew it could be awkward to campaign as a bachelor even though he was known by friends to have a serious interest in women. So he was looking, really looking. Jackie Bouvier was a great friend of (my wife) Martha's and mine. We immediately thought of her. She was very good looking, very bright, and rather elegant. We thought she might be the one and we were right.

They met at a very small dinner in our house in Georgetown. The spark was immediately struck, and it kept the romance alive through months in which JFK was away tending to his base in Massachusetts.

Credit for the next phase really belongs to Martha, because Jackie was already engaged to a nice fellow from Manhattan. This was not, it appeared, a hot romance, so Martha urged Jackie to invite JFK to escort her to the Dancing Class, a Washington social ritual. The evening clearly went well and this was the beginning of a courtship that went on to the alter. That was in December (of 1952) and they were married in September.

I talked to him the night before he left for Texas. Something nudged me to call him to say goodbye. I didn't normally do that. I called about nine o'clock at night and found him in a very, very good mood. He gave no hint of foreboding. He had often talked to me about how easy it would be to kill a president. He believed an assassin would have no problem if he (the assassin) really wanted to do it. But this fatalistic sense was not on his mind the night before he left for Texas.

We talked of the political scene. His old friend Abe Ribicoff in the Senate had made a rather sharp criticism of him in a speech on the Senate floor. It was reported in the press and I saw it.

And I asked Jack in our last talk, "Why is Abe knocking you?"

"That's easy," he laughed. "Abe wants to be the first Jewish president and that's a long alley with no cans to kick."

(On November 22, 1963) I was in my office banging out a story on a typewriter. The news came over the wire service. It was a huge shock. My first thought was to go see Bobby. But then I thought he would have all kinds of people swarming around him. So I just sat there and thought about all that Jack would have liked to have done and about Jackie.

I didn't cover the funeral. In fact, I did not cover anything involving Kennedy. That was a problem for a newspaper man—a very personal friend was the president of the United States. I made a decision: Nothing mattered except his success in the White House. I don't think I wrote about anything that was not already made public. I had no desire to exploit the friendship.

That night, we all went out to Bethesda Naval Hospital while doctors did the post-mortem. There were many friends and family there, and all seemed weighted with a glum sense of shock. JFK's death was a huge loss for me and for his friends. In all my conversations with JFK, he had never dwelled on negative gossip regarding individuals. He seemed to me in his private moments to nurse no animosities. In dealing with almost everyone, JFK was fun. He stood for politics at its best.

Kennedy was a model for politicians. In terms of issues, I don't think he really had the time to do a lot of things he wanted.

In the days before he was killed, he was in very good spirits. But in our conversations, there was one thing really on his mind—the fact that he had been betrayed by Israel on nuclear weapons. He had just learned that one of the people who worked in the development of the Israeli bomb came to the CIA and told them. And the CIA told the President. The issue never blew up and he never talked about it publicly. But Kennedy was absolutely furious. He was raging mad. He felt it was a personal betrayal.

He said, "I've done everything I can to help these people, and this government gave me no hint about what they were up to. Not one hint. And I want to tell you one thing. As long as I am president, they will never build another bomb, because I'm going to have inspectors in their laboratories all the time to insure they're not producing another bomb. There will be no second Israeli bomb." He was really firm, really angry. It was the first time I ever saw him this angry.

Our conversations centered on this development for much of the last two or three weeks of his life. For him, it was a big issue. But it was the kind of issue a politician facing an election would not take to the public.

He talked about it (death) several times with me. I suppose any president would because assassination is an obvious hazard. But we had a talk about it in September before he was shot, I remember, up on the boat off Hyannis Port. It was just interesting that we would discuss it at some length. I mean, you know, subjects like what Lyndon would be like as president. He, by the way, told me that he liked LBJ very much.

He had that kind of mind that he was always talking about all the eventualities. I mean, on that same afternoon he talked about what he was going to do when he got out of the presidency. He said he thought he'd like to be ambassador to Italy if a friendly regime was in power. He thought that would be a good place because Jackie would like it, because he would be out of the country, and therefore, the man who took the presidency wouldn't be in his way.

I do remember one time in Middleburg he was driving along a back country road, and a car sped by the Secret Service car and by us. And he was for a moment shaken and he said, "The Secret Service should have blocked that car." But to cover his concern, he joked, "Charley, that man could have shot you."

❧ Benjamin C. Bradlee
Journalist

"We all rose, stricken and uncomfortable, as (Jacqueline Kennedy) came slowly toward us. When she got to Tony and me her eyes brightened a little, she raised her arms and then lurched into my arms, and sobbed. Then she turned to me and said, 'Oh Benny, do you want to hear what happened?' And then quickly added, 'But not as a reporter for Newsweek, *okay?'"*

I have to confess, I'm not a great historian. And John Kennedy and I did not discuss substantive issues of foreign policy.

I knew John Kennedy accidentally and, with a few exceptions when it was just the two of us playing golf, we got together as a foursome socially—he and his wife and me and my wife. I rarely saw him alone.

Excerpt from *Conversations with Kennedy* by Benjamin C. Bradlee, copyright © 1975 (Used with author's permission):

> As best I can now remember, that first moment came on the afternoon of a sparking late summer day in 1958. My wife and I bumped into the Kennedys during an afternoon walk in Georgetown. Already casual acquaintances, they now were new neighbors. We talked then for an hour or so in their garden, a few doors from our house, and we drew each other as dinner partners later

that night. The subject of those conversations—like so many that followed—was the private lives and public postures of politicians, reporters, and friends.

Our friendship just happened. It was never calculated. I didn't follow any script. We had a great time together. If I had any contribution to his life, it was that we did not have to worry about newspapers or issues. It was a friendship.

Excerpt from *Conversations with Kennedy* by Benjamin C. Bradlee, copyright © 1975 (Used with author's permission):

The sledgehammer news that President Kennedy had been shot came to me while I was browsing through Brentano's book store on my lunch hour. First it was the barely distinguishable whispers of incredulous pedestrians, then all too finally it was the AP ticker in the Newsweek bureau on the twelfth floor of the National Press Building around the corner. It's not enough to say that you can't believe these terrible things as they happen.

Late in the afternoon, Nancy Tuckerman, who was Jackie's social secretary, called to ask Tony and me to come to the White House. . . . About 9:00 Nancy Tuckerman told us that Jackie—and everyone else connected with the slain president—were going directly from Andrews Air Force Base, where Air Force One with the new president aboard would land, to Bethesda Naval Hospital. A final autopsy on the president's body would be performed there, and Jackie was apparently determined to stay as close as she could for as long as she could . . .

The next seven hours have stayed blurred in my mind for all these years, except for the moments right after Jackie entered the hospital suite on the arms of the Irish Mafia in the form of Larry O'Brien and Kenny O'Donnell, men she had never really understood or appreciated, but to whom she turned and clung now, strong men from the Irish political side of the dichotomous

Kennedy, whom Jackie had never met on equal terms, but who now seemed to comfort her more than any of the rest of us.

Her entrance, announced to us by the flashes of photographers' bulbs many stories below us, into that dreary hospital green room is scarred on my soul for the rest of my life. Her pink wool suit was copiously spattered with the blood of her dead husband, when she had cradled his shattered head in her lap. She looked so lovely, I remember thinking incongruously. But a closer look showed her to be dazed, moving ever so slowly, with eyes apparently not taking all of us in.

We all rose, stricken and uncomfortable, as she came slowly toward us. When she got to Tony and me her eyes brightened a little, she raised her arms and then lurched into my arms, and sobbed. After a minute or so she pulled back and greeted Tony in the same way. Then she turned to me and said, "Oh Benny, do you want to hear what happened?" And then quickly added, "But not as a reporter for Newsweek, *okay?"*

I felt badly that she obviously felt she had to be that careful in that awful moment about the old problem and was about to proclaim my innocence as usual, when she started telling us about the actual shooting. I can remember now only the strangely graceful arc she described with her right hand as she told us that part of the president's head had been blown away by one bullet. She moved in a trance to talk to each of us there and to new friends as they arrived, ignoring the advice of friends and doctors to get some sleep and to change out of her bloody clothes. Those were some kind of dreadful badge of the disaster she had been through, and no one could persuade her to remove them.

I was asked to be an usher, and as a result, I walked from the White House to St. Matthew's Cathedral as part of the procession. I remember that walk very, very well.

Excerpt from *A Good Life: Newspapering and Other Adventures,* by Benjamin C. Bradlee, Copyright © 1995 (Used with author's permission):

> *In the weeks after Kennedy was assassinated, Tony and I spent a couple of emotional weekends at Atoka, the Kennedys' country house in Middleburg, Virginia, with Jackie, trying with no success to talk about something else, or someone else. Too soon and too emotional for healing, we proved only that the three of us had very little in common without the essential fourth.*

If people read the book *Conversations with Kennedy,* I think they will realize that I'm not a great historian. Quite simply, a friend of mine got elected President of the United States.

∞ Robert F. Kennedy Jr.
Nephew, environmental activist

"(T)here had been a sense of foreboding even within our family as he and Aunt Jackie prepared for the trip. Jack made an unscheduled trip to Cape Cod to say goodbye to my ailing grandfather. The night before the trip, Mummy found Jack distant and brooding at a dinner for the Supreme Court justices."

(NOTE: This reflection was published previously by *The Huffington Post*. Used with author's permission)

On November 22, 1963, Mummy picked me up early from Sidwell Friends School in Washington, D.C. Driving home to Hickory Hill in Northern Virginia, I noticed that all the district flags were at half-staff. Mummy told us that a bad man had shot Uncle Jack and that he was in heaven.

Daddy's friend and former football teammate, Dean Markham, a Justice Department Rackets Division Attorney, picked up my little brother David at Our Lady of Victory. "Why did they kill Uncle Jack?" David asked him. Dean, an ex-marine, combat veteran, known as the toughest linesmen on the "GI-Bill Squad"—the toughest football team in Harvard University's history—wasn't tough enough to field that question. He wept silently all the way to our driveway.

When I got home, Daddy was walking in the yard with Brumus, our giant black Newfoundland, and Rusty, the Irish Setter. We ran and hugged him. We were all crying. He told us, "He had the most wonderful life, and he never had a sad day."

Neither Beck, Hannity, nor Savage nor the hate merchants at *Fox News* and talk radio can claim to have invented their genre. Toxic right-wing vitriol so dominated the public airwaves from the McCarthy era until 1963 that President Kennedy, that year, launched a citizen's campaign to enforce the Fairness Doctrine, which required accuracy and balance in the broadcast media. Students and civic and religious groups filed more than five hundred complaints against right-wing extremists and hate-mongering commentators before the Federal Communications Commission.

The Dallas, Texas, airwaves were particularly radioactive; preachers and political leaders and local businessmen spewed extremist vitriol on the city's radio and TV stations, inflaming the passions of the city's legions of unhinged fanatics. There was something about the city—a rage or craziness, that, whether sensible or not, seemed to have set the stage for Jack's murder. The *Voice of America*, half an hour after the assassination, described Dallas as "the center of extreme right wing." The Texas town was such a seething cauldron of right-wing depravity that historian William Manchester portrayed it as recalling the final days of the Weimar Republic.

"Mad things happened," reported Manchester. "Huge billboards screamed 'Impeach Earl Warren.'" Jewish stores were smeared with crude swastikas. Fanatical young matrons swayed in public to the chant, "Stevenson's going to die—his heart will stop, stop, stop and he will burn, burn, burn!"

The mercantile elite that ruled the city carefully cultivated the seeds of hate. Radical-right broadsides were distributed in public schools; the Kennedy name was booed in classrooms; junior executives who refused to attend radical seminars were blackballed and fired.

Manchester continued: "Dallas had become the mecca for medicine show evangelists of the National Independence Convention, the Christian Crusades, the Minutemen, the John Birch and Patrick Henry Societies and the headquarters of right wing oil man, H.L. Hunt, and his dubious activities. . .The city's mayor, Earl Carroll, a right wing co-founder of the John Birch Society, was known as "the socialist mayor of Dallas" because he maintained his affiliation with the Democratic Party."

Dallas's oil and gas barons who routinely denounced JFK as a "comsymp" (Communist sympathizer) had unbottled the genie of populist rage and harnessed it to the cause of radical ideology, anti-government fervor, and corporate dominion.

Uncle Jack's speech in Dallas was to have been an explosive broadside against the right wing. He found Dallas's streets packed five deep with Kennedy Democrats, but among them were the familiar ornaments of presidential hatred; high-flying confederate flags and hundreds of posters adorning the walls and streets of Dallas showing Jack's picture inscribed with, "Wanted for Treason." One man held a posterboard saying, "you a traitor [sic]." Other placards accused him of being a Communist. When public school PA systems announced Jack's assassination, Dallas school children as young as the fourth grade applauded. A Birmingham radio caller declared that, "Any white man who did what he did for niggers should be shot."

As my siblings and I visited the White House to console my cousins John and Caroline, a picket paraded out front with a sign "God punished JFK."

Jack had received myriad warnings against visiting the right-wing Texas city. Indeed, there had been a sense of foreboding even within our family as he and Aunt Jackie prepared for the trip. Jack made an unscheduled trip to Cape Cod to say goodbye to my ailing grandfather. The night before the trip, Mummy found Jack distant and brooding at a dinner for the Supreme Court justices. He was very fond of Mummy, but for the first time ever, he looked right through her.

Jack's death forced a national bout of self-examination.

In 1964, Americans repudiated the forces of right-wing hatred and violence with an historic landslide in the presidential election between LBJ and Goldwater. For a while, the advocates of right-wing extremism receded from the public forum. Now they have returned with a vengeance—to the broadcast media and to prominent positions in the political landscape.

ᏂᎤ Christopher Kennedy Lawford
Nephew, author, filmmaker

"Jack Kennedy overcame serious health problems and that's in part what made him great. We often forget that."

I was very young when my uncle was around, but I have recollections of him coming to visit my parents in Los Angeles when I was growing up on the beach here. I do remember the 1960 Democratic convention. I went to the convention when I was five years old. My mom was a delegate. I remember being amazed by this enormous spectacle in the LA Sports Arena.

I remember sitting in a chair and then later being awakened in my uncle's hotel room. I was sitting on his bed and my uncle sat down and said he had just been nominated to be President of the United States, that it was going to be a very hard job, and that he wanted my help. I responded that I would help him, but that I was kind of tired right then, and I wanted my mom to take me home.

My uncle had a lot of energy obviously. We were a big Irish family; there was a lot of laughter. When he came to my home, we would go swimming in the ocean. I got to raise the presidential flag when he came to our home. People would gather outside our fence and try to look into our home. There was always a sense that he was very important and that people were very attentive to him. Everyone was always energized when he was around.

I remember going to Washington and being in motorcades with my uncle. I got carsick once and threw up on his assistant, Kenny O'Donnell.

I remember November 22 very vividly. I was in school—St. Martin's Roman Catholic School. I was treated very well by the nuns there; it had nothing to do with me and everything to do with my family. I was in class and these women came to the door and they looked distraught. There was obviously something going on. They kept looking at me. I didn't know why. Then they motioned me to come over. They said something about my family. I don't remember if they said the family member was hurt or dead. But whatever it was, it was very bad.

I thought they might have been referring to my grandfather, Joseph Kennedy. He was old and I remember, as a kid, you think those are the people who are going to die. My uncle was way too energetic, way too young, and way too full of life to be dead. And, at that age, I did not understand shootings.

Obviously, this was a big deal. They asked me if I wanted to go home. I said "No," because it did not occur to me that I would want to go home. Later, at recess, we played stickball, and I remember being very prolific in my hitting that day. There was a certain energy. Up until then, nobody really focused on me. That kind of attention, that energy, is powerful. People were paying attention to me in a way that energized me. There was a level of concern, and in my family, that pity, any self-pity we never really went down that road. That sense of wanting to take care of me, I didn't want any part of.

I later went home that day, and my mother was obviously unbelievably affected by this. I don't remember my father's reaction. There were a lot of people in front of my house. I went outside and walked among them and began to get a feeling of tension, which I did not particularly like. Then later, my mother asked me if I wanted to go to the funeral. I was having a friend spend the weekend and I did not want to disappoint him, and so I said, "No," not really grasping what I was saying "no" to.

I understood there was something big going on, but at the time, I thought it didn't really have anything to do with me. Also, there was a certain amount of denial about death and what death really was. It was the first death I ever experienced. I must say that for a long, long time, I really regretted that decision, in the sense I had really let my family down, my mother down particularly. I felt bad for many, many years. In hindsight, it was selfish. I was thinking how I did not want to disappoint my friend. That gives you a sense of a kid's viewpoint. My sister Sydney went to the funeral with my mother.

My uncle was very smart. I later went to Cuba and produced a film on the Cuban Missile Crisis called *Thirteen Days*. Obviously, Cuba played a big part in my uncle's presidency and in this country's more recent history. There were weapons of mass destruction in Cuba. The Soviets would have attacked. (Then-Cuban President Fidel) Castro told me that he had given orders to his field commanders that if American planes came, they were to rush to the missile sites and yell to the Soviet troops, "Fire the missiles! Fire the missiles!" The Soviets, Castro said, in the panic of it would have fired the missiles.

His legacy—the promise of it, the youth of it, the vigor of it—was something people respond to. But substantively, his legacy includes his commitment to the arts, to mental health issues, to those things I care about. In terms of the civil rights movement, poverty—all the things that Lyndon Johnson was able to create in the Great Society—were legacies of my uncle. Those things are missing today. We have a country today where people are so concerned about their own dwindling assets, they can't seem to get out of their own way and think about anyone but themselves. It's a shame. My uncle's legacy of "Ask not what your country can do for you. Ask what you can do for your country," is a theme that has gone by the wayside. It's really unfortunate. Unless we get back to the things that made us great, our country will die on the vine.

My uncle struggled with a lot of illness and a lot of issues with regard to those illnesses. We grew up with this ethic and it came from him: in order to achieve great things in life, you have to overcome something great. He ascribed to that and he passed that on to us. There are millions of people in our society who have struggled with great things and they are marginalized. They've dealt with poverty, or mental health issues, or addiction issues, and they are not considered assets to our society. Jack Kennedy overcame serious health problems and that's in part what made him great.

We often forget that.

❧ Frank Mankiewicz
Peace Corps director in Peru, president of NPR, press secretary to Robert F. Kennedy

"We've got a president who stays up until midnight watching television."

I was about to go to Peru as the first director of the Peace Corps in that country. That would have been 1962, and I was waiting in Washington because there had been an armed overthrow of the elected government in Peru, and we were withholding the volunteers until democracy was restored. Meanwhile, President Kennedy was in the process of visiting every government agency just to say "hello" and be seen. And he got around to the Peace Corps, which would have been January or February of '62.

We all gathered in the auditorium, across the street from the White House in the Chamber of Commerce building. And (Peace Corps Director) Sarge Shriver asked me if I would stay on the platform and sort of entertain the troops while he went across the street to the White House to escort the President.

So I was telling some stories about my early visits to Latin America, and pretty soon there's a big commotion at the back of the hall, and here comes the president with Sarge Shriver. Photographers. Spotlights. He comes down the aisle, comes up on the stage. And Sarge is introducing him to people, and he says to the president, "This is Frank Mankiewicz. He's our director in Peru."

The president shook my hand. Then he stopped and looked at me and said, "I saw you on Mike Wallace's show last year talking about Peru."

And I thought, Jesus, huh? We've got a president who stays up until midnight watching television.

But I was very impressed with him. He was very tan, very fit, very energetic. He had that quality of talking to someone or listening to them as though they were the only other person in the room, or indeed the country. A very serious listener.

(On November 22) I was then in the second city in Peru, called Arequipa. We had some Peace Corps volunteers there. I was walking on the street, probably a block or two from the Peace Corps office, headed somewhere. And I noticed a big commotion. People talking. A man came toward me weeping. Physically crying.

And I stopped him, and I said in Spanish, "What's happened? What's going on?"

And he said to me, "The president's been shot."

And I said (and this is all in Spanish), "You mean President Belaúnde?" who was, of course, the president of Peru.

And he said to me (in Spanish), "I wish it were." A Peruvian. I always found that a very, very impressive response. Not because he wished ill of their president.

And so I then rushed back to the Peace Corps office, and we started hearing reports on short-wave radio . . . I told the rest of the volunteers. I checked with Washington—how serious this was. And we simply called off whatever activities we had, and I made an effort to try to get the volunteers together. We missed the funeral, and of course, there was no TV.

I went back to Lima to go to the (U.S.) embassy as quickly as I could. I remember spending time with the ambassador. On the following Sunday morning, I was at the embassy and the ambassador came in, maybe from church service or something, and he said, "I've heard the most horrible news. Someone had killed Lee Harvey Oswald in the Dallas police station." That was the first I had heard of that.

I was inspired by President Kennedy then and I think I remain so. He was our president. He was from our generation, which was quite a change. Presidents up to then had always been father figures. Here was a man who was a few years older than I. He fought in "our" war. Like

10

me, he was a World War II veteran. Young, vigorous. Thinking about the same things we were, and I think that was what contributed largely to my—and I think my cohorts'—inspiration by President Kennedy. Here was a guy who had been to school when I was. He left school, went into the service. Fought in the service. Came out; graduated. He was one of our guys.

I think his legacy is pretty good. I know there's a lot of preoccupation with scandal now. A lot of things have happened in his family. But on the other hand, here's an extraordinary family. I'm not sure anyone (in the family) since Joe Kennedy has devoted more than an hour to personal aggrandizement—to making money, to the American dream of becoming a rich person. I think they all have a strong social instinct. I know Robert Kennedy's kids all do. It's quite an extraordinary family.

We (Robert Kennedy and I) met once again in Panama. In those days, when you flew from Washington to Lima, you had to stop in Panama for re-fueling. The stop in Panama was usually for an hour and usually between two, or three, or four o'clock in the morning. I was having a meeting of all my country directors in Panama at the time, and I happened to read in the local paper that Kennedy was going to be coming through on this flight early the next morning.

So, I thought, I'll go down to the airport and say, "hello."

So, at three o'clock, maybe two forty-five, I showed up at the airport, and there's the airplane. And, of course, there was no security, I just walked over. And there were a couple of newspaper reporters there.

They said, "When's the press conference?"

I said, "I don't know about any press conference. But I'll find out."

So, I went up on board to the plane. (The airline) had fixed up two of the overhead compartments into berths. Robert Kennedy was in one and Ethel was in the other—in pajamas. So I came on board and I told him about these reporters, and he started to get out of bed and get dressed. And somebody said, "There's no press conference scheduled. They just showed up."

And he said to me, "If I don't come down to the press conference, who gets hurt the most, those reporters or their publishers?"

I said, "Undoubtedly, the reporters will get hurt."

He said, "That's what I thought."

He started to get dressed. And then one of his staffers said to him, "Senator, why don't you stay here? Stay in your bed, and we'll bring the reporters on board. And you can have the press conference right here. And that way, you won't have to get up and get dressed."

Robert Kennedy looked at me and said, "What do you think of that?"

And I thought, "There's a key question here."

I didn't have a lot of time to think, but I'm very happy to say that I said to him, "Senator, I think that's what President De Gaulle would do."

He laughed. And said, "Yeah, I agree. C'mon."

So he got up, got dressed, and we went down and had a little press conference. If he had done the press conference in his pajamas, I don't think we ever would have stopped hearing about it.

❧ John Seigenthaler Sr.
Journalist, author, First
Amendment historian

"(John Kennedy) poured me coffee, and then he
was standing with the pot in one hand and his
cup in the other, and said (to his brother Robert),
'So that's it, General. Let's grab
our balls and go.'"

MY first encounter with President John F. Kennedy was in the spring
of 1957 when I was a reporter for the Nashville *Tennessean* assigned to
Washington. My assignment included covering the hearings of what
was called the Senate Select Committee on Improper Activities in
Labor and Management.

I thought (and my view was shared by many correspondents covering the nation's capital) that Jack was in a class by himself—an intellectual, who also was a street-wise politician, having been elected to
the U. S. House of Representatives, and subsequently to the Senate—
and who was ambitious to run to succeed President Eisenhower in the
White House.

I was not alone among the reporters who put him in a class by
himself. Thinking back on it, I realize that while my sense of that was
a "first impression," it did not come with an initial handshake or as
a result of a few casual conversations. It was, really, an impression,
strengthened and confirmed gradually, as I got to interact with him
while he was in the Senate.

Later, in 1958, I was a Nieman fellow at Harvard, and by the time I arrived in Boston in September, Jack was running for reelection to the Senate. Already the press was speculating that this race for the Senate was a prelude to a 1960 run for the White House.

Our Nieman class—twelve journalists from across the nation and five from abroad—urged me from the first day to try to get Jack to come sit in on one of our weekly afternoon wine-beer-and-cheese seminars. There was some hesitation about it. It took a couple of phone calls to Ted Reardon, Jack's administrative assistant, but finally Ted called back. Jack accepted the invitation. And he came.

In fact, he showed up a bit early that afternoon, and it was a mark of the man that he was interested in knowing about my classmates. Where were they from? What news organizations did they represent? What was he or she like? As the session started, and we began to put questions to them, I noted that he would begin his responses by addressing the questioner as "Mister Turner" or "Mister Morgan" or "Mister Parasuram." That kept the session rather formal, but still, his humor sometimes self-effacing, was calculated to set a tone that resulted in our questions beginning, "Senator" or "Mister Kennedy." Perhaps half the class was his age, a couple perhaps his senior, and some of their questions were pointed. But I thought his demeanor set the tone throughout: formal, respectful, friendly.

A few years later, I watched him during presidential press conferences, and thought back to that session with my Nieman class. He knew many of the journalists popping questions in those press conferences on a first name basis—but still it always was "Mister." And he had that same self-effacing sense of humor that let him laugh at himself as well as with others. He would take a tough question, respond with a wry comment, and, as the wheels turned, he would craft a substantive answer. It was a natural gift—this "think while you talk"—one shared by few politicians I have observed.

The Nieman Fellows seminar that afternoon was terrific for all of us. We were happy that he did not seem at all pressured to leave. When it was over, I escorted him out to a waiting car, and he said, "I'm going to be moving around the greater Boston area during my campaign, and if you have any additional time while you are here at Harvard, any time you would like to ride with me, I'd be glad to have you along."

I took him up on it. On one occasion, we were stuck in traffic in Boston, and Johnny Powers, who was a member of the Massachusetts legislature and quite an astute fellow, told the driver, "When you get to the next corner, pull over." Powers tapped Jack on the shoulder and said, "Jack, look up ahead. That's Mr. McCaffrey painting his house, and he is the key to this neighborhood. You need to have a conversation with him. Just a quick hello."

The senator got out of the car, went to the ladder, and called up to the fellow. The old man looked down, at first seeming puzzled, or harassed. Sort of irritated, he called down, "What is it? What do you want?" Maybe the sun was in his eyes. He didn't recognize him. (This was the first time I ever noticed Jack had any problems with his back. He started up the ladder with great care and took those steps one at a time and very slowly, under some stress—one foot up, and then the other; one foot up, and then the other.)

He had taken a few steps up when the old fellow finally recognized him and said, "Oh, Jack, Jack Kennedy! I'm coming down. I want to see you." And down he comes, Jack now backing down, still feeling some stress. Then they were on the sidewalk, shaking hands and into a conversation about how the campaign was going. Jack says something like, "You ask me? I'm asking you. How are we doing?"

Within minutes, passersby and people in the neighborhood started flocking around them, and it turned into a street corner rally. The U.S. marshal got out of the car and had to direct traffic. Jack had a ball. Mr. McCaffrey would introduce him to people and say, "This is so and so, and his brother, he was in the Navy like you." Or he would say, "This is Pat Egan, and his brother Joe or Uncle Charlie, you remember, is the head waiter (or maybe dishwasher) at such and such restaurant." And Jack would say, "Oh yes, I've eaten there." Or, "I remember him." It was warm and funny to watch. As (House Speaker) Tip O'Neill later said, "All politics is local."

I returned to the newspaper in late October, 1959. During this period, Jack Kennedy's plans to run for president were rapidly moving forward. Jack's formal announcement came in early January, 1960—no surprise to anyone since the media had been reporting it for weeks in advance.

By spring, Bob (Robert Kennedy) was calling, asking if I would be interested in coming to work with him in the campaign as his administrative assistant. There finally came a point when I felt I needed a change, and in late June, I called Bob to ask if he still was looking for an administrative assistant. He was. The new editor, knowing that I was grousing (as were several of my colleagues), granted me a leave from August through the November election.

Immediately after the election, Jack took some vacation time in Florida, and one day while playing golf, ran Bob's name up the flag pole as a possible candidate for attorney general. William Lawrence, *The New York Times* reporter in the golf foursome, wrote a story about the possibility, and it drew negative editorial responses including one from *The Times* that complained he had never practiced law as a litigator and had limited experience, except for his work as an attorney in the Senate. It was also reported—accurately—that Joseph P. Kennedy favored the idea, which did not contribute to any groundswell in its favor.

Jack was in the process of naming members of his cabinet and did so every couple of days from the small elevated front porch of his house in Georgetown. One afternoon, Bob asked me if I could devote the next day to driving him to several appointments he had made with various veterans of Washington political life. It would be a tight schedule and take the entire day.

I was staying with Bob at Hickory Hill, and we left the house early. His first appointment was with Harry Truman at the Mayflower Hotel on Connecticut Avenue. I circled the block for half an hour while he talked about his future with the former president. When he got back in the car, it was apparent that it had not gone the way he had hoped. Next, we went to the Supreme Court building where he spent almost an hour with his friend, Associate Justice William O. Douglass. It was clear that Bill Douglass had made him no happier than Truman had.

Then, to the Senate office building where he saw, separately, John McClellan and Bill Fulbright. He seemed no happier. Next, we stopped at the Justice Department (in those days the FBI headquarters was there), and he spent a half-hour with J. Edgar Hoover. Finally, he stopped at the law office of Clark Clifford, and then we headed home. The meetings had not gone well. On the way home, his spirits were down. He was disconsolate. The "wise old heads" he talked with that day (with one exception) did not tell him what he had hoped to hear—that he should become attorney general, or even go to work in the Defense Department. The exception came from Hoover. "He wasn't sincere about it," said Bob. "I could tell. He just wanted me to tell Dad and Jack that he was for it. He was just being political."

Finally, he decided that he would not do it, and that he would call his brother and tell him. Just before he picked up the phone, he said, "This will kill my father." And, so he called his brother and told him he wouldn't do it. He recited the whole series of visits to his brother, Jack, who then said to him, "Well, don't tell me now. I want to have breakfast with you in the morning. Come to the house."

Bob invited me to accompany him next morning. When we walked in, the president-elect was coming down the stairs, smiling. We went in toward the back of the house to the breakfast table. When we were done with our biscuits, eggs, and bacon, Bob says, "Now, can we talk about my situation?"

They were facing each other across the table; I was sitting on Jack's left, Bob's right. The president-elect reached over and grabbed my wrist, and for ten seconds he had eye contact with me and said, "Have you heard the arguments for and against this thing?" And he began to tell me—but now he was talking directly to Bob, their eyes locked. Then he looked at Bob and said, and I'm paraphrasing, "I have named the Cabinet, and I know some of the members. Some I do not know. I have known Rusk casually, but never had any intimate dealings with him. I know Stu Udall—we served in the House together." He went down the list. Then he said to Bob, "There will be times when I need the unvarnished sense of someone who is not interested in anything except the success of my presidency. There will be difficult times." He mentioned civil rights and organized crime. He ran through a list of critical issues and again added, "I need someone who has an interest in the success of my administration."

He went on for about ten minutes. He was direct and to the point—and he made the point in strong terms directly to his brother. It was clear. He needed Bob.

He then said to me, "Do you want more coffee?" He went into the kitchen and came back with the coffee pot. He poured me coffee, and then he was standing with the pot in one hand and his cup in the other, and said, "So that's it, General. Let's grab our balls and go." We got up, and as we walked back out to the front porch, the president-elect told him to come back the next day and they would announce it.

I had told Bob I did not want to work in the administration but wanted to return to journalism. Now he asked me to rethink that decision and come to work for at least a year as his administrative assistant in the Department of Justice. I agreed that very night to do it. I never regretted it.

The oral history projects I have participated in over the years since their deaths have included my reflections on that breakfast meeting at the president-elect's house. One of the revisionist historians on the Kennedy family, C. David Heyman, grossly distorted the account as I recorded it. He wrote that the meeting with me had been contrived by the two brothers, and that they were play-acting, assured that as a journalist I would write it for publication and repeat it to other journalists.

To believe him, you have to accept that Robert Kennedy took those trips to President Truman and the rest on the previous day, and that they "arranged" the phone call the night before—just for my benefit. Both of them knew, of course, that I was not a journalist at the time, had not worked as one for many months—and the fact is that I would not do so for at least 18 months more. Had I leaked what had transpired to some journalist (and I could have done so) both brothers would have considered it a breach of friendship, and I would have forfeited the opportunity to share future confidences with either of them.

On November 22, I was in my office at *The Tennessean*. A reporter from the AP came in. He had a torn strip from the AP wire machine and said, "John, you should read this." I read it and flared with anger and said, "If this is somebody's idea of a joke, it is sick." The reporter burst into tears and said, "I wish it was a joke." I remember it vividly.

That night, the night of the autopsy, I got a call from I believe it was John Nolan at the hospital (Bethesda Naval Hospital), and he said Ethel would like to talk to me, and he put her on the line. Ethel said, "Could you come up?" And I said, "Well sure." I planned to come, but I just didn't want to get in the way. (The next day) I went to the

White House. It seems to be there were all sort of strange people in line as I was going through: Southern governors who really had been knocking Jack Kennedy's ass off for years. I went through the line and I was coming out the back of the foyer and I ran into Ethel. She told me where Bob was. He was in another part of the White House, upstairs. I remember my first impression was that he looked to me like a man who is just in intense pain; he looked like a man who hurt, I mean, you know, just physically hurt. He was glad I was there. He wanted to know if there was anything he could do for me, and I wanted to know if there was anything I could do for him. It was largely small talk; there wasn't really anything to say.

By this time, I was the editor of the newspaper, and we had a suite of offices on Connecticut Avenue. I was on the office's balcony with three members of my staff as the funeral procession came by. I did not march in the procession to St. Matthew's Cathedral. I did go to the cemetery and was on the periphery of the crowd. Almost everyone there was in tears. Looking back, the images are so vivid on television and in the newspapers. It is difficult to know what I took in visually and what became the lore of that funeral.

Having worked in that administration and then having the opportunity to be there, and living with the memories of some of the encounters like a visit to the White House for a birthday party for Caroline, you live with those memories. After all these years, the New Frontier is almost a cliché. But for those of us who worked in the 1960 campaign, the whole concept was very real to us. It was not political rhetoric. We knew quite well the civil rights challenges. The economy was sluggish, and internationally, there was a sense of lethargy. We took it very seriously. We felt deeply that it was vitally important to "get the country moving again."

To me, Jack Kennedy's legacy is that his life and his administration served as a model for governance by politics—in the best definition of the word. He looked at politics as an honorable profession. Any journalist who lived during that time or who has watched videos of his press conferences cannot come away with any other sense. He unconditionally loved the role of public service. For me, Jack will always be the happy warrior.

SECTION SIX:

Journalists and Commentators

⚜ Eddie Barker
KRLD Dallas,
first journalist to confirm
Kennedy's death

"John Kennedy was the darling of the press. To an extent that no other man who has held that office has enjoyed that. . .Let your own imagination create good or evil."

ON November 22, 1963, I was assigned to cover President Kennedy's speech at the Trade Mart for both KRLD radio and television. I realized something was wrong when the people supposedly coming in for the luncheon didn't come in. Up at the head table everything was very much in order, but no one was coming in to sit.

Excerpt from *Eddie Barker's Notebook* by Eddie Barker and John Mark Dempsey © 2006 (Used with author's permission):

> It was shortly before one o'clock central time. President Kennedy's arrival at Dallas's Trade Mart had been delayed. . . . Suddenly sirens were audible as the president's car and a parade of accompanying vehicles sped by the Trade Mart. We knew where they were headed: Parkland Hospital, where the most serious trauma cases were treated.
>
> I knew a doctor who was a member of the staff at Parkland Hospital and who happened to be at the

Trade Mart for the president's speech. Like the rest of us, the doctor realized something wasn't right, went to a pay phone, and calmly placed a call at 12:35. An acquaintance in the emergency room matter-of-factly told the doctor that the president was dead when they brought him through the door. Of course, the president was not officially pronounced dead until 1:00 p.m., but the information my doctor acquaintance received more closely reflected the reality of the situation.

My friend saw me struggling to maintain a coherent broadcast with the limited information available, walked over, and whispered in my ear words that would shock the world and stay with me for a lifetime:

"Eddie, he's dead."

Those words sent a cold chill running down my spine. I didn't want to believe them, but the source was too good.

I then made a decision that has caused a lot of comment in the years since that strangely brilliant Friday afternoon. I told an audience that included the whole CBS network that a reliable source had confirmed to me that President Kennedy was dead. What I didn't know was that my shocking report caused a lot of anxiety as CBS News headquarters in New York. Walter Cronkite, holding the story at arm's length, repeatedly gave me, the local newsman, credit for saying the president was dead. As the minutes went by, Walter was generous in crediting me with the story, making sure the local reporter was given the credit he deserved. And the history books take note of the fact that CBS News stuck with the story of a reporter they knew and trusted.

Once a reporter, you're always a reporter. My God, I was told this, and I had to do something with it. Because it was pretty much straight from the horse's mouth, I went ahead and used it. I had been so close to CBS with various stories whose origins were here in Dallas. I was a known entity and the people in New York, including Walter, would say, "Well, if Barker says it, it's correct."

John Kennedy was the darling of the press. To an extent that no other man who has held that office has enjoyed that. I think you have to look at the time he served. Let your own imagination create good or evil. He was so popular—even in Dallas—so many thought the world of him. He missed the mark, but had he had the full run at it, he would have ranked up there with the most important presidents in the history of the United States.

But he was cut short.

❦ Tom Brokaw
NBC News

"And I suppose I matured in that twenty-four hours, over those couple of days. I think I became more realistic as a journalist and saw the larger screen. And the consequences of daring action and the evil that can come, even to America. I do think it was a seminal time for me."

(JOHN Kennedy) matched all my impressions because he was very cool and elegant. When his brother (Robert) came (to Omaha), it was different. He was rumpled, and his shirt was frayed, and his hair was messed, and he was very combative in an exchange with reporters.

There was this enormous generational shift. This was the World War II generation that had been forged by that war. They represented such a profound change from the generation of FDR, Harry Truman, and Dwight Eisenhower.

There was youthfulness about them that we could identify. They were in their forties—Kennedy and Nixon for example.

For most of us in working class America, we had our nose pressed up against the glass of the Kennedys. They had a lifestyle that we could not imagine. It was F. Scott Fitzgeraldian in its own way. And they brought enormous energy to the campaign obviously. I remember first being aware of them when Bobby was counsel to the Senate Racketeering Committee and hearing that distinctive New England accent. We didn't hear that on a regular basis because television was just coming of age. And wherever we lived in the country, we could hear the different dialects now because they played out on that little screen every night. So the Kennedys brought dash, distinctive accent, and enormous wealth and lifestyle to parts of the country that we could not imagine.

In photography, they talk about a first and second generation print. I think we're in about the fifth generation now. And there are still people who were inspired by John Kennedy, who, even if they were not alive when he was president, know the ringing words, "Ask not…" and the whole "Camelot" concept still plays, I think, for a lot of people across the country.

But we've moved on from there. And there have been many people since then. Ronald Reagan came along and inspired an entirely different generation in an entirely different fashion. There's a Reagan generation as there was a Kennedy generation. We keep evolving in our politics and our reaction to it. There is an entire generation of social conservatives and entrepreneurial people in this country who were inspired by Ronald Reagan. They were in college when he was the president. And now they are in their late thirties, early to mid-forties and they make up a lot of this country. They got interested in politics because of him.

(Regarding the impact of television coverage of the assassination) I don't think I turned to friends and said, "This is a new era." But we were bound together by that screen. And we could watch the state burial and common grieving that was going on across the country on that screen. We had not seen anything quite like that. When FDR died, and he made that long train ride back across the South, that was primarily in Movietone News and still pictures. But this played out live. You were wedded to that screen.

I remember being in church on Sunday morning when Lee Harvey Oswald was shot. The priest came out and said, "What have we come to? They've now shot Lee Harvey Oswald." The church pretty well vacated, and we all ran home to watch the replay of it. And then I went to the office. The television set was, if you will, the centrifuge for the country. Everybody drew from it in some fashion.

I was just a bit player. I was in Omaha, and I was racing around the city getting reactions. I did broadcast it for the NBC audience in Omaha because the network was dark for local programming. I also remember the Midwestern governors were meeting in Omaha at the time. Mitt Romney's father, George Romney, was there. And he was a Republican. Big strong executive. And we went down to catch his reaction coming out of a conference. And my cameraman said to him, "Governor, I'm just so sorry." And Romney walked over and put his arms around him and said, "We're all so sorry." And I thought, at that time, "This goes up and down the generational ladder and across the country."

And I suppose I matured in that twenty-four hours, over those couple of days. I think I became more realistic as a journalist and saw the larger screen. And the consequences of daring action and the evil that can come, even to America. I do think it was a seminal time for me.

I think (John Kennedy's) legacy is in the boldness of his rhetoric and declaration, and the transition from one generation to another. Legislatively, there's not a lot you can look at. He wasn't there that long. I really do believe he brought younger people into the arena. And made the public arena a really attractive place for the adventurous, for the young. His offspring, politically speaking, were front and center of the anti-war movement of the sixties. Al Lowenstein and people like that who stepped up.

So I think his legacy is mostly in the memory of the dynamism he seemed to bring to the office. And the people that he would attract to high office. He made it honorable to go to Washington and a calling, if you will, for people of all stations of life.

✎ Bob Clark
ABC News, only journalist to cover assassinations of both John and Robert Kennedy

"We had no idea the president was going to the hospital. When we got there, we were permitted to run up next to his car. He was lying in the back seat with his head in Jackie's lap. That's the first we knew he had been shot. It was a horrific sight. I will never forget it."

I started covering politics in Washington in 1948, and presidents, beginning with Eisenhower's first day in office in 1953. Both President Eisenhower and President Kennedy were very good at handling the press. Eisenhower gave direct, responsive answers; Kennedy made a little more of a game of it. He gave clever answers. I would put Eisenhower at least as equal with Kennedy.

On November 22, 1963, I was the back-up ABC reporter in Dallas, back up to Bill Lawrence, who was on vacation. I was selected as the network pool correspondent and was placed in the pool car for the motorcade. That car was just a few vehicles behind the limousine Kennedy was in. I was directly under the window where Oswald was shooting from when the shots rang out.

The shots were loud and clear, though we had no idea Kennedy had been hit. Merriman Smith of UPI, who was the senior wire service reporter, was in the car. He was a gun fancier and said, "Those are shots."

He was permitted to sit in the front seat of the car and grabbed the only phone in the vehicle. Jack Bell, the AP reporter, didn't make an objection, but soon realized "Smitty" was going on and on and keeping him from filing (a bulletin). So, as we were nearing the hospital, Bell was reaching forward trying desperately to grab the phone out of Smitty's hand.

We followed the motorcade as fast as we could. We had no idea the president was going to the hospital. When we got there, we were permitted to run up next to his car. He was lying in the back seat with his head in Jackie's lap. That's the first we knew he had been shot. It was a horrific sight. I will never forget it. Moments later, they (hospital staff) brought out gurneys for Kennedy and the Texas governor John Connally.

I went back to Love Field and witnessed the swearing in of Lyndon Johnson, but that weekend, did not cover the funeral. I was working the story from ABC's offices on Connecticut Avenue in Washington and watched the procession as it went by on the way to St. Matthew's Cathedral.

ℰ Sid Davis
Westinghouse Broadcasting Company, NBC News, witnessed swearing in of Lyndon Johnson

"What I reported in the pool report were the first words flashed to the world that Lyndon Johnson was sworn in as the thirty-sixth President of the United States."

I first met John Kennedy when I began covering the 1960 campaign. I don't recall exactly my first trip out with Kennedy, but I covered Kennedy for most of the 1960 campaign, and I covered Nixon for eight weeks.

The campaign for the nomination started a few months into 1960. I would follow Kennedy here and there, not on a regular everyday basis. But as the year progressed, I went out more and more with the candidates. And he was one of them. I went to West Virginia to cover the primary. It was key to getting Kennedy the nomination.

Both the Bay of Pigs and the Cuban Missile Crisis were important to Kennedy's career, important to making him the president he eventually came to be. The attack on the Bay of Pigs was a dreadful mistake. A serious, grievous mistake. An embarrassment to the United States, and a lesson for John F. Kennedy. That Cuban operation took place within a few months after Kennedy became president. It was April of 1961. Kennedy had no role in planning the Bay of Pigs. It was a holdover from Eisenhower. It had been planned by the CIA, and poorly planned. No air support. No ground troops from the United States. Independent observers were very nervous about it, but the CIA assured Kennedy that they could pull it off.

What's interesting is that later, President Eisenhower was astonished that Kennedy would undertake the thing. Immediately after the Bay of Pigs disaster, Kennedy looked for cover. He was embarrassed, and of course, the papers were all critical of what he did. So he met with President Eisenhower at Camp David. I went up for the meeting. They allowed us about twenty feet from the two of them as they took a walk. There's a great picture of Eisenhower and Kennedy taking a walk on one of the beautiful paths.

Eisenhower questioned Kennedy about how he went into the operation. "Did you ask how many troops there were? Did you ask about air support? Did you ask that? Did you do this?" And Kennedy said, "No" to every one of the Eisenhower inquiries. Mr. Eisenhower said, in effect, "How could you have started this thing if you had not asked these questions?"

We did not know of this conversation until years later. So, that led me to believe that Eisenhower was not in on the planning for the Bay of Pigs. It was a CIA operation. They obviously were doing it in secret and might have been afraid to bring it before Eisenhower, so they waited until '61 when Eisenhower was gone.

The Cuban Missile Crisis came a year later and was probably the most fascinating thing I covered, besides the assassination. My recollection of the night JFK addressed the nation, Monday, October 22, is that I was in the Oval Office behind one of the areas where the cameras were when Kennedy walked in to deliver his crisis speech that there were Soviet missiles in Cuba. He entered the room holding a sheaf of papers. He seemed a bit nervous before he went on the air, but as soon as the red camera light flashed, he was very cool, very tough. After the speech, he was surrounded by Ted Sorensen and others. My recollection is that I was the only pool reporter in the room. Pierre Salinger chose me, and I thought, "Gee, look how fast I've risen." Well, the reason they chose me was that every other reporter who had any sense did not want to watch the speech at the White House. They wouldn't get much. They wanted to be at their office typewriters and teletypes, so they could file stories immediately.

The brilliance of John F. Kennedy was evident and was displayed in its finest detail during the thirteen days of the crisis. His wisdom and his handling of it, a potential conflagration, was brilliant, despite being this young, forty-five year old facing the generals at the National Security Agency and General Curtis LeMay, who was a World War II hero, sitting across the table from JFK. Of course, Kennedy had been a hero in the Navy with his PT boat. The other fortunate thing for Kennedy was that he had his brother in the room. When they say blood is thicker than water, they mean it. Kennedy looked around the room to see who was with him and who was not, and they—the National Security Council—were not entirely with him. But every time JFK looked at his brother Bobby when a question came up, Bobby would shake his head one way or another, usually in disagreement with most of the generals.

The options were: bomb, invade, blockade. The military people wanted to bomb, and then invade. And Bobby was urging to take the lesser of the more dangerous options. Kennedy held his ground and said, "No, we'll go for the blockade. It won't be World War Three." And when he made his speech on Monday night, the twenty-second of October, the most important paragraph in that speech that caused Khrushchev to cave in was something Khrushchev apparently had never figured on putting missiles in Cuba. In JFK's speech you'll find a paragraph that says, "It shall be the policy of this nation to regard any nuclear missile launched from Cuba against any nation in the Western Hemisphere as an attack on the United States, requiring a full retaliatory response upon the Soviet Union." Brilliant, is the only way I can describe the moment.

The U.S. would not only target Cuba, it was the entire Soviet Union open to a nuclear attack. At that point Khrushchev is said to have panicked: "Why didn't we know that this is what they would do?" But Kennedy put Khrushchev on notice that any action against the United States would be considered an action by the Soviet Union and not by Fidel Castro. I felt that was the most important part of the speech. And then, of course, the Russians started treading water with their ships heading toward Cuba, or turning back, leading to a removal of the missiles in Cuba. The boil had been pierced. The crisis was over.

In November of 1963, we first went to San Antonio—I still have the press badge—then we went to Houston, then to Fort Worth, then to Dallas and from Dallas, President Kennedy was to go to the LBJ Ranch for a barbeque. The Kennedys were going to spend the night at the ranch, and come back to Washington on Saturday.

I was seven or eight cars behind the presidential limousine, in press bus number one. It was a city bus and probably carried thirty or more people. All reporters. This was mostly the national press. The crowds at the airport were warm and enthusiastic. Very admiring. That's the way it was all the way into town. It was a beautiful day. Jackie had on that beautiful, they called it raspberry-colored, wool suit with the pillbox hat. She was radiant. She was enjoying herself. She had had some serious personal problems in August of that year. They lost a child, two or three days after he was born, Patrick Bouvier Kennedy. So, she was coming out for the first time. We were rounding Elm and Houston streets and that's when the shots rang out. Our press bus, being seven or eight car lengths behind the presidential limousine, would have meant that we were about eighty feet behind JFK. With the presidential limousine being ahead of us that meant that Oswald, leaning out the window of the School Book Depository Building had to fire at an angle. It just so happened that the reason we heard the shots so clearly was because we were right under the window.

So I got to the hospital and went toward the emergency room area. The top had been put back onto the presidential limousine. But I could see blood on the back seat. I could see the flowers Mrs. Kennedy had carried lying on the back seat. And I could see the suit jacket of Clint Hill, the Secret Service agent, on the seat. He had taken his jacket off to cover the President's head.

By that time, the Kennedys had been removed and taken inside the hospital. I was told to get upstairs. I tried to get into the emergency room and was thrown out. So I went upstairs, found a telephone, and I called my office. I told them what was going on and filed my story. I had attended the news conference at the hospital at approximately ten after one, Central Standard Time. Kennedy was shot at 12:30. Malcolm Kilduff, the deputy press secretary, who deserves a lot of credit for the way he handled himself that day, told us at a brief news conference that, and I'll never forget the words, "John F. Kennedy died at one o'clock, Central Standard Time today here in Dallas. He died of a gunshot wound in the brain. I have nothing further to say."

So I ran to the phones, started filing. I filed the story, did some Q & A's and color, and then a White House staffer grabbed me by the shoulder and said, "We need you immediately. We need a pool."

I said, "I haven't got time. I'm on the air."

And he said, "I'm telling you. We're desperate. We need you right now. Tell your office you're coming with me."

So I said, "Bye."

They raced us out to Love Field in an unmarked police car. About eighty miles an hour. No siren, no nothing. We got to Love Field, and we were told the Secret Service was bringing the casket aboard the airplane. They had removed four seats to get the casket into the rear of the plane. It was a huge casket. It weighed about eight hundred pounds.

We were brought into the cabin used by JFK as a conference room. Vice President Johnson was already in the compartment. There were a lot of people. The room was humid, sweltering hot. The scene was somber. LBJ was calm, reserved, deliberate, asking people to do certain things as he prepared to take the oath. They brought a federal judge from downtown Dallas, Sarah Hughes. Johnson turned to his secretary, Marie Fehmer, and said, "Would you ask Mrs. Kennedy if she would like to stand with us?"

Marie went back to the rear of the plane where the casket was located with Mrs. Kennedy beside it. Marie asked Mrs. Kennedy what the Vice President asked her to do, and Mrs. Kennedy said she would like to attend, but that she needed a few minutes to compose herself.

We waited a few minutes. We were anxious, because the Secret Service wanted to get the president and the plane out of Dallas immediately. No one knew whether it was a conspiracy or not. In a few minutes, Mrs. Kennedy came into the cabin, and of course, everybody was awestruck. Women and men burst into tears. Jackie came into the room still wearing the same suit with blood on her skirt and stockings. Blood covered her right wrist, where she had held JFK's head. She was obviously in grief, but knew what was going on. She wished to be at the swearing-in ceremony. I think it was very important for her to be at the ceremony. Her presence was and remains a symbol of the nation's unity at this sad time. It took a great deal of courage for her to leave the casket, even if it was for a few minutes.

Johnson placed Mrs. Kennedy to his left, his wife to his right, and told the judge to proceed. The oath took twenty-eight seconds. Only forty-five words.

One of the three of us had to brief the rest of the press still in downtown Dallas. I was told there were only two seats on the airplane back to Washington. And that I would have to flip a coin to see who would stay—me or Chuck Roberts, the *Newsweek* reporter. Merriman Smith, because he was a wire service reporter, was entitled to one of the two seats. And the other seat could go to Chuck or myself. And I said, "Chuck, I'm not going to flip for the seat, I'm going to get off and give the pool report."

In all selfishness, if I gave the pool report at Love Field, I could then file my own story with my office, and have an eyewitness account of the swearing in of the new president. If I had stayed on the airplane unable to file, I would have been airborne for almost three hours, and my office would have been waiting. And would not have heard from me until I had arrived back in Washington. It served me well in that I got to file my own eyewitness account that no one else had. What I reported in the pool report were the first words flashed to the world that Lyndon Johnson was sworn in as the thirty-sixth President of the United States.

LBJ's behavior was magnificent. There have been stories to the contrary. It's baloney. Not true at all. Lyndon Johnson was calm. He was respectful to the Kennedy family. He understood the gravity of the situation. And his behavior for the next few months and years on behalf of the country and the Kennedys was magnificent. It was among LBJ's finest hours. He knew what to do. He brought a grieving nation together. And he would be exemplary in the civil rights bills and social welfare legislation he got approved, including voting rights and Medicare.

The Pan Am press charter took off about 9 or 10 o'clock. We arrived in Washington at about one in the morning, I went right to the White House, and I was asked to broadcast the arrival of the casket following an autopsy at Bethesda Naval Hospital. It took what seemed forever. I went on the air somewhere around four o'clock, Saturday morning, November 23. There were about three hundred or four hundred diligent, curious people outside the White House gates peering in. The body was brought to the North Portico in a Navy ambulance. Mrs. Kennedy did not want the body in a hearse.

Small kerosene lanterns were placed along either side of the driveway. It was an eerie and sad scene, but so appropriate. The leaves had fallen off the trees. It was late November. A chill cooled the night; temperature somewhere in the forties. The ambulance moved very slowly. An honor guard marched ahead of the ambulance in funeral cadence, slowly stepping up the driveway. I could see Mrs. Kennedy through the ambulance's window, sitting with the casket. Stoic, somber. She had helped make some of these arrangements. Closing the broadcast, I made the mistake of trying to quote poet Robert Frost. Frost was Kennedy's favorite poet. He had spoken at Kennedy's inauguration. And Kennedy used to quote from Robert Frost during the 1960 campaign, "Walking By Woods On a Snowy Evening." It closes with, "The woods are lovely, dark and deep, but I have miles to go before I sleep. And miles to go before I sleep."

I tried to repeat those words as a tribute, and I didn't get through it. I cracked up on the air. What amazes me is how many people across the country heard me at four-thirty in the morning breaking down and wrote me letters. Very kind people. Some of them were college classmates I hadn't seen for years.

For the weekend, I covered everything that had to do with the White House. I stayed at the White House through the following Monday.

I didn't see animosity between the Kennedy and LBJ staffs. You could understand the sadness of the Kennedy people. They had just lost their hero. They campaigned with him. They took him to the presidency. And they had such an exciting future to look forward to in running the country. But it all went away. It was destroyed by one guy with a $14.95 rifle.

JFK left a promising legacy. In education, the arts, in Head Start for children. He was planning civil rights legislation that probably would have been tough to get approved were it not for Lyndon Johnson. It would have been tougher for Kennedy. Johnson, a Southerner, was able to break down barriers. He was a master parliamentarian, probably the best among all our presidents.

I think Kennedy's presidency left a remarkable legacy. The Cuban Missile Crisis changed our relationship with the Soviet Union, leading to a nuclear test ban treaty. JFK's remarks in his inaugural speech, "Ask not what your country can do for you. Ask what you can do for your country," still reverberate.

Kennedy was intelligent, witty, and sensitive. He and Mrs. Kennedy were as glamorous as the famous of Hollywood. Because he was in office only two and a half years, he did not have time to fulfill the great agenda he had hoped for. But his vision of America's greatness is lasting.

✑ Nicholas Gage
Writer for *The New York Times* and other publications, author

"Kennedy was a groundbreaker in many ways. First, he was the first non-WASP to be elected president. . . . I don't think Obama would be there today if Kennedy had not opened the way."

I met John Kennedy in 1963 when I won the Hearst Foundation National Journalism Award. It was a tremendously inspiring experience for me, because I had come to the United States fourteen years earlier without knowing a word of English and eventually won this national prize for the best published writing by a college student. It was presented at the White House by the President of the United States. It made me feel that anything was possible in this great country.

Excerpt from *A Place for Us* by Nicholas Gage © 1989 (Used with author's permission):

> We were ushered into a richly decorated waiting room and then joined by Kenneth O'Donnell, the president's director of appointments. Finally he said, "The president is ready to see you now," and led us into the Oval Office.
>   I blinked in the bright sunlight and saw the imposing figure of John Kennedy standing in front of his desk, holding out his hands in greeting. Then I heard a commotion, and turned around to discover several

dozen reporters with cameras and microphones pointed toward us. They were all shouting, flashing light bulbs, waving, and calling to me as if I were Cary Grant disembarking from the Queen Elizabeth II: "Look this way, Mr. Gage"; "Smile, please"; "How do you feel, meeting the president?"

After posing until the photographers were satisfied, Kennedy shooed most of them out of the room and spoke to each of us individually. He was relaxed and seemed to be enjoying himself, perhaps because his first job after leaving the Navy had been as a reporter for the Hearst Corporation, and he enjoyed the company of journalists and Randolph Hearst. He obviously had been briefed on our backgrounds, and made much of the fact that he and I were both from Massachusetts. "You're getting a great start with this award," he said to me. "You're obviously a much better reporter than I was. I was pretty bad, wasn't I, Randolph?"

Hearst told him briefly how I had come to America as a war refugee and managed to learn English, enter journalism school, and work my way through college with a combination of academic scholarships and part-time jobs.

"And you're doing all this so you can become a reporter?" Kennedy asked. "Why do you want to be a newspaperman?"

"Just a masochist, I guess," I answered, because I couldn't think of any way to encapsulate all my reasons in a few words.

Everyone laughed as if this was a pearl of wit, and it was widely quoted in the newspapers the next day. The quarter-hour we spent in the Oval Office passed in an instant.

On November 22, 1963, only six months after my visit to the White House, I was studying for my master's degree at Columbia University's Graduate School of Journalism. We were in a class and one of the students came in and said, "President Kennedy's been shot and they've taken him to the hospital."

We all got up and rushed to the Teletype machine. We read with great horror that he had been killed. All of us were stunned. We stopped whatever we were doing. A group of us went to a local bar to try to drink, but I couldn't even swallow. We thought the whole world had collapsed. There is no tragedy that does not produce something positive. I wound up marrying (one girl with us)—Joan Paulson—and we are still married forty-two years later. When the news came over the teletype machine, she tore off the story and still has it.

I watched the news that weekend with Cronkite and read Tom Wicker's stories in *The Times*. Later, Wicker came and spoke to our class, and subsequently, I worked with him at *The Times* as an investigative reporter.

Kennedy was a groundbreaker in many ways. First, he was the first non-WASP to be elected president. He opened up the possibilities for other Americans to become president. I don't think Obama would be there today if Kennedy had not opened the way. Second, he generated optimism. Historians would say that other presidents accomplished more in similar periods, but I don't think anyone created such a feeling of optimism and well-being in the country as Kennedy, at least in the sixty years I've lived in this country.

And the way he stood up to the Soviet Union showed his fierce opposition to authoritarianism. I was a refugee from the Communist civil war in Greece, where the Communists executed my mother for arranging the escape of her children so they wouldn't be taken to indoctrination camps behind the Iron Curtain. Kennedy was someone who had the right values, and he projected those onto the nation and world.

✐ Bob Jackson
Dallas Times-Herald, captured
Pulitzer Prize–winning image
of Jack Ruby shooting
Lee Harvey Oswald

*"All of a sudden someone (Jack Ruby) stepped out
from the right, and the thought flashed in my
mind, 'He's blocking my view!'"*

ON November 22, my assignment was to go with our chief photographer, John Mazziotta, to photograph the arrival (of the president and Mrs. Kennedy at Love Field). I got some good pictures of them there. It was kind of a struggle. He decided to go over to the fence and greet people. It gave us a good photo op. We (myself and the other photographers) were kind of jammed in there, and as he moved along the fence, we had to back up and step on each other.

I was in the eighth car behind the president. It was a convertible, and we were sitting up on the back of the back seat. Tom Dillard, chief photographer of the *Dallas News*, was sitting next to me. I had an engraved invitation to his luncheon (at the Dallas Trade Mart) where he was to speak. That event was the rest of my assignment.

(Later) we had gotten around the corner and we heard the first shot. Then two more shots closer together. We were facing the Texas School Book Depository Building. I looked up there and there was a rifle on the window ledge. And I could see it being drawn in. And I said, "There's a rifle!"

Dillard said, "Where?"

And I pointed out the empty window to him. Of course, he took a picture of that. I have an empty camera in my lap and wondering when I should try to reload it. On the Nikons in those days, the back wasn't hinged. You had to take the back off the camera, put the film in, and stick the back of the camera back on. That made it hard. The car was moving, and I didn't want to drop the back off the camera and lose it. So I wasn't able to do anything just then. So as we got to the corner (in front of the building), I just looked at the scene off to my left: the grassy knoll, people covering up their kids; people running. I saw the president's car disappear under the overpass and then Johnson's car. A cop rode his motorcycle up the slope of the grassy knoll; he jumped off, and the motorcycle kept going until it fell over. And he ran to the door of the building and another policeman joined him there. They went inside.

I soon found out the president had been hit.

I saw that the traffic, which had been held up at the corner of Houston and Elm, the police are letting the drivers go. So the traffic is coming toward me, over the evidence, any evidence that happened to be there. And I thought, "Why are they (police) letting these cars down there?"

Two other photographers and I flagged down a car. We told this lady we needed to go to the hospital. We got into her car—just about the point where Kennedy had been hit. She pulled onto the on-ramp on the Stemmons Freeway, and a motorcycle cop was there, stopping traffic and checking everyone. We explained who we were and that we needed to get to the hospital. At that point, I overheard a conversation on the officer's radio, and someone said, "But we don't know where the shots came from." And I said, "Hey, I know where the shots came from." So he took my name and my phone number at the newspaper and let us go.

(The driver) took us to the hospital. But, because I had not stayed in the motorcade, I did not have the access I could have had. I was kept back with the crowd behind the hospital's emergency entrance. In the meantime, I heard on another police radio that an officer is down in Oak Cliff. I remember commenting to someone, "I wonder if that has anything to do with what just happened?" But then I thought, "Surely not, because whoever did that (the shooting of the President) is in custody." Sure enough, that's what it turned out to be.

Sometime between one o'clock and one-thirty, we got the announcement the president had died. The word spread outside soon after it was announced inside. I never got inside the hospital; never needed to, really

Eventually I got back to the newspaper office. To this day, I don't remember how I got there. I ran my film, and eventually I went to the Dallas Police Station, and I was there into the night. I was able to shoot images of the police bringing (Lee Harvey) Oswald down the hall. I also shot images of his wife Marina and his mother Marguerite. If I had known then what was going to happen Sunday morning, I would have shot images of everything I possibly could in the hallway. If nothing else, for the record. Jack Ruby was there as well.

At one point on Friday night, I wormed my way between Marina and Marguerite and the elevator door and I got several frames, including one really good close-up of their faces, showing the strain on them. I was tempted to just back into the elevator when the doors opened, but I realized there was no way the police would allow me to do that. But I thought about it.

On Sunday morning, November 24, we had one photographer stationed at the county jail awaiting Oswald's arrival there. I was the "Sunday man" on duty and the other photographer called me on Saturday night asking if I would cover the transfer of Oswald at the Dallas Police Department. I said, "Sure." I knew I would be at the police department and thought, "What if somebody makes an attempt on his life? What if something happens? What if he (Oswald) never gets to the county jail? What if . . . ?"

The other photographer wanted to be at the county jail, where people had been putting hundreds of flowers at the entrance, and he probably was thinking in the back of his mind, "That's the place for the picture." And it was! If Oswald had made it there.

So finally, the police said, "We're bringing him (Oswald) down in about five minutes, so you have five minutes to get in position. We don't want anybody moving around when he appears." So I picked my spot which gave me a clear shot. I pre-focused the camera at about eleven feet. I must have checked it ten times! I expected it would be a pretty routine shot. It's a matter of the police escorting the prisoner toward you. Except in this case, it was a little more historic.

All of a sudden someone (Jack Ruby) stepped out from the right, and the thought flashed in my mind, "He's blocking my view!" At the same time, the car to take Oswald was backing up. It already should have been in place. I remember leaning against the fender at the time it (the car) stopped. I was leaning a bit to my left because this person (Ruby) on the right was coming out. All of this, of course, was quick. Instantaneous. He (Jack Ruby) took a few steps and "bang."

And I punched the shutter at the right time. It could not have come together any better. I could not have planned it any better. It just happened and I guess it was meant to be.

After the shooting it was pandemonium. One cop ran over the car—from the hood to the trunk—and jumped into the pile. The next thing I know is that I am being shoved back by a plainclothes detective and I remember saying, "Get your hand off my camera!" He was really upset, and another policeman next to him had to calm him down.

We waited until they brought the ambulance in—about five minutes. I was able to get a lucky shot when they put him (Oswald) into the back of the ambulance. I was holding my camera in the air and pointing it down. His shirt was pulled up and there was no blood. The bullet was lodged inside him.

In the spring of 1964, when the Pulitzer Prizes were announced no one in the newsroom broke out the champagne. It was the newspaper's first Pulitzer. The photo didn't really change my life. I got a twenty-five dollar a week raise. And it made getting another job easier. I never had to show a portfolio again.

John Kennedy's legacy? I guess it's the space program and how he pushed for that. I was not a Kennedy lover. My family were Eisenhower Democrats. I was not into politics in 1963, and so I can't rave and rant about what a wonderful person he was. He was certainly charismatic and he brought the presidency closer to the people.

He was tough. Look at what he went through in the Pacific. I've read the account of the PT 109 sinking and that certainly prepared him for politics and for running the country, for going through crises, like the Vietnam War. He was an interesting character and I certainly think a lot more of him than I do of his younger brother Teddy.

❦ Marianne Means
Writer for Hearst newspapers

*"He wasn't simple. You couldn't see through him.
He had his own thoughts in his own head and he
had his own stuff."*

MY husband (then boyfriend) was the head of the student foreign affairs group (at University of Nebraska). We got ourselves assigned to go down and pick up (Senator) Kennedy and Ted Sorensen at the airport, because we had arranged for him (JFK) to come. He was a hot ticket then. He was (being considered as) a vice presidential candidate. So, we sat around at the airport, picked him up, talked to him on the way to school, and then, when we got back to the airport (after JFK's speech), the plane was late, of course, so we sat around and talked some more. We talked about how we, and I in particular, wanted to go into journalism. And he (JFK) said, "Well, when you come to Washington, look me up."

Being naïve, I took him at his word.

My boyfriend (and later husband) and I came to Washington. I knew three people on Capitol Hill who turned out to be very useful. One was John Kennedy, one was Ted Sorenson, and one was Evelyn Lincoln, who was his (JFK's) secretary. (Sorenson and Lincoln) were from Nebraska and being from Nebraska was a big asset.

John Kennedy was engaging. He was charming. He didn't know what to do with me, so he transferred me to Sorenson. And then to Evelyn. I ended up as an executive assistant to the editor of *Broadcasting* magazine. It turns out I was his secretary and I hated it. But one of the guys there told me about an opening at the *Northern Virginia*

Sun, and I worked there as the woman's editor. That was the only job they were willing to offer me at the time. Kennedy got elected and (several staff members) left and went into the (new) administration.

I met the bureau chief of the Hearst papers. He was allowed to hire two reporters, and he picked two non-threatening people—the son of a friend of his and me. So that's when I started working at the Hearst papers and that's where I felt comfortable for the rest of my career, almost fifty years with Hearst.

(Kennedy) was the first president I had ever covered, and I had nobody to judge him against. I watched him. He muffed the Bay of Pigs, obviously. He had to live with that; it was his big mistake. But the rest, he did very well. Of course, he really didn't have much experience. He had been in the Senate, but nobody really knows until you're there (in the presidency). He was always so self-confident, in public, and when I was around. He was always genial, confident, and comfortable.

There was the trip to Vienna to meet Khrushchev which turned out to be a disaster. (Press Secretary Pierre) Salinger lied to us about the meeting, claiming it went well. I also went to Germany when he made his "Ich bin ein Berliner" speech. It was very emotional. Huge crowds had gathered to see him, waving hankies and flags. Then we went to Latin America for a conference. Huge crowds.

And I went to Dallas.

I was in the first press bus. Smitty (UPI's Merriman Smith) and Jack Bell of the Associated Press were in the car behind him (and Vice President Johnson). I was in the front seat of that press bus. And I remember hearing the shots, but I didn't know what a rifle shot sounded like.

But one of the guys, I think it was Bob Pierpoint (of CBS News), said, "Those are rifle shots. I'm leaving." All the motion was on the grassy knoll. People were falling on their children because everybody thought the shots were aimed at the grassy knoll because they came from the (Texas School Book Depository) Building. Another thing we did not know was whether this was a mass conspiracy by the Soviets. We were deep in the Cold War then, and the Secret Service had to get Johnson out of there.

The second car, which had Johnson and Ralph Yarborough, sped ahead. So the cars sped ahead rapidly, and we could see what was happening, but we didn't know a damn thing. I remember everyone else in the press corps turning and running toward whatever transportation they could find. We had proceeded on to the Trade Mart because we didn't know what else to do. Of course we got there and there was not a sign of Kennedy.

I got into a car with a couple of other guys. I was one of the first to get (to Parkland Hospital). Everybody was milling around, not knowing anything. But Yarborough and (Congressman Jack) Brooks were standing outside the hospital crying. We knew this was bad.

So we had to hang around until finally Mac (Malcolm) Kilduff (Deputy Press Secretary) came out and told us what to do and where we were to go and to sit in a certain room, and we went like the sheep we were. Kilduff came in and told us (JFK was dead), then we all had to go find phones. And I was fighting over a phone with some nurse at a desk. And I said, unfortunately, "This is all Goldwater's fault." And she got very mad at me. We were all so damn emotional.

We were gathered there (at Parkland) and they wouldn't let us out until Johnson and the casket had gone to the airport. All because they thought it might be a Soviet plot.

The press plane was sitting at the airport, and Air Force One was sitting at the airport—both were highly guarded. So, with all our press credentials and so forth, they wanted us out of the way. They hustled us to the (press) plane. And gave us Bloody Marys and things to calm us down.

Some people were crying. Mostly me.

When they went (the passengers on Air Force One), then we went. We all went to Andrews (Air Force Base) and went our merry ways. My boss said, "I'll see you at the office." Click. (Over the next three days) it was very traumatic. It's all kind of a blur.

His brothers knew him well. And maybe a few of his old buddies, like Red Faye (friend from PT boat training in WWII; later appointed by JFK to serve as Undersecretary of the Navy). Certainly nobody like me. Presidents become very private. Once they become elected, they (presidents) don't know whom to trust. So they tend to trust the people they knew before they became presidents.

He (JFK) wasn't simple. You couldn't see through him. He had his own thoughts in his own head and he had his own stuff. He wasn't simple. No president is, including Barack Obama.

He lifted the spirits of the country. He came in after Eisenhower, who had been going along, treading along in the old, tired ways, rehashing World War II, and so forth. He was young and vibrant. And Jackie was gorgeous. He filled the city (Washington) and the country with new hope. And that's why it was so devastating when he died.

Covering JFK consolidated my reputation in the Hearst Corporation—that a young woman could actually handle all this. And that was important. There were no examples to follow; we had to cut our own way. It's inspiring to cover a president as a young journalist. You know his inner circle. You get all this inside information. And you can handle it well. It was inspiring and it was much fun.

✑ Michael Medved
Author, syndicated radio show host, commentator

"Everyone was screaming and you didn't know why. But you did know why. . . It was an echo of November 22, 1963. The screams that night seemed to have started in Dallas."

I first saw John Kennedy in October of 1960. I was twelve years old, and my parents allowed me to cut school from Dana Junior High School in San Diego where we lived. Senator Kennedy came to San Diego for a midday rally at Horton Plaza. I got there early, so I was up close, the front row, maybe one row back. When he came out to speak it was very exciting. There are, of course, two things you remember. First, his hair. At the time, his hair was famous. It was much fairer than what you saw on black and white TV. On TV, his hair looked dark. It was actually a sandy, light brown color. And second, he was slender, really slender. As we all know, television adds weight to a person.

I saw him again in 1962 in San Diego, when he delivered a speech at San Diego State College. My dad taught at San Diego State. I was a huge Kennedy enthusiast. And I recently found my notebook from that period. It has a very carefully hand-lettered "Kennedy for President" message on it. Of course, I spelled his name wrong—"Kenedy." I was a political geek as a kid.

In my book, *The Shadow Presidents*, my chapter on Jack Kennedy was based on the wonderful cooperation of Ted Sorensen. Writing that book—and the interviews I did with extraordinary people like Sherman Adams, Clark Clifford, and Dick Cheney—made me a Republican. Sorensen, for the rest of his life, continued to feel hero worship for John Kennedy. I'm very positive toward Sorensen; he was a very effective aide to JFK. But the Jack Kennedy whom Ted Sorensen described did not come off well at all. I was struck by the detail that I had never heard before. Like the fact that Kennedy never carried money, or a wallet for that matter, so when it came to meals, drinks, and other expenses, Sorensen and other staff members were expected to shell out for everything.

I don't think Jack Kennedy deserved the adulation he received—and still receives—from the American public. It always stuns me that polls of our greatest presidents rank Kennedy quite high. In some of the recent polling, Kennedy is placed at the top of the list as the greatest president we've ever had.

Kennedy relied on Sorensen in a different way than other presidents have relied on their chief aides. The funny thing about the Kennedy Administration is that so much was based on imposture. I learned this for the first time from Sorensen. Part of my youthful hero worship of John Kennedy had been based on the idea that, "Oh, the Eisenhower Administration was that of a really old, dumb guy." Rather, with Kennedy, there was this image that he loved culture, as demonstrated by having cellist Pablo Casals perform at the White House. I learned from Sorensen that John Kennedy did not like classical music. In fact, he fell asleep during the concert. He liked Sinatra. There's nothing wrong with that. But that was part of the imposture.

Most striking about the Kennedy inner-circle is that everybody was part of this grand imposture, such as conveying the idea that Kennedy was a devout Catholic. Not. And that he was mad crazy in love with his beautiful wife. And was an ideal family man. And was the picture of health. It just wasn't true, but the American people were led to believe it all was.

On November 22, 1963, I was a junior at Palisades High School in class and an announcement came on the PA system. The initial announcement by the principal was that the president had been shot and wounded, and he had been taken to a hospital. The implication was that he was going to be OK. For the rest of the day, there was not a lot of school work getting done. It was shortly afterward that the announcement came through that the president had died—and it was that announcement that produced gasps, tears, and hysteria.

I remember I got a ride home that day from Jean Hernandez, the English teacher who was closest to me at the time. She was compassionate because I was so upset; she commented that it was a terrible time for our country. Like a lot of people, my parents initially thought that because it occurred in Dallas, the assassination must have been associated with the far right and segregationists. The assumption was that there were dark forces at work in our country.

My fascination with the presidency—what presidents could do, presidential greatness—was all tied up with John Kennedy. I have one of those flashing campaign buttons with that fabulous profile of him, and on the other side, it reads, "A time for greatness." I used to do Kennedy impersonations. I saved for and bought Vaughn Meader's album "The First Family." It was a huge bestseller. I tried to emulate John Kennedy, but of course, I could not. I admired him, and the whole idea of the Peace Corps, public service. The line "Ask not what your country can do for you . . ." in the inaugural address. . .I was a textbook example of someone who was completely taken up with that.

Today, I'm torn about John Kennedy's legacy. In the conservative world in which I function, it's become commonplace to suggest that John Kennedy would be a Republican today. He was pro-tax cuts. He clearly was pro-business. And he supported a strong defense, and he had a strong foreign policy. But it's tough to ignore his support for New Deal notions and his advocacy of Medicare and other dramatic expansions of government.

The question of his legacy is complicated. On one hand, part of his legacy was reinvigorating the competitive juices in the United States, making the nation feel more zesty and youthful, his call to American greatness. I think that was positive for the country, but it unfortunately involved a denigration of the previous two terms of Ike. In truth, any contrast between Kennedy and Eisenhower—except the ability to impress people on TV—shows Eisenhower as a greater, more successful president. Of course, Eisenhower never had the favorable congressional dispensation that Kennedy had. Kennedy was not in office long enough. But the Kennedy-Eisenhower contrast between style and substance as a national leader changes my outlook substantially. Eisenhower clearly wins over Kennedy.

I was a junior in college during Robert Kennedy's presidential campaign. I got a leave of absence from Yale and went to work in the California primary. I was there at the Ambassador Hotel and was right in front of the podium. I'm heard at the end of his speech yelling, "We love you, Bobby!"

Then, of course, he went into the kitchen, and you couldn't see anything and you really couldn't hear. The kitchen was too far away. Then, there was a scream. It started in the kitchen, moved into the front of the hall, then to the back of the hall, then back again. It was one, long wail.

Everyone was screaming and you didn't know why. But you did know why. Everyone knew what had happened. You didn't have to be told. It was an echo of November 22, 1963. The screams that night seemed to have started in Dallas.

෨෧ Al Neuharth
Author, founder
of *USA Today*, the Freedom
Forum, and the Newseum

"Kennedy congratulated (the Mercury Seven astronauts) and then said, 'Do you guys think we can go to the moon and back in this decade?' (Alan) Shepard said they all looked at each other and exclaimed, 'Sure!' . . . Then they left and got together for a beer and said to each other, 'Is he nuts?'"

I first met John Kennedy when he was in the Senate in the mid-fifties. I was in the Washington bureau for the *Miami Herald*, part of the Knight News organization. I covered him, though I did not get to know him very well. I thought he was a smart, cocky, young guy. When we met with senators—either individually or in groups—some stood out and some didn't. He was certainly one who stood out because he was a bright guy.

On November 22, 1963, I was in Palm Beach Florida attending the Inter-American Press Association convention. He had spoken to that group earlier that week before he went to Dallas. In that address, he did a good job of relating to the members of the association, which included leading people from Latin America, as well as the United States. I don't recall any specifics of the speech, but I do know that he was a hit.

We all just kept our eyes and ears on Walter Cronkite. My recollection of Cronkite and the TV coverage is much clearer than any
newspaper coverage of the assassination. It was all intrigue and sticking
to the tube until Cronkite told us he was dead.

John Kennedy was a visionary and he was politically astute. My
clearest memory of him is in connection with the space program. I
was friends with all the original astronauts. I had started a magazine
called *Florida Today* and was up at Cape Canaveral quite a bit for the
launches, including the first one Alan Shepard rode up in. Later, when
John Glenn made his orbit, Kennedy had the astronauts to the White
House. Shepard often told the story that Kennedy congratulated them
for what already had been done and then he said, "Do you guys think
we can go to the moon and back in this decade?"

Shepard said they all looked at each other and exclaimed, "Sure!"
So they talked about it some more and assured him of their interest in
that program. Then they left and got together for a beer and said to
each other, "Is he nuts?" Because none of them believed we would be
in a position to do that. They hoped it could happen, but none of them
thought it could.

I don't know that I could say I was influenced by John Kennedy. I
was certainly impressed by him. I like to think I was not too influenced
by any public official. But I was impressed by him as much—if not
more—than any other president. Maybe Eisenhower might be slightly
ahead of Kennedy.

What is John Kennedy's legacy? I am a bit prejudiced, being a
Space Coast guy. His space program impressed me more than anything
else he did. But today, decades later, it sure as hell is being compro-
mised significantly.

✑ Bob Schieffer
CBS News

"I've always had this theory that the most successful politicians are the ones who master the dominant medium of their time. . . . He changed the presidency forever. I still think nobody has mastered it quite the way he did."

I never met John Kennedy, but my brother, who was in high school at the time, went down to the Hotel Texas (on the morning of November 22) and stood outside. When (Kennedy) came out to greet the crowds, he actually shook hands with the president. He was one of the last people in Fort Worth to do so, just because he happened to be standing close to the limousine.

My wife—we were not married at the time—and her father attended the breakfast that morning (where JFK spoke). She heard the president, she heard Lyndon Johnson, and she saw Jackie Kennedy when she came in and the president remarked, "Nobody wonders what Lyndon and I wear."

My wife's father was a big Democrat. He had been a big supporter of John Connally. In fact, when she was growing up, John Connally lived across the street from her family.

The night before was such a big night in Fort Worth, but I was in a bad humor. I was the night police reporter at the *Star-Telegram*. There's nothing like having a big story in your town, and you're not a part of it. I had asked if I could cover it (JFK's visit) and the editors said, "No," that the political reporters and the chief of our Austin bureau would be doing the story. Kennedy came to town and got this overwhelming welcome. He landed at Carswell Air Force Base, and ten thousand people showed up that night just to see him and Air Force One, and then the president motored into town to the Texas Hotel.

We had decided to keep the press club open beyond closing time for all the members of the White House Press Corps. To us local reporters, these were celebrities. Presidents didn't travel that much in those days. There was this "coffee house"—an after-hours joint. I didn't get off work until three in the morning and I would often go down there. I was a well-known figure there. A lot of evenings, the night city editor and I would go there. They served coffee, but if you were a friend of the owner, they served you this Kool-Aid spiked with grain alcohol. They gave it away. It's a wonder it didn't kill us all. His place was well known. This was in the days when San Francisco was the headquarters for the beatniks—Allan Ginsberg and the counter-culture. Fort Worth felt like it was on the cutting edge because we had our own "coffee house." The waitresses wore underwear; that was their costumes. By today's stand-ards, their outfits would be seen as bikinis.

It had quite a reputation, and some of these White House reporters had heard of it and told us, "What is this thing? We've got to see this!"

So Phil Record, the city editor, and I, we led a delegation down to this place from the press club a couple of blocks away. There were also some Secret Service guys there, too. I will preface this: If they were drinking, I never saw it. I don't think they were, quite frankly. But, of course, they were all off duty. My group—the White House Press Corps—stayed until after the sun rose. And we did have a few drinks. And we all had a fine time and then we all went home (or back to hotels).

That's why I was sound asleep the next day when my brother woke me up. I had not been asleep all that long, I was in a total fog, and he told me, "You'd better get up. The president's been shot." I didn't believe it. At that time, we did not have all these horrible school shootings and these other violent incidents. We didn't know what had happened.

Excerpt from *This Just In: What I Couldn't Tell You on TV,* by Bob Schi-effer, © 2003 (Used with author's permission):

I got dressed as fast as I could, grabbed my black felt snap-brim Dick Tracy hat, and roared off in my two-seater Triumph TR-4 sports car. As I parked in the lot of the Star-Telegram office, the radio confirmed the worst: The president was dead. It was as if someone had hit me with a hammer. At once, I was stunned, hurt and embarrassed. Stunned, because such violence was unthinkable in those days; hurt and embarrassed, because it had happed in our home state. Why did something like this have to happen and why did it have to happen in Texas?

. . .When I got back to the city room, the confusion was worse than ever. . . I hadn't even removed my hat when I settled behind a typewriter and picked up one of the ringing telephones. In all my years as a reporter, I would never again receive a call like that one. A woman's voice asked if we could spare anyone to give her a ride to Dallas.

"Lady," I said, "this is not a taxi, and besides, the president has been shot."

"I know," she said. "They think my son is the one who shot him."

It was the mother of Lee Harvey Oswald, and she had heard on the radio of her son's arrest.

"Where do you live?" I blurted out. "I'll be right over to get you . . ."

The fact that Lee Harvey Oswald's mother called, everybody thought it was unusual, but not that unusual. The local newspaper was so much a part of the community.

Excerpt from *This Just In: What I Couldn't Tell You on TV,* by Bob Schieffer, © 2003 (Used with author's permission):

The drive to Dallas took about an hour, and when we reached the police station, Bill (Foster, the newspaper's automotive editor) let us out and said he would join us later once he parked the car. Hundreds of reporters had converged on the station, most of them in a hallway where the detective offices were located. Since I was wearing the Dick Tracy hat, it was easy for me to pass for a plainclothesman. There was a uniformed cop behind a counter in one of the offices so I approached him and said, "I'm the one who brought Oswald's mother over from Fort Worth. Is there someplace she can stay where she won't be bothered by all these reporters?"

The officer guided us to a small space that seemed to be some kind of interrogation room and said, "How's this?" I said thanks, and settled Mrs. Oswald in and went into the hallway to see if I could help our guys. . . . Never once did anyone ask who I was. As the evening wore on, Oswald's wife was brought to the police station and an officer asked me if we would mind if they let her share the room. I told them I saw no problem . . .

Toward dark, Oswald's mother asked Detective Captain Will Fritz if they could visit Oswald. Fritz agreed, and led us into a holding room below the jail. The group included Oswald's wife, his mother, an FBI agent and me. I would soon be face-to-face with the man who was being charged with killing our president. Whatever Oswald said, this would have to be the story of a lifetime . . . We had only been there a few minutes, but to me it seemed like an eternity and I could feel my heart beginning to beat faster, when the FBI agent casually asked, "And who are you with?"

I had watched veteran interrogators bluff their way with a suspect by answering a question with a question, and with my best imitation I sort of half snarled, "Well, who are you with?"

The agent seemed a little edgy now. "Are you a reporter?"

Now I was really pushing it: "Well, aren't you?"

It was at this point that I believe I received my first official death threat. The embarrassed agent said he would

kill me if he ever saw me again. Or at least that seemed to
be what he was saying.
I was already leaving as he said it.
It would be the biggest story I almost got but didn't,
and I went back to the crowded corridor and blended
with the rest of the reporters. For the next two days, I
would just be part of the crowd.

Truth be told, covering this story did not really boost my career. I was in Dallas. I wrote some stories about it. What really changed my career was when I went to Vietnam in 1965. That was the turning point.

Jack Kennedy figured out how to use television. I've always had this theory that the most successful politicians are the ones who master the dominant medium of their time. The founders were all great writers and that's how people got their news in those days. They got it in the written word. Franklin Roosevelt was the first politician to really understand radio. Before he came along, when a politician would be on the radio, he would speak as if he were addressing a crowd of forty thousand people at Madison Square Garden. Roosevelt figured out there would be three or four people sitting around the kitchen table or the living room listening to the radio and he spoke directly to them. He was so effective.

Television came along and Eisenhower didn't understand it, didn't know what to do with it. He held news conferences, but they were so afraid he might say something untoward or start World War III that they never broadcast his news conferences until his press secretary, Jim Haggerty, reviewed the transcript.

Kennedy came along and he had this great wit and verve. He was so good. He changed the presidency forever. His mastery of television. The way he could answer questions off the cuff. They were broadcast live. I still think nobody has mastered it quite the way he did. It's hard to say anyone was better on television than Ronald Reagan. But Kennedy could do the interview. He could do the press conference. He could make a speech. He was just better at all of it.

Television is no longer the dominant medium. We don't know where people get their news now. Television is still a powerful force, there's no doubt about that. When you add up the total number of people who watch the (network) evening news every night, it is still a very large group—probably thirty million people. There were nearly sixty million people who watched the debate I moderated last year. We do three or three and a half million every Sunday morning on *Face the Nation*. Television is still influential, but when we start our evening news now, we assume that most of the people turning it on already know what the news is. They've heard it on the radio; they've gotten it on the Internet; they've gotten it on cable. So you can't say anymore that television is the dominant medium. Everything has changed. The whole communications revolution. We don't know where it's going, but we're dealing with a totally different world. It's 24/7.

The good news about Twitter and other social media is that you no longer need a charismatic leader to lead a revolution, as we saw in Egypt. The bad news is that all the nuts now know where other nuts are, and they can find validation in their cause, no matter how bizarre.

Kennedy set a tone and a style for the presidency. He brought glamour to the presidency. He made a lot of young people want to take part in public service and serve their country. But the fact is, he was not there for very long, and as far as his accomplishments, they were not extensive. The person who got the most done was Lyndon Johnson. Perhaps, Johnson would not have been able to do it if it had not been for Kennedy's death. He (Johnson) got the civil rights programs passed. Had it not been for Vietnam where he made a mistake, he would have been remembered as one of our great presidents.

Kennedy's brother Bobby really disliked Lyndon Johnson. He didn't want (Johnson) on the ticket in the first place. They (RFK and LBJ) never healed that breach. They (JFK and RFK) didn't treat Lyndon Johnson very well as vice president for whatever the reasons, but it was Johnson who got done what Kennedy proposed.

✍ Sanford Socolow
CBS News

"The press corps knew he was a flagrant womanizer, and the American people never got a hint of that. . . . The theory of the day was, which sounds specious when you think about it now, if it did not interfere with his professional or civic duties, his (the president's) private life was out of bounds for us."

I shook John Kennedy's hand once. It was an event at the White House. It was brief—"Hello, glad to meet you." Something like that. I was enthralled, as most people were, by his youth, his vigor, his handsomeness. He seduced a lot of us (members of the press) of whom I am one.

For instance, one of the first things he did, which caused quite a stir in my memory, was allowed live coverage of his news conferences, which up to that point had been a no-no. Eisenhower allowed television news coverage of his press conferences after they had been vetted. But with Kennedy's live press conference there was an air of excitement and thrill to them. People anticipated he might goof. Don't forget, this was the height of the Cold War. The thrill that went through the press corps, I just can't dramatize enough. And, of course, that thrill influenced news coverage.

If you examine it, you'll find the coverage was unbelievably positive. From all corners. Beyond what would be expected. Let's get down to the down and dirty of it: The press corps knew he was a flagrant womanizer, and the American people never got a hint of that. That's one example of how his image was distorted by the press.

The Carlyle Hotel was the hotel Kennedy used when he came to New York. I was very friendly with Bob Pierpoint, now deceased, who was the White House correspondent for CBS, so when they came up (to New York), I would go to the press room at the Carlyle to meet Bob for drinks and dinner.

I remember Pierre Salinger, the news secretary of the day, would come into the room and say, "The lid is on," which was jargon for there would be no new developments for the rest of the day or the evening. "You guys can go out and get drunk. I promise you nothing's going to happen while you're gone. The president has gone to visit his friend Mrs. Smith over on Fifth Avenue."

So we (journalists) would go on to have drinks. We knew at the time that Mrs. Smith was one of his amours.

The theory of the day was, which sounds specious when you think about it now, if it did not interfere with his professional or civic duties, his (the president's) private life was out of bounds for us.

What changed was the so-called credibility gap (term referring to public skepticism first used to describe LBJ's policies on Vietnam). And Nixon with Watergate. People discovered the government was lying to them. This was, of course, post-Kennedy. That changed everything.

On November 22, 1963, I was on vacation in upstate New York with my then-pregnant wife. We had just arrived in Dutchess County and were having lunch at a down market diner. Somebody burst into the diner and yelled, "The president's been shot." I didn't believe it. It was beyond comprehension to me. But I decided I ought to check, so I went to a nearby pay phone, and I couldn't get through to CBS. The CBS switchboard was dead in the water because of the overload. I explained to my wife; she was very understanding. We went back to the house we were staying in, packed up, and drove back to New York. Our vacation was maybe six or seven hours.

I drove her home and went to the office. By the time I got there, it must have been seven or eight in the evening. And I was there for the next four days doing all sorts of odd jobs. I got only a few hours of sleep over the next four days.

Those of us in the trenches did not reflect on the momentousness of the events. We were so busy doing the nitty-gritty of getting information out and researching. Looking for people to interview. Feeding Cronkite, and then later Charles Collingwood, who spelled him. Things were so frantic and so out of control. If you're doing your job, there is no time to reflect.

I remember the big disappointment—I cannot dramatize it enough—that we were not on the air when Oswald got shot Sunday morning. We were in some form of ordinary, routine programming. I cannot remember what it was. This was an era with only three networks. NBC, which carried it live, their regular programming was *The Today Show*. They were live from Dallas. They lucked out and we at CBS were just beside ourselves. I was in the newsroom and within seconds of it happening (shooting of Oswald), we were on to it.

At the convention center to which Kennedy was headed (the Dallas Trade Mart) there was a fellow named Eddie Barker, then the news director of the CBS news station in Dallas and who owned Dallas, and Dan Rather, then the most junior member of the CBS news staff. He had been assigned to work with Barker at the convention center and be Barker's "bat boy," doing whatever Barker needed. Eddie was the first news man to learn that Kennedy was dead (from a physician standing near him who had called Parkland Hospital). Eddie told Dan Rather. Rather called in to the Cronkite news room and told them Kennedy was dead. Cronkite rejected that as not being substantial enough to put on the air. Barker and Cronkite were close friends, and Cronkite later that day put Barker on the air.

We came out of this exhausted. Totally drained. Journalists at that time, especially the good ones, were not very reflective. Cronkite, in his heyday, was not a reflective person.

Several years after the assassination, Cronkite published his memoir, *A Reporter's Life*, which was a huge bestseller in its day. Sometime after the book came out, I got a call from Bob Pierpoint who, as I said, was a very close friend of mine. He was beside himself, really upset.

I said, "Bob, what's the problem?"

Bob said, "I just read Cronkite's book."

I said, "So what?"I personally didn't think much of Cronkite's book.

He said, "Sandy, on the day of Kennedy's assassination, he's got Dan Rather at Parkland Hospital. Sandy, I was at Parkland Hospital. Dan Rather was at the convention center."

We're talking about the first edition of the Cronkite autobiography. Sure enough. There were repeated references of Rather at Parkland Hospital.

So I went into Cronkite's office, and I said, "Walter, we've got a problem. In your book, you've got Rather at Parkland Hospital and it was Pierpoint."

And he said, "Get out of here. What are you talking about?"

"What I'm talking about," I replied, "is that on the day Kennedy was shot, Pierpoint was part of the White House entourage. He was at Parkland Hospital. Dan Rather was at the convention center."

It turned into a very heated conversation, with Cronkite finally dismissing me, shouting at me.

"I don't want to talk about it anymore, goddamn it, it was Rather at the hospital, not Pierpoint."

At one point, Cronkite said, "I can see it in my mind's eye."

I said, "Walter, we didn't have the technology in those days to have a remote at the hospital in such quick time."

He dismissed me. We had a very angry display.

I retreated. CBS had published a four-volume text of everything that was said over the four days of coverage, and what was seen on television. I proudly went home and pulled up volume one, day one. Sure enough, you go through it and there it is: Pierpoint, Pierpont, Pierpoint. At Parkland Hospital. There is hardly any reference to Rather. So I brought it into Cronkite the next day, and I laid it on his desk and said, "You've got to read this."

And he looked at it. And I must say, his lips paled right in front of me. He shouted at his assistant to get Pierpoint on the phone. He spoke to Bob and he groveled. He was dismayed. He promised Pierpoint it would be changed in subsequent editions. He apologized to Pierpoint over and over again for the horrendous mistake.

As I was leaving the office, Cronkite said to me, "You know, in a courtroom under oath I would have sworn it was Dan Rather."

The moral of that story? I no longer believe any memoir I read. If the most trusted man in America could make that mistake of memory, you can't trust anybody's memory.

What is John Kennedy's legacy? He saved us from nuclear disaster. We should all be grateful that we did not have a nuclear exchange with Russia over Cuba, though he did start our bad investment in Vietnam.

✑ Al Spivak
United Press International, participated in the Kennedy-Nixon debates in 1960

"(During the campaign, there) were young teeny-boppers who would go running after his open convertible in the motorcades. And they would leap up and down as he drove past. Somebody in the Kennedy entourage named them 'the jumpers.'"

I first met John Kennedy when he was in the Senate. I covered the Labor Committee. I also covered the campaign of 1960 and got to know him well, because I was traveling with him on his family's airplane. It was a twin-engine Convair, "The Caroline."

I was a "press pooler" as a wire service reporter. I thought he was bright, capable, and charming, and as the campaign wore on, I thought he was "out-campaigning" Richard Nixon. I also had met Nixon in 1951, shortly after I arrived in Washington, and got to know him during his Senate days, and occasionally covered him when he was vice president.

I watched the first debate on television, and I reacted the way most people did. On television, Kennedy came across much better than Nixon. There was, of course, the contrasting opinion that on radio, Nixon came through much better.

After the first debate, the public response to Kennedy on the campaign leaped up by quite a bit. There were larger, more enthusiastic crowds. And people eager to see him; to touch his hand. That's when the so called "jumpers" came into existence. These were young teeny-boppers who would go running after his open convertible in the motorcades. And they would leap up and down as he drove past. And somebody in the Kennedy entourage named them "the jumpers." It was like the reaction young girls gave to Frank Sinatra in his heyday. A lot of that for Sinatra may have been staged, but I don't think it was staged in the Kennedy campaign. It didn't have to be. The crowds for Nixon were more subdued. But then, he ran a more subdued campaign.

And Kennedy was on the attack. He was attacking an incumbent vice president and an incumbent administration. If you review the transcripts of those campaign speeches, he hit it hard. My favorite line from his stump speech was the characterization of the Republicans: "They remind me of the elephants in a circus parade. They lock their trunks onto the tails of the other elephants and they all march around in lock-step."

On November 22, 1963, I had just returned to my apartment in Arlington, Virginia, after an extended vacation in Europe. I had been in my apartment for only ten or fifteen minutes when the phone rang, and it was the number two man in our Washington bureau, Grant Dillman. He said, "Thank goodness you're back. Don't unpack. Kennedy has been shot and we want you to go to Dallas." Not too long after that, Grant called me back and said, "You're not going to Dallas. Kennedy's dead. But you are going to Andrews to cover the arrival of his body on Air Force One."

At Andrews, there was an eerie scene. It was dark and there was a rope stretched across a press area so reporters could see the plane well as it taxied up. Before the casket was removed, Merriman (Smith), who had been on Air Force One as a pooler, got off and rushed over, looking for whoever was there from UPI. He saw me and he handed me his copy and said, "Phone this into the office." He had written a story, a follow-up to the assassination. He had been the only wire service reporter on Air Force One. He covered the swearing-in of Johnson, and he was able to interview people on the staff.

During the funeral, my job was to cover the cemetery. I was dictating the graveside ceremony to a typist, play-by-play, and at a certain point there was a flyover of Air Force jets. Several years later, the young lady to whom I had been dictating said to me, "Do you remember breaking down when the airplanes flew over?"

I responded, "I did nothing of the sort."

She said, "Yes you did. You choked up. And you had to say, 'Wait a minute.' And it took several minutes before you got back and started dictating some more."

I said, "I have no memory of it."

But thinking about it more and more, I am convinced that I did choke up. I choke up very easily. I also recall bagpipers performing. Anyone who would not choke up at that is made of iron.

Kennedy's legacy is one of inspiration. He inspired the country through his speeches—not only his inaugural address, but other speeches as well. He came in as a younger president than the nation was accustomed to. And he loved to use the word "vigor."

He performed magnificently during the Cuban Missile Crisis, and I think he started then to get his stride. Prior to that he felt, I am convinced, that Khrushchev "did him dirt" to coin an old phrase, and JFK felt that it was his job to protect the country and the world against Khrushchev. That was a great achievement. It kept the country out of a Third World War.

✑ Stan Stearns
United Press International, captured iconic photo of John Kennedy Jr. saluting his father's casket

"One exposure. A roll of thirty-six exposures, only one exposure, that's it."

I was a pool photographer for a state dinner one evening at the White House. And they put me in some anteroom, waiting for the entertainment, the famous cello player, Pablo Casals. So I'm in this ante waiting and President Kennedy walks in there. And there's nobody in there but me.

I'm like about to pee in my pants. I mean, I'm a twenty-year-old kid.

And he takes his coat off, and he calls me by my first name. I don't know how he remembered that. I was shocked. And he says, "Stan, would you mind adjusting my corset?" And I'm in the back, tightening up the laces on his corset.

He leaves, and I said, "God, I need a drink." So then, I guess it was a half hour or so later, the entertainment started. And they brought me into the ballroom.

On November 22, 1963, I was out at the Bowie (Maryland) golf course. I was on the seventeenth green, putting for birdie. And the pro came out there and he says, "Stan, I think you need to come with me, the president's been shot."

I said, "I'm sitting here putting for birdie."

I thought he was pulling my leg, because he knew the guy I was with, we had a heavy bet going on. Well, I went back with him to the pro shop, called my boss George Grayling in Washington, and he says, "Thank God you called. Get out to Andrews Air Force base as soon as you can. The plane left Dallas and they're en route." So that's when I started with the four-day funeral.

The most memorable image is Jackie with the blood on her legs, the big martyr, to prove to the American people. Jackie was in another world. Jackie set the motive. Hairstyles, fashion. She redecorated the White House. She was like the first queen, the only queen we ever had. And Jack was like a prince. It was different times.

She was a promoter. She used to hide the kids all the time, didn't want their publicity, didn't want them in front of photographers. But she would always bring them out at a strategic time. Her timing was unbelievable. And then nothing would happen for a couple months. But she timed it.

So I'm looking at the blood on her legs, and I'm making all the pictures. This is front page all over the world. It might have been fifty to sixty feet. It was quiet; you could drop a pin on that runway. Nobody said anything. And you could see Bobby look like he was almost in tears, Lyndon got out of there real quick. But I'll never forget the blood-soaked Jackie. In fact, one of the magazines in France, or somewhere else, I forget, they blew up her leg, just from the skirt down.

As far as the funeral, in my estimation, she would outdo Cecil B. DeMille. She copied all this stuff from the Lincoln funeral, I mean everything. And then the flame at the grave site had to be blue, because that was Jack's favorite color. The whole world stopped. Everybody was glued to that TV set. And I worked the full four days. I think I caught a two-hour nap once at the White House.

It was myself and an AP photographer who were chosen to walk from the White House with the entourage, with Jackie and all the world leaders, who walked from the White House to the church. And we walked out in front, to the side, and made pictures along this route. So when we got to the church, there were seventy or eighty other photographers. And I got under the rope, and there's no place to go. It's like sardines. And I wind up right next to a fellow UPI photographer Frank Cancellare.

So we agreed that I was just going to concentrate on Jackie, and he was going to photograph everything like I wasn't even standing there. So they come out, I'm looking through the finder at her, her expressions. Next thing you know, she reaches down, whispers in (John Jr.'s) ear, the hand goes up, click, and it's over.

One exposure. A roll of thirty-six exposures, only one exposure, that's it.

So I made that one exposure, and I'm supposed to go with the entourage for the funeral. And I ask Frank, I said, "Did you get the salute?"

And he says, "What are you talking about?"

I started asking every photographer I could get my hands on, did you see the salute? They all said, "What are you talking about?" They didn't see it. So I'm supposed to give my film to the motorcycle courier to go back to the office. And I said, "Man, I know how good this picture is." So, I decided, I'm going to walk this back to the office myself. So I walked off the job.

The office was on Thirteenth and L streets. Well, I was just talking to myself, there's nobody there. And I'm talking to myself about how much this picture would be worth. And if I walked off the job, and if I sold it to *LIFE, TIME, Newsweek, Paris Match*. Then I said, "Well, if I did that, they would sue me and get all the money back, and then I'd be in the headlines and nobody would hire me." It was just a passing thought that went through my head.

So I get in the office, and my boss sees me. I thought he was gonna pass out. I never saw a man that angry, and that wounded.

I said, "George, I've got the picture of the funeral."

He says, "Are you shitting me? Because we've got twenty-five photographers. Look at this film right here. It looks like confetti." I never saw a guy that mad. And about that time, the big boss from New York walks over and he grabs me by the shirt collar and he says, "You son of a bitch, you better have the picture or you're fired on the spot."

And I said, "Frank, take your hands off of me."

Then George says, "Give the film to the kid and let him develop it."

I said, "No, not in that crap that we develop it in." I said, "This is a big enlargement, we've got to have fine grain developer." They all look at me like I'm a crazy man. So I go outside, I get in a cab, and I go down to the camera store, and I buy fine grain developer. I come back. I've got to fix up the chemicals. It takes time. I've got to cool it down, because you mix it up with hot water. So I go in the darkroom, and I develop this film.

One image. I look at it with a magnifying glass on the light box, and I'm gleaming from ear to ear, because I know I've got it. So I wash it properly, I dry it properly, I put it in a little plastic sleeve, and I walk outside. And they start to grab this thing.

I said, "Just everybody relax." And I walked over to my boss and I handed it to him.

And he takes a magnifying glass, and he looks at it and he says, "Holy shit, he does have *the* picture of the funeral."

❧ Richard Stolley
LIFE magazine, negotiated the rights to the only film of the assassination

"Then we see frame 313. . . . I've been in journalism almost seventy years, and that is the most dramatic moment I can recall."

MY connection to John Kennedy before his death was quite limited; my connection after his death was quite strong.

I remember November 22 as if it were yesterday. I was in the LA bureau when I heard that John Kennedy had been shot. We got the news over the AP teletype. The first bulletins were not stories—just fragments of sentences: "shots heard in Dealey Plaza;" "presidential limo speeds up." I'm not quoting here, just trying to give a sense of what we were reading on the wire. Soon, it was clear that something terrible had happened: "Kennedy believed wounded," or something like that.

I called New York instantly and they were watching the same thing. I asked, "What can we do?" My editor in New York replied, "How fast can you get to Dallas?" The answer was that there was a National Airlines plane in an hour. I grabbed (correspondent) Tommy (Thompson) and two photographers and said, "Let's go." We heard on the car radio just outside LA airport that Kennedy had died.

The plane was crowded with journalists. The pilot kept us informed on the flight about developments in Dallas and told us the police had arrested someone named Lee Harvey Oswald from Irving, Texas.

Tommy turned to me and said, "I know the cops in Irving, let me go after that part of the story." And I said, "Godspeed."

Once we landed, Tommy took off for Irving with one of the photographers. The other photographer and I went to the Adolphus Hotel, where our bureau receptionist had booked us a suite. I had been there maybe two hours when I got a phone call from our stringer, Patsy Swank, who had been at the Dallas Police Department all afternoon. Another reporter had called her and said, "Patsy, I just picked up a report from a cop that a Dallas businessman was in Dealey Plaza with a movie camera, and I'm told he photographed the assassination."

I asked, "What do we know about the photographer?"

She replied, "My friend just pronounced the name to me. He didn't know how to spell it. Zapruder."

I had never been in Dallas before, so I picked up the Dallas phone book—a phone book at that time was a very important research tool. I ran my finger down the Z's until I found the name, spelled exactly as she had pronounced it to me. Z-A-P-R-U-D-E-R, Abraham.

So I started calling. No answer. It was about six o'clock in the evening. At eleven o'clock I was still calling, and finally, this weary voice answered. I identified myself and asked if other reporters had contacted him. He said, "No." He had been out having the film processed all evening long. I asked if I could come to his house and see it. At that point, he was exhausted and full of grief.

He said, "Come to my office at nine a.m."

I got there at eight. His office was just a few steps from Dealey Plaza. Zapruder looked slightly annoyed that I was so early. He was just about to show the film to two local Secret Service agents. But he said I could join them. He showed it to us in this small windowless room. Eight-millimeter film is tiny—only about a quarter of an inch wide. The image we saw was not larger than a small television screen. He beamed it onto a white wall. You see the motorcade turning right into Dealey Plaza, and then it takes a sharp left. There were some cops on motorcycles out in front, then the limo disappears behind a big road sign. When it comes out, Kennedy's fists are at his throat, and you can see Governor John Connolly starting to fall off the jump seat, his mouth opening up in pain. The president is still clutching his throat. Jackie is looking at him quizzically.

Then we see frame 313. The whole right rear of the president's skull explodes, a plume of blood and brain matter.

All three of us grunted when frame 313 came into view. I've been in journalism almost seventy years, and that is the most dramatic moment I can recall. I was overwhelmed, and immediately understood what an important piece of photography this was. I was determined not to leave that office without that film for *LIFE* magazine.

Other reporters showed up. He showed them the film. I stayed away from them. Then Zapruder called us all into the hall outside his office. He said he realized they all wanted to talk to him about purchasing film rights, but, "Mr. Stolley was the first person to contact me, so I feel obliged to talk to him first." He invited me into his office, and of course, the other reporters went nuts. There were no TV people among them. There was *Saturday Evening Post*, AP, several newspapers, and a newsreel. This was less than twenty-four hours after the president's death. Dan Rather and the other TV people didn't appear until Monday. That may seem astonishing, but TV news was only beginning; it had gone from fifteen to thirty-minute nightly broadcasts just a few months earlier.

Zapruder and I sat down and negotiated. He was a canny businessman, and he knew the value of what he had. I determined that very early on. We didn't have to bullshit after that. But he was also deeply concerned about the possible exploitation of the film. He realized how incredibly grisly and sensational it was.

He told me he had had a nightmare the night before, after the assassination. In it, he was walking through Times Square in New York, back when Times Square was particularly sleazy, and a guy in a pinstriped, double-breasted suit was on the sidewalk urging people, "C'mon in, folks, and see the president get shot on the big screen!" Zapruder said he woke up almost in tears. It haunted him.

I was able to assure him that *LIFE* would not exploit this film. I said, "You know *LIFE* magazine. *LIFE* has a reputation for graphic photography presented with taste." In the end, that factor was very important.

We kept raising the ante, and I got up to fifty thousand dollars. I said, "Mr. Zapruder, that's as high as I am authorized to go. You'll have to excuse me so I can call New York."

The other reporters were banging on the door and shouting. I could see this was making him exceedingly nervous. The thought of going through this negotiation process with representatives of half a dozen other publications was weighing heavily on him.

He looked up at me and said, "Let's do it."

I had spoken with one of the *TIME-LIFE* lawyers the night before, and he told me how to compose a basic contract. I sat down at a desk in Mr. Z's office and typed out a six line contract for print rights only. We both signed it, and his business partner signed it as a witness. He gave me the original film and one copy. He had made three copies, and had already sent one to the FBI and another to the Dallas police department.

It was amazing the Secret Service agents didn't confiscate the original that morning. Astonishing.

I got those two little reels and said, "Do you have a back door to this place?" Thank God he did, so I was able to sneak out and leave poor Mr. Z to go out and tell that hallway full of extremely angry journalists that he had just sold the film to *LIFE* magazine.

I sent the original to Chicago by courier. We were on a tight deadline, and *LIFE* had set up a makeshift office at the plant where the magazine was printed. Normally, we would assemble all the editorial material for an issue in New York and put it on a train for Chicago and Donnelley, the printing company. The one copy of the film went to New York. The editors there watched it, called me Sunday, and said, "This is an incredible piece of film. We now want all the rights." I called Zapruder, and he seemed so relieved to hear from me. He said, "Meet me in my lawyer's office tomorrow."

Meanwhile, a small staff of editors in Chicago was putting the film's images into the magazine in black and white because the plant could not print color that fast. And they did not use frame 313 out of deference to the Kennedy family.

In that frame, the brain matter is spilling forward, which proves fairly conclusively to me that there was no shot from the grassy knoll because it would then be going in the opposite direction. The editors were all set to close the magazine Sunday morning when Oswald was shot. So they had to rip open that issue and start all over again.

Tommy Thompson meanwhile had found the Oswald family, and it was an exclusive. He called me on Saturday and said, "I got them. Nobody else has. We've got to hide them."

We did. We put them in a suite under an assumed name at the Adolphus Hotel. It was Marina, the two babies, Lee's brother Robert, their mother Marguerite, and a Russian interpreter. The Secret Service called us and demanded to know where they were, claiming, "We've got to protect them." I denied any knowledge of their whereabouts. The agent got extremely profane with me, and I finally said, "If I tell you where they are, will you promise me you won't tell any other reporters. I'm very serious about this." He said, "I promise."And he kept his promise.

I think they moved agents into the hotel near the family immediately, and the following day, Sunday, after Oswald was killed, they whisked the family to a motel on the outskirts of Dallas.

The day after that, Monday, I went to the office of Mr. Z's attorney, Sam Passman, and that's where Dan Rather comes in. He was there and saw the footage for the first time. I knew Dan. I had covered the South for four years and had seen him on a few racial stories working for CBS. He later wrote in *The Camera Never Blinks* that he was dismayed when *LIFE* magazine walked into the office because he knew we had "deep pockets." He saw the film and left. He had been authorized to offer ten thousand dollars for film and broadcast rights.

I went into Passman's office with him and Zapruder. I offered another hundred thousand dollars for the film and TV rights, and we ended our negotiations in about fifteen minutes. Zapruder asked that the amount not be revealed. I promised I would not.

After that meeting, I never saw Abe Zapruder again, although we did speak on the phone once or twice. Time Inc. had agreed to split whatever revenue it made selling rights to the film after recouping the one hundred fifty thousand dollars, and he called to ask how sales were going. At the time, I realized that he had given all his copies of the film to law enforcement agencies, and I asked if I could send him a good first-generation copy. He said no, he did not want the film in his home.

The film almost didn't get made. Zapruder had not brought his camera to work that day. His secretary badgered him, saying, "Mr. Z, it's not every day that the president comes through the neighborhood."

All Dallas, including Oswald, knew the motorcade route because it had been published in the local papers. It was raining that morning, so Zapruder left his camera at home. But he drove back home and got it. Then he went to Dealey Plaza and found the one spot where he could film the whole thing from beginning to end.

You can see an almost imperceptible jerk three times in the film—three shots. The first shot missed. It was fired when the limousine was the closest to the sixth floor of the Texas School Book Depository Building where Oswald was hiding. The second shot was fired, from Zapruder's vantage point, when the limousine was behind the road sign. And the fatal third shot came two or three seconds after that.

Ever since, I am frequently asked how I managed to obtain the film. Part of the answer came years later when I was speaking with Zapruder's business partner, whom I had no recollection of meeting even though he signed the first contract as a witness. It was that tense a situation. He asked me, "Do you know why you got that film?"

I said, "What do you mean?"

"Do you know why you got it instead of all those other people in the hall?"

And I said, "Well, we paid him fifty thousand dollars."

He said, "No, he could have gotten that and maybe more from somebody out in the hall."

I said, "Well, *LIFE's* commitment not to exploit the film was important."

He replied, "No question that was important to Abe. But do you know why YOU got it?"

I said, "I give up."

And he said, "Because you were a gentleman."

On a lot of assignments you have to be a son of a bitch. But on this one, my instinct was not to go out to his house the night before. I considered it, because, in the end, there were not a lot of people who would say no to *LIFE* magazine. But I realized this was something none of us had ever been involved in before.

John Kennedy's legacy is mostly spiritual, not substantial. Those of us who were around remember him with fondness and such "what if" longing. He never really got a chance to do very much. But there is one exception. I covered the South during four years of school desegregation. Kennedy tried to get civil rights bills through Congress, but there was no way in hell those bills were going to be passed. Lyndon Johnson, who was the most fascinating human being I ever met, did get them through.

Kennedy knew what the country needed and was blessed by having a vice president, whom he probably didn't like very much, and of course, Bobby Kennedy hated, who had great influence in Congress. I was in the Senate gallery when the 1964 Civil Rights Act was passed, a truly historic moment. Senator Everett Dirksen, who was from my hometown in Illinois, rallied the moderate Republicans, of whom there were still some then, to vote for the bill. Of course all the Southern Democrats voted no. It was an amazing example of how politics works. Kennedy realized that the civil rights bills were essential and just, and he was their spiritual leader. But the credit for their passage belongs to his successor.

✑ Sander Vanocur
NBC News and
ABC News

*"During the Cuban Missile Crisis, we were very
close (to a nuclear war). I had been told that in
case of an evacuation of the President and his
family to wherever they were going, I was to be
the TV pool correspondent and go with them.
And I didn't know how to explain this to my
wife."*

I first met John Kennedy at Midway Airport in Chicago, and as luck
would have it that day, Nixon and Kennedy were both there changing
planes. It was 1958 or 1959. I was based in Chicago and one of them
had a book, it might have been Kennedy's *Profiles in Courage*, and I was
sent to the airport to get an interview with him.

What I knew about him at the time I had learned from my college roommate at Northwestern University, Newton Minow, an Adlai
Stevenson law partner. He was urging Adlai not to run again for the
presidency in 1960, but rather to give his support to Kennedy. That
was kind of difficult because Stevenson was a good friend of (Eleanor)
Roosevelt. She didn't like Kennedy because she didn't like his father.
She once said, I think, "I do wish the senator from Massachusetts
would, from time to time, show a bit more courage and a little less
profile," referring, of course, to Kennedy's book.

Catholicism was the most important issue in the 1960 election. In 1928, Al Smith (a Catholic) had run and lost to (Herbert) Hoover. The joke was, at the time, when the election was over, Al Smith sent a cable to the Pope, and all it said was "Unpack." But (in 1960) the Catholic issue was still very strong and not entirely in the South. Kennedy made the decision to speak to the Greater Houston Ministerial Association one week before the (first) Kennedy-Nixon debate in Chicago. And he did very well. Later, Kennedy and Nixon spoke at the Al Smith Memorial Dinner in New York. I can't even say it was a bipartisan event because Cardinal Francis Spellman was in charge and Spellman didn't really like the Kennedys. The audience was mostly Republican, anyway.

After the first debate in Chicago in 1960, in which I was one of the journalists asking questions of the candidates, I went up to the podium and took a yellow legal pad on which Kennedy had made notes. It's now in the Newseum in Washington, DC. Both Kennedy and Nixon left almost immediately after the debate. During the broadcast, Nixon had a little sweat on his upper lip, and he would glance once in a while at Kennedy as if—and I am being a bit subjective here—seeking approval. Kennedy hardly ever looked at Nixon; he looked straight at the camera. We later learned Kennedy had a perpetual tan to hide the pallor from taking prescription drugs for Addison's disease. We didn't know it at the time and had we known it, I'm not sure we would have reported it. Different kind of ethics then.

Later, in 1962, at the end of the Cuban Missile Crisis, Kennedy had a press conference in the White House Situation Room and after he spoke, I went to where he had been standing. There was a yellow legal pad on which he had written one word five times and had circled it: "Berlin." I went to grab it, and Kennedy's military aide, Major General Ted Clifton, put his hand on my wrist and said, "Sandy, that's for the archives."

During the Cuban Missile Crisis, we were very close (to a nuclear war). I came home one night and my late wife asked, "Are we going to war?" I said, "I don't know. I need a drink." I had been told on Tuesday, after Kennedy's address to the nation on Monday night, that in case of an evacuation of the President and his family to wherever they were going, I was to be the TV pool correspondent and go with them. And

I didn't know how to explain this to my wife. Anyone who says they knew there would not be a war, don't believe it. I was scared. I didn't know what to do. I probably would have stayed with my family.

Later, when I visited Havana for an event commemorating the crisis, I came away with how angry the Soviets were at the Cubans for getting them into this, and how angry the Cubans—at least Fidel Castro and his brother—were because they thought the Soviets had collapsed at the strong stance Kennedy had taken.

Newt Minow was a friend of Sargent Shriver, who married Kennedy's sister Eunice, and one night I attended a cocktail party at the Shrivers' apartment. The old man (Joseph P. Kennedy) came up to me and introduced himself. That is where he said, "I keep telling Jack that television is very important and that (he) ought to pay more attention to you guys in television, than in the press."

The old man was more alert to the possibilities of television than Jack Kennedy was. Jack eased into it. He really was our first television president.

This continued with Kennedy after he was elected president. We in television thought the guys who had the best entry into the White House were Benjamin Bradlee at *Newsweek* and Hugh Sidey at *TIME* magazine. Also, Kennedy was a close friend of Bradlee. They were neighbors. Hugh Sidey had an in because *TIME* was very influential, terribly powerful at the time. And *LIFE* magazine, too.

Covering the Kennedy White House was not a day at the beach because television had not come into the dominant position as it has today. After Kennedy and Jackie arrived at the White House, I think it was the day after the inauguration, he took her on a tour, and in the press room, he introduced her to Merriman Smith of UPI. He said, "Jackie, this is Merriman Smith of the United Press. He owns the place."

On November 22, 1963, I was in Los Angeles. I had been asked by Robert Sarnoff, David's son, who was running the West Coast office of NBC, to be the speaker at a dinner. The next day I was playing tennis, and someone leaned out an apartment window and said, "Kennedy's been shot."

I took the first flight I could to Dallas. Air Force One had already left and so I flew then to Washington.

On the next day, Saturday, I was at the White House standing on the small street between the West Wing and what was then referred to as the "Old State Department Building," now called the Eisenhower Executive Office Building. I was facing down toward the Potomac outside the office of (Kennedy's National Security Advisor) McGeorge Bundy and out came Kennedy's rocking chair. And about ten minutes later, in came a saddle on a stand. Visually, nothing could illustrate more forcibly the change.

Now I have to say, President Johnson was very gracious and kind to Mrs. Kennedy in getting her through this.

The Kennedys were made not just for television but for still pictures as well: the image of Kennedy clapping while his children are jumping in the Oval Office; the image of John-John peeking out from the desk. The Kennedys were a good story.

Kennedy's legacy is generational. He and Nixon, even though they lived during Roosevelt's presidency and the New Deal, represented the post-World War II generation, symbolized by the GI Bill of Rights.

It was almost like central casting gave us Jack and Jackie. And their beautiful children.

SECTION SEVEN:

Political Figures

✑ Barry Goldwater Jr.
Member of the United States House of Representatives, businessman, son of U.S. Senator and 1964 Republican presidential nominee Barry Goldwater

"They talked about running against each other, and instead of wasting a lot of money, decided to travel around the country together, stop at different towns and cities, and debate each other."

I met John Kennedy as a young high school student. I was visiting my father at the United States Capitol. He and my father were talking, and a photographer took a picture of me taking a picture of the two of them. That was my only personal connection with the president. It was probably 1956.

My father and I talked about his expected campaign against John Kennedy in 1964, and I overheard many of my father's conversations about it. My father and JFK were good friends, having served together on the Senate Labor Committee (Senate Select Committee on Improper Activities in Labor and Management, also known as the "McClellan Committee"). He would spend time at the White House from time to time, sitting in the president's rocking chair, talking politics and sipping whiskey.

They talked about running against each other, and instead of wasting a lot of money, decided to travel around the country together, stop at different towns and cities, and debate each other. It would have been very entertaining and would have set a high standard for future campaigns. They ought to do that today.

Excerpt from Barry M. Goldwater oral history interview for the JFK Library and Museum, recorded January 24, 1965 (Pages 16 and 23):

> ". . . And I never will forget this—and God, I hope they don't play this for a long, long time—he came in and he had a little cigar in his mouth, you know, those little cigarette cigars. He looked down and he said, "Do you want this (deleted) job?" I said, "Hell, no."
>
> (On whether Goldwater believed he could have defeated JFK in 1964): "Well, I felt that I could, frankly. And I think that he felt that I had a chance. The tide was turning against him at the time he passed away. Certainly he couldn't have carried the South. The business fraternity was against him. I felt that I had a fair to middling chance of defeating him. I wouldn't have bet a lot of money on it . . . Kennedy would not have been afraid to debate as Johnson was . . . I imagine he (JFK) would have agreed to go along with me in town after town and have personal debates on the subjects and the issues. Johnson was afraid to get out of his shell. In fact, he never talked about an issue in his life. Kennedy enjoyed that kind of thing and I really looked forward to a campaign against Jack.

On November 22, 1963, I was on the floor of the Pacific Coast Stock Exchange, as a broker and trader, with two telephones to my ears. I was watching the ticker tape. In those days, stock brokers learned to read the ticker tape, so when the market opened, you never took your eyes off it. And it (the shooting of the president) was announced over the ticker tape. I saw it just as it came across. I was in the middle of a trade which I had to complete, but then I got a call from my dad. He was actually calling about the funeral of my grandmother. And he told me he had heard the president had been shot. We didn't talk much about the president; we were focused more on my grandmother's funeral.

I think the difference between Kennedy and my father was their attitudes toward a strong defense and to react to situations the United States was confronted with in a strong and decisive manner. He was critical of Kennedy for not being more reactive and forthcoming on stopping the missiles in Cuba. Kennedy had an indecisive factor that my father did not appreciate.

Excerpt from Barry M. Goldwater oral history interview for the JFK Library and Museum, recorded January 24, 1965 (Pages 25 and 26):

> *"(New York Senator Kenneth B. Keating) and I together had been pointing out on the floor of the Senate since June of that year that there were missiles in Cuba, that we should be doing something about it. In fact, I wrote down on a piece of paper flying back from Arizona after Labor Day that year that on or about the middle of October Kennedy would do something about Cuba and I gave it to Sam Shafer of Newsweek. And Sam, like you guys do, he printed it.*
>
> *But Kennedy could have pulled this confrontation off at any time and he should have done it earlier. I don't hesitate a moment to say, as I've said before, I feel it was a politically motivated operation and it certainly cost the Republican Party a lot of seats in the House of Representatives. There's no question of that. I'll never forget for four or five days I was just like a fish out of water—what the hell could you say? You had to back your president—it was the right act. He didn't go far enough or long enough with it. I think at that time we could have completely toppled Castro and we wouldn't have had to have any bloodshed on our part about it.*

A lot of people judge presidents incorrectly. The most important attribute of a president is to be a leader, and through communications to the nation, move us in certain directions and rally the spirit of the American people to get together and solve problems, to get together and support initiatives. I was not around then, but Franklin Roosevelt had that same knack. I'm not sure if he was on the same level of a JFK or a Ronald Reagan, but he certainly made strong efforts to communicate to the American people in a non-partisan way.

In regard to Kennedy's legacy, the only thing that stands out is the Cuban Missile Crisis and that's a mixed bag. As a result, you wouldn't necessarily give him high marks. He wasn't in office long enough to do much else. The other thing I recall—and Republicans like this— he advocated reducing taxes. A main point of the Republican philosophy—get the government off people's backs and out of their wallets. I respect that and JFK's message—"A rising tide lifts all boats." He was successful in building the nation's economy.

He stood out—and he still stands out—as an admired and respected president. More so than the others who came after him.

◈ Gary Hart
Member of the United States Senate, Democratic presidential candidate

"He was going in to see the President with two guns!"

I saw John Kennedy twice in campaign appearances in the fall of 1960. I was a graduate student at the time and happened to be with some friends in New York City. We were in midtown Manhattan. There was a lot of excitement: campaign signs, leaflets being handed out. And he was making one of his first appearances after the Democratic convention in the fall campaign.

In those days, my recollection is that the conventions were held, but people didn't do very much in August, unlike now. The official campaign started after Labor Day. This would have been the first ten days or so in September. The event was a rally of supporters at the Waldorf Astoria Hotel ballroom, and we walked into the hotel, went up to the second or third floor to the ballroom, and more or less just walked right in. You obviously could never do that today. We were midway back in the crowd over on the edge. I remember it vividly. At this event and with others in the campaign, he usually ran an hour or two late. It was supposed to start at three or four in the afternoon. There were some preliminary speeches; a lot of standing around; a band playing.

Finally, the curtains parted and out he came. Of course, he was an extraordinary looking man. Not someone you would mistake for anyone else; very tanned and Hollywood looking in a way.

He had a manner about him that was almost shy. He always looked a bit startled when he would walk out and see a bunch of people yelling and screaming. He had a seven-minute campaign speech: "Let's get this country moving again." It was kind of standard rhetoric; all the sayings people wanted to hear. And that was it and he was gone. People stayed and cheered and clapped.

The next time I saw him was the Sunday morning before the election. He had a big rally at Madison Square Garden on Saturday evening. Then he made four or five stops through Westchester County at rallies, then two or three stops in Connecticut, well into the night. He was due on the New Haven Connecticut green at about 9 o'clock Sunday morning. My wife and I went down there fairly early, around 8:30, and within minutes the green filled up. It was solidly packed. People were on every side street you could see. I think the crowd estimate was seventy-five thousand to one hundred thousand people, which was monstrous for a campaign at that time.

My principal impression was the degree to which he inspired my generation toward public service. A lot of people thought it was politics, but he never said, "Run for office." He always said, "Give something back to the country."

It was a broad challenge toward public service. I entered law school the next year and graduated in '64 and went into three years of government service in Washington. For my class, the class before us, and maybe one or two others, the thing was not to go to a Wall Street firm, but to go to Washington and work in government. I attribute that to John Kennedy. It traces back to the ancient Republic. He read a lot of literature from the Greek and Roman eras. He knew the theory of the Republic was citizen involvement and civic virtue. He conveyed that and I think was the last president to really do so.

Of course, I recall vividly where I was on November 22. That was the fall of my senior year of law school, and so we were interviewing for positions for when we would be graduating the following spring. Law firms were coming to the campus to interview people. Ironically, I had an interview at two o'clock that afternoon with a partner from a Denver law firm, Holme, Roberts, and Owen, a very well-established firm.

At the time, my wife and I managed one of the international houses on Prospect Street up on the hill, and it was a fifteen minute walk downtown. I had the television on and was getting dressed up for the interview. The news came on, and of course, later the famous Walter Cronkite announcement. So I just went through the motions. I walked down the hill and was in a state of "auto-pilot." It was unbelievable. I went to the room where the interviews were being held. The lawyer, who subsequently became a very good friend of mine, had just heard the news. I introduced myself and sat down.

Neither one of us said a word for fifteen or twenty minutes. Then, I thanked him for his time and left.

The most important lessons (JFK) learned in office dealt with the Cuban Missile Crisis, as well as the confrontation with Soviet leader Khrushchev during their first summit meeting. The general consensus was that he (Kennedy) got overpowered. He was stunned at how blunt and demanding Khrushchev was and how little respect he paid to Kennedy. Kennedy came out of that saying to his close friends that he realized the seriousness of the Cold War.

He was very much an international president, as demonstrated by the famous trip to France and meetings with De Gaulle. Given who he was, and his background, and his family, he was by no means a novice in the ways of the world and international relations. He had traveled.

He had met a lot of important people, so it wasn't like this was a new set of experiences for him. But when he walked into the Elysee Palace, he was President of the United States, so that had to have made a big difference. I would imagine that the two shaping experiences of his presidency were the meetings with international leaders on the international stage and the civil rights struggle, how bitter it was given Southern sentiments.

Regarding the Cuban Missile Crisis, he was a war veteran and had enormous respect for senior commanders, but not necessarily the hawkish ones, such as Curtis LeMay—not only their willingness, but their eagerness to go to war in Cuba, really sobered him. And their underestimation of what it would take to overthrow Castro, I think it caused him to understand that he couldn't take somebody else's word for events on the ground, whether they were in intelligence or the military.

The concept of public service, as Kennedy spoke of it, is not prevalent today. The theme needs be re-echoed by leaders and particularly new leaders—young leaders who can inspire idealism. Idealism is an interesting phenomenon.

I've described myself as the oldest and last living American idealist. I tell student audiences to take a look because when I'm gone, there won't be any more. Idealism is something that, if it occurs to people at all, it usually occurs in their late teens to mid-twenties. Why that period? Because if you're going to have any spirit or sense of idealism—meaning that we can make improvements to make our society better—it's going to be in the period when you're old enough to understand what that takes—a commitment to service, a belief that things can be improved, but also before you get life's burdens, meaning families, mortgages, and careers. It really is an appeal to a window of young people—that's what the Peace Corps was about. It resonated with a few people over that age, but by and large, in that younger group.

You can't be against government and then challenge people to be involved in government. And that's an appeal of Republican ideology.

What will it take to inspire people into public service? Dynamic young political leadership that issues the challenge. There's no magic to it; there's no secret formula. It's the theme and the reiteration of the theme and providing opportunities to fulfill it. One thing I tried to do in the late seventies and early eighties was to promote different forms of national service. This was a kind of update of the Peace Corps concept. Kennedy not only said, "Give something back," but "Here are a variety of ways you can do it, including internationally." And I think you have to do both; you have to say, "Give something back and here are some ways that it can be done." By the way, not just in the national arena, but at the state and local levels as well.

The question of John Kennedy's legacy is so complex. I would rank him very high because of that intangible of appealing to idealism which cannot be qualified, cannot be measured, by any normal political science measurements. He had a profound impact on this country, at least in my generation. It hasn't survived much beyond that, and my generation is moving on. So I worry about that for future generations.

His legacy is not only the tangible events like the Cuban Missile Crisis and his very important American University speech, probably the most important and historic speech he gave. It was visionary. But it is also—in those brief three years—his inspirational contribution. And it was unique. I don't know American history well enough to know whether a Teddy Roosevelt sixty years earlier inspired that kind of activism. Of course, there was the Progressive Movement at the time. As historian Arthur Schlesinger commented, there are "waves of reform" and those, generally, are periods of idealism and social improvement.

I would like to believe that if he had a chance to see what some of the people he inspired went on to do, that he would be very pleased. That is to say, a lot of people did go into the Peace Corps, the military, and had brilliant careers in government and diplomacy. A few of us got ourselves elected to office. The greatest rewards of my service are the people who have helped me, and then have gone on to do great things themselves. And some in political life and some, quite often, in other humanitarian causes. There have been an extraordinary number of them.

One last story. I got to the Senate in 1975 and was immediately appointed to the Select Committee to Investigate the Intelligence Agencies of the U.S. Government. It came to be called the "Church Committee," after Senator Frank Church of Idaho. Shortly after we began our work in the spring of 1975, the CIA started to turn over a lot of files having to do with attempts to assassinate foreign leaders, particularly Fidel Castro. We got deeply involved in that—how decisions were made and who made them. Was it John Kennedy? Was it Robert Kennedy? We spent endless hours on that. But in the process, we talked with a CIA deputy director of operations, who later became the director of the CIA, Richard Helms. We were trying to find out who had access to John Kennedy during that period, 1961 and 1962 principally, because the efforts to assassinate Castro ended with the Missile Crisis resolution in October of 1962.

In a meeting, Helms said, "On my way out of the Oval Office in a planning session, the president asked me to stay behind and I did. He said, 'Dick, I've been reading these Ian Fleming books on 007,' which Kennedy made famous. And he said, 'Do we have a 007?'"

Helms said he had to think a while and he responded, "'Well, not in the way those books portray, but one of our principal agents has a lot of exciting stories to tell.' And Kennedy said, 'Bring him around. I'd like to meet him.'"

His name was William Harvey. Harvey become famous for digging the tunnel from West Berlin to East Berlin under the East Berlin phone exchange and tapping into Soviet telephone conversations for quite a while. And when the Soviets found out about it, they got tipped off and sent a whole bunch of people down the tunnel to West Berlin. Harvey was manning a machine gun at the other end of the tunnel ready to kill them if they came over.

Physically, however, he looked like the opposite of Sean Connery.

So we—the members of the select committee—called Harvey in to ask him if he ever met Kennedy. He said "Yes." And we said, "Tell us the circumstances."

He said, "Dick Helms took me to the White House and we were waiting outside the Oval Office. The door was guarded by a Secret Service man. We waited a few minutes, and Helms came over to me and whispered in my ear, 'Bill, you're not carrying a weapon, are you?'"

And Harvey whispered back, "Of course I'm carrying a weapon. I always carry a weapon."

So Helms goes to the Secret Service man and says, "This man with me is one of our top agents at the agency, and he tells me he is armed."

The Secret Service guy turns pale and goes over to Harvey and says, "Mr. Harvey, you're not going in to see the president with a weapon."

Harvey reaches under his arm, pulls out a forty-five and a shoulder holster, and gives it to the Secret Service agent. So they sit for two or three more minutes. And Helms had a terrible idea. He went over and whispered to Harvey, "Bill, you don't have any other weapons, do you?"

And Harvey whispered back, "Of course I do. I always have a back-up weapon." And the Secret Service guy took a derringer off of Harvey's ankle holster.

He was going in to see the president with two guns!

❦ Ken Hechler
Member of the United States House of Representatives, state official from West Virginia

"JFK and his campaign family spent so much time in West Virginia (during the 1960 primary) that West Virginia became a household name. (He) said that 'West Virginia' was the third word that his daughter Caroline learned to pronounce."

I first met John F. Kennedy in 1947. I was teaching at Princeton University and took a group of my students to Washington. He talked to us in his congressional office. The students and I were not impressed with the off-hand manner in which he answered questions. Believe it or not, shortly thereafter, those same students interviewed Richard Nixon and were impressed with the directness of his answers.

In 1960, Senator Kennedy was trailing Hubert Humphrey midway in West Virginia's primary presidential campaign because of his Catholic religion. Ironically, Kennedy overcame this deficit with his crisp and direct answers to the media's questions, in contrast to Humphrey's over-expansive and drawn-out detail. Because Humphrey talked so much, it was often said of him: If you asked him what time it was, he would tell you how to build a watch!

When I was a congressman, I once was flying into Charleston on the same plane with Senator Kennedy. The county Charleston is in is called Kanawha which is pronounced "Ka-*naw*-wa." As I walked up the aisle of the plane passing by Senator Kennedy, I heard him softly repeating "Ka-*naw*-wa" over and over. Kennedy wasn't going to mispronounce the name as so many others often did.

Ultimately, Kennedy was able to articulate that he supported the Constitution of the United States and convinced West Virginians that he would adhere to the principles of peace and justice and would never let his religion interfere with his Americanism.

During JFK's campaign he visited Huntington, West Virginia, home of then-Marshall College, which would not allow him to campaign on their campus. So I let him stand on the hood of my Chevy. JFK and his campaign family spent so much time in West Virginia that West Virginia became a household name. He said that "West Virginia" was the third word that his daughter Caroline learned to pronounce.

The head of the Logan County State Democratic Executive Committee was Raymond Chafin. For years he had been a machine boss who dictated the way elections would swing. Raymond told me a story about meeting with Kennedy's national organizer, Larry O'Brien, and being asked what it would take to get Raymond on board, so to speak. Raymond told me he said, "Oh, about thirty-four." Later a suitcase was delivered that contained thirty-four thousand dollars, not the thirty-four hundred that Raymond had meant!

On the day that President Kennedy was assassinated, I was in my congressional office in Huntington preparing remarks for an address I was scheduled to make later that day in the town of Spencer. My address was on the leadership and influence of President Kennedy. During the preparation of my remarks, I received a phone call from the chairman of the Roane County meeting stating, "Turn on your television set. President Kennedy has been assassinated in Dallas."

We went ahead with the meeting as scheduled, and I talked about the President's legacy. I said that "A compassionate heart and courageous spirit have been stilled."

Along with millions of Americans, I was inspired with John F. Kennedy's brilliant inaugural address: "Ask not what your country can do for you. Ask what you can do for your country." These stirring remarks inspired millions of Americans to join the Peace Corp and dedicate their lives toward helping their fellow Americans in areas like civil rights, health care, and programs to assist poor or under-privileged people.

✒ Pete McCloskey
Member of the United States House of Representatives, attorney

"I said, 'Chuck, your boss is very impressive. If he can inspire a Republican to help him in a national cause, that's real leadership.'"

IN June of 1963, I was thirty-five and sitting in my little Palo Alto office and I get a telegram. It says, "Would you please join me and other distinguished leaders of the bar in the East Room of the White House at three o'clock Thursday? Signed, John F. Kennedy."

Of course I got on a red-eye flight and was the first one in the room at two-thirty in the afternoon. The room soon filled up with older lawyers. I recognized some of these older California lawyers.

They were with the big firms. There were, maybe, twenty I knew. They seemed surprised to see me, because I sure as hell did not rate with these fifty and sixty-year-old distinguished lawyers.

We sat in a semi-circle, and I believe there were about three hundred lawyers. There was a rostrum with the great seal of the presidency. Pretty soon, in comes the president with Lyndon Johnson on one side and Bobby Kennedy on the other. I didn't think much of Kennedy up to that point. I was a Republican. I didn't like the idea of appointing your brother as attorney general. That's nepotism.

The president opened with a very humble statement. He said, in close to the following words:

"Gentlemen, people think the President of the United States has great power. But there are things the president can't do. And there

are things he can't do that you men can do . . . What I'd like to ask
you to do is to help me. To do something I cannot do. I'd like you
to go back to your communities and form committees of black and
white lawyers. I'm not asking you to represent black people, but
to act in a capacity so that when blacks have a legitimate griev-
ance in your community, you make sure they can communicate
with the power structure: the mayors, the chambers of commerce,
the bankers. So that they can get redress or at least seek a means
of redress for their grievances. If you can do that, you can help
remove a problem which is going to occur in every city in this
country, as the blacks move into the inner-cities and the whites
move into the suburbs."

And then we all went into the Rose Garden and shook hands with
the president and went away. I walked out of the Rose Garden about
three feet in the air and went to see my friend Chuck Daly in his office
in the West Wing.

I said, "Chuck, your boss is very impressive. If he can inspire a
Republican to help him in a national cause, that's real leadership. I've
never thought about politics, but I think someday I might want to run
for Congress. Who should I talk to?"

He said, "Nobody will talk to you around here. You're a goddamn
Republican. But there's one guy who may give us some problems
around here someday."

He picked up the phone and his secretary got this person on the
phone for Chuck. Daly talked to the guy, saying, "I have this guy who's
got a crazy idea to get into politics." He handed me a slip of paper and
said, "He'll see you if you stick around until tomorrow at four o'clock."

The man who was advising me was John Lindsay, who later became
mayor of New York City. It was clear the White House thought John
Lindsay might be a threat to the Kennedy dynasty—Jack, Bobby, and
Teddy in that order. I tried to talk him out of becoming a Democrat
when he was mayor of New York. John and I stayed friends until the
day he died.

Here's how I was invited to the meeting at the White House.
Chuck is one of my closest friends in the world. We served together
in the Marines in Korea. He worked in the Kennedy White House. It

turns out Chuck had sat in on a meeting about this forthcoming conference on civil rights and Bobby Kennedy was present. The attorney general remarked, "We have a lot of lawyers coming, but they all seem to be Democrats. Doesn't anybody know any Republican civil rights lawyers?"

Daly piped up and said, "I know two." That was me and my then partner Lewis Butler, who later became an assistant secretary at the Department of Health, Education, and Welfare under Nixon, and the first person to quit the Nixon administration over the invasion of Cambodia in 1971.

On November 22, 1963, I was in San Mateo County Superior Court arguing an important case and the big utility company Pacific Gas & Electric was on the other side. There were four or five lawyers at the counsel table at one end. We had a visiting judge from one of the mountain counties. He was about seventy-five or eighty years old. At about eleven forty-five, I was in the midst of the final argument and the bailiff, sitting at the rear of the courtroom, came up to the judge and handed him a slip of paper. The judge said, "Hold up your argument, young man. Gentlemen, I've just received news here that President Kennedy has been shot. Now, please continue your argument."

I lamely finished the argument. At noon, I ran out of the courtroom, got in my car to go back to the office, turned on the radio, and by that time, it was clear Kennedy had died. I couldn't face it. I really couldn't face it. So, instead of going back to the office, I drove home and went to sleep.

I felt a tremendous sadness when Kennedy was assassinated. He had given the nation great hope. He inspired not just me. He inspired a whole generation of people in his inaugural address. Here was a young guy coming out of the war, having been wounded in the war. He was a war hero. I had the feeling he never would have sent troops to Vietnam. Lyndon Johnson came in with this Texas, "Bring the coonskin home" attitude.

Walter Mondale
Vice President of the United States, member of the United States Senate, 1984 Democratic presidential nominee

"There still is a horrible sense of loss nearly fifty years later. We were robbed."

I first met John Kennedy in 1958. He was coming through Minnesota in his first effort to seek the presidency. He spoke at the annual DFL (Democratic-Farmer-Labor Party) dinner. I was awed by him. He was eloquent, although he was still learning how to speak with presidential timber. For young people especially, he was inspiring: his strength, youth, and his embrace of the need for change. It all hit me where I lived; most people in the room were impressed. I was affected because, at that time, I was a young man and thinking about going into politics.

Of course, I met him many times after that.

Excerpt from *The Good Fight: A Life in Liberal Politics*, by Walter F. Mondale © 2010 (Used with author's permission):

> *"I thought his inaugural address (in January 1961) was one of the finest political speeches of our generation. I believe that the stirring phrase he used—that America would 'pay any price, bear any burden' to advance the cause of liberty—was an enduring source of inspiration to the country."*

That (statement) really hit me and encouraged my interest in politics. The one caveat or adjustment I would make more than fifty years later, after Vietnam, Iraq, and Afghanistan, is "be careful." We've gotten into some bad wars and we've been ignorant about what we were getting into. These were toxic environments, and they've been tragic for us.

Kennedy had come to Duluth, Minnesota to speak at a conference on forestry in late September of 1963, a few weeks before the assassination. He stayed overnight at the Duluth Hotel. A bunch of us were sitting in his room, including Hubert (Senator Hubert Humphrey) and McCarthy (Senator Eugene McCarthy). All of a sudden, a loud foghorn went off. And the president said with a big smile, "Will this be running all night?" The answer, of course, was "Yes." I don't think he got a lot of sleep that night.

On November 22, 1963, I was serving as Minnesota's attorney general and sitting in my office in the State Capitol with Nick Coleman, a leader in the state legislature and an old friend. I had agreed to be Kennedy's re-election campaign chairman for the state. Nick and I were working on the campaign when my secretary came in and said, "I don't know how to say this, but I just heard the President's been shot. You'd better listen to the radio."

So we turned on the radio and heard the news that he was dead. It was one of the saddest moments of my life. The man we were working for was just gone.

Excerpt from *The Good Fight: A Life in Liberal Politics*, by Walter F. Mondale © 2010 (Used with author's permission)

> *"After Kennedy's assassination, I believe we had moral momentum. And in the White House we had Johnson and Humphrey—masters of Senate procedure and brilliant legislators. We could have passed nearly anything we wanted. The Senate has never moved so fast in its history. The Elementary and Secondary Education Act, which established the first federal aid to poorer children, was reported to the Senate floor on April 6 and passed on*

April 9. The Voting Rights Act—reported on April 9 and passed on May 26. Medicare, reported to the Senate on June 30 and passed nine days later. The Immigration Act of 1965—a landmark bill that did away with the old country-of-origin quotas—was reported on September 15 and passed seven days later. It was like driving in a hailstorm—Johnson kept hitting us with one bill after another.

"Some years later, in a talk at the University of Minnesota, I called that period of my career the 'high tide' for American liberalism. It was as if we took the intellectual heritage of Franklin Roosevelt, the moral inspiration of John Kennedy, and a decade of pent-up demand for social change and converted them in a social reality."

I think we had the moral urgency of personal involvement for social change in the United States. There was a generational restlessness. Things had been sluggish for a long time. I think of Kennedy's line from the inaugural address, "God's work must truly be our own."

I think John Kennedy was denied a complete legacy. His commitment to civil rights, to Medicare, to health care, and even to environmental causes, were all part of his vision for America. And then, he was killed. I still think about him and that sense of urgency, the way he was able to take what we consider to be the noble causes of social justice and make them appealing by the way he carried himself, by the way he made compelling arguments for social causes.

There still is a horrible sense of loss nearly fifty years later. We were robbed.

❧ Jim Wright
Speaker of the United States House of Representatives

"It was the strongest emotional roller coaster I've ever experienced. We had been so happy that morning."

FROM my first encounter with then-Senator John Kennedy, I was very favorably impressed. I was a member of the House of Representatives and hosted a fifteen-minute TV program in my community, Fort Worth. His was one of my earlier interviews. I had just finished reading his book *Profiles in Courage* and had been impressed with it. We did a thirty-minute interview.

After the interview, I made a pledge: Anyone who was a senior in high school, or a student in a college and university, who would write a two-page or five-hundred word essay on his or her favorite character in American history, I would send them an autographed copy of John Kennedy's book.

In those days, the author's price for a book was about two dollars; brand new on the shelf, the book was about five dollars.

I was able to give away a bunch of those books, and John Kennedy autographed each one personally. The books were first editions. Later, I gave more of them to other people—faculty members of schools, students, and others I knew would appreciate them. This was long before I dreamed he would be a candidate for president. But you can image the value attached today to those books.

I was impressed with his willingness to sit down for the interview. The spontaneity of the man, his engaging personality, and his ability to speak freely and with a strong measure of conviction on important issues. He was very much impressed with Sam Houston, who was a hero of mine. I developed an attachment to him and a friendship for him long before I ever imagined he would be a candidate for president.

Kennedy's magic was spontaneous and inspired people. He had the ability to say something that would be lasting, to grasp an idea or something that had been said, and to make a comment that would be memorable. He had a peculiar capacity for humor—especially self-deprecating humor. He was the first man I ever knew who actually seemed to enjoy jokes made upon himself. He didn't just tolerate it; he made something out of it.

Early in 1960, after he was an announced candidate for the nomination, I attended the annual Gridiron Dinner in Washington. As was the custom in those days, they had professional actors portraying various characters in skits calculated to embarrass. Just before Kennedy was to appear, (they had chosen him to be the spokesman for the Democrats) was a skit capturing the most vulnerable spot in Kennedy's armor. The actors portrayed Kennedy out among crowds with a huge sack of money, and loosely scattering the money around, purchasing votes.

Kennedy had no idea this was coming. When the skit ended, the spotlight came upon him, and he was expected to make some response to this "vote buying." He reached in his pocket, pulled out a piece of paper, looked at it, and said, "I have just received a telegram from my wealthy father. It says, 'Dear Jack, Don't buy one vote more than necessary. I'll be damned if I'm going to pay for a landslide.'" You can imagine how that captivated the audience.

In 1960, when he was campaigning in West Virginia, there was talk that Kennedy, never having been poor a day in his life, would not have any way to understand the problems of poor people. Not sure if this really happened, but he told me that after a campaign speech, a grizzled old coal miner came up to him and said, "Senator, there's just one thing I want to tell you. That stuff those have said about you about never being poor, don't let that bother you none. I've been awfully poor, and I can say, you've not missed a damn thing."

Kennedy's Catholicism did not match in intensity the Cold War with the Soviet Union or other tensions in the world as an issue. And, thank God, it was not nearly as pivotal an issue as it had been in 1928. In the intervening years, I believe there had become a growing recognition that people had over-reacted and over-played their hands.

Kennedy did a great deal to help cultivate that calm among some poorly educated Protestants. I admired so much his courage, standing there in Houston before those prominent Protestant ministers from around the country. Bearing his breast, he told them exactly how he felt. It was a beautiful speech. I could sense a sensible mood among these people. They seemed content.

They seemed to recognize that some people of their faith had over-reacted. And that hostility had no place in this campaign. It still lingered, though, among some people. I made a statement afterward that Kennedy reminded me of Daniel in the lion's den. A few of my constituents got angry at me, accusing me of comparing Protestant ministers to lions. They were just looking for something to get shook up about.

I'm glad I lived during the presidency of John F. Kennedy. It was a time when a man could have heroes and be unapologetic.

Excerpt from *Balance of Power: President and Congress from the Era of McCarthy to the Age of Gingrich,* by Jim Wright © 1996 (Used with author's permission):

> *On that Friday morning, which today seems like an eternity ago, it would have been hard not to feel that the nation and this man who so perfectly symbolized it was their finest hour. . . . After his speech to the Fort Worth Chamber of Commerce, we flew to Dallas. . . . En route from Carswell Air Force Base to Dallas Love Field aboard Air Force One, I talked with President Kennedy. Someone had shown him a copy of the* Dallas Morning News *which contained a scurrilous display advertisement accusing the president of treason. What a boorishly rude and inhospitable thing! Any self-respecting newspaper, I thought, would have rejected such a vulgar advertisement on the day the president of the United States was visiting the city. Kennedy was puzzled by the extreme right-wing fanaticism that seemed to pervade*

the upper echelons of Dallas. What made the twin cities,
Fort Worth and Dallas, so different, he asked.

I was in the motorcade—probably six cars behind the president. I heard the shots ring out. I thought at first it was a twenty-one gun salute. We were heading north toward the Texas School Book Depository Building where Oswald leaned out the window and shot him. We turned the corner and I saw the fallen president's body slump over. Suddenly, Jackie was on her knees crawling on the back of the car. Then the Secret Service agent jumped onto the car, pushing her down and throwing himself over both of them. Then the car rushed onto the highway toward the hospital. We followed it. I arrived as they were taking the president in on a stretcher. I looked into the back of the limousine and saw pools of blood and thought it must be fatal.

It was the strongest emotional roller coaster I've ever experienced. We had been so happy that morning. It was so triumphant to have the president appear in our town. He didn't ask for money. He didn't ask for votes. He spent his time thanking the citizens of Fort Worth for their service helping the nation's defenses over the years from the time of our municipal birth as a territory on the prairie saving the settlers from the ravages of the savage Comanches.

It was a marvelous speech. He said kind things about me, and his words impressed this young congressman. To have his president, in his town, talking to his people.

Then, of course, at noon time we plunged into the depths of despondency. I don't know of anything career-wise that has rocked me as much as that tragedy. At the time his death was confirmed, we didn't know that Oswald had been arrested. I was worried it might be a conspiracy. My place was to stay in my home town until I found out what was going on. Of course, I flew back to Washington later that weekend for the funeral and burial.

Excerpt from *Balance of Power: President and Congress from the Era of McCarthy to the Age of Gingrich,* by Jim Wright © 1996 (Used with author's permission):

For several days most of us moved about in a cloud.
The trip back to Washington. . . . long queues of people,
which streamed through the Capitol all Saturday night
and into Sunday to pay respect at the casket as it lay in
state in the rotunda. . . . the little boy, John, unaware of
the finality of what had happened to his father, saluting
the flag . . . the long, slow march to Arlington Cemetery
. . . all this burned itself into our memories.

John Kennedy was a great inspiration. He gave us hope, hope in which Americans can still take pride. I will always be grateful to have had the privilege of knowing him.

SECTION EIGHT:

Those with Humorous, Poignant, Quirky, and Tragic Encounters and Connections

✒ Patricia Baillargeon
Assistant to Eleanor Roosevelt

"After almost an hour, he obviously just couldn't bear being a bystander any longer. He threw down his cane and went running onto the field. My first thought was, 'If your back is that bad, how can you do that?'"

IN mid-1953, I started working for Eleanor Roosevelt at the United Nations Association in New York City, and a few months later, the weekend of January 30-31, 1954, I was visiting a friend in Washington, D.C. That Sunday morning, longtime friend from Washington State, U.S. Senator Henry ("Scoop") Jackson, took me to breakfast at the Mayflower Hotel and then to the "Red Mass" held annually for government leaders at St. Matthew's Cathedral when Congress convenes.

President and Mrs. Eisenhower were there, as well as many judges, senators, and representatives—including Senator John Kennedy and his wife Jacqueline. Although there was no opportunity to meet the senator after Mass, I was to have such an occasion later that day.

It was the custom for Senator Jackson and other Senate colleagues and staff members to gather in Georgetown on Sunday afternoons to play touch football. So a couple hours after the cathedral service, we joined his group at a Georgetown playfield. Jack Kennedy and his brother Robert had just arrived and "Scoop" introduced me to them before he ("Scoop") and Robert went into the game. I was more formally dressed for traveling on the train, which I did later that day, back to New York.

Senator Kennedy, who was walking with a cane, was not dressed for football either. So he and I stood on the sidelines and visited. We talked about current issues, the United Nations, and touched on various lighter subjects and I greatly enjoyed our conversation. After almost an hour, he obviously just couldn't bear being a bystander any longer. He threw down his cane and went running onto the field.

My first thought was, "If your back is that bad, how can you do that?"

But, of course, we know now that it was that bad. He was to have serious surgery later that year. After about ten minutes, he returned to the sidelines and quickly grabbed his cane. He obviously was in pain.

In a letter to my parents in Seattle dated February 2, 1954, all I said of John and Robert Kennedy was, "They are most attractive." Rather an understatement. My impressions of Jack Kennedy that afternoon were that he was extremely vigorous and delightfully bright, energetically involved in the issues of the day. He connected with people individually; he had a sparkle. To use today's vernacular, he had charisma. To a young woman in her twenties, he was very handsome and I enjoyed his sense of humor. And he laughed a lot.

It was in the Senate dining room a few weeks later that I again saw Jack Kennedy. I was in Washington for a day, and Kennedy said he remembered me. We had a very friendly chat and my first impressions were reinforced. I saw Senator Kennedy and later President Kennedy several more times, but always with groups of various sizes.

In 1960, after winning the Democratic nomination, Senator Kennedy continued his efforts to acquire Mrs. Roosevelt's endorsement. He knew how invaluable it would be in the tight race against Richard Nixon. Finally, Mrs. Roosevelt was ready to express her support for the senator and a date was set for a private meeting the second week of August in Hyde Park. The day before the meeting, Mrs. Roosevelt's granddaughter tragically was killed falling off a horse. Senator Kennedy offered to postpone, but Mrs. Roosevelt kept the appointment. Although I was not in Hyde Park that day, I can envision the two of them having luncheon alone at a table by the corner window in Mrs. Roosevelt's living room at Val-Kill Cottage.

The very last time I saw him was at a distance during his visit to Seattle in November of 1961, when he delivered a speech on foreign policy. President Kennedy was here to commemorate the one-hundredth anniversary of the University of Washington. His remarks, more than a half century ago, are of special interest in today's world:

> *"We must face problems which do not lend themselves to easy or quick or permanent solutions. And we must face the fact that the United States is neither omnipotent nor omniscient—that we are only 6 percent of the world's population and that we cannot impose our will upon the other 94 percent of mankind—that we cannot right every wrong or reverse each adversity, and that, therefore, there cannot be an American solution to every world problem."*

Late in the evening of November 21, 1963, I returned to Seattle from New York City after attending a meeting of the Rockefeller Panel on the Performing Arts, a group of national leaders preparing a report assessing the arts in America. I had been asked to issue a press release in Seattle about the panel's work. So, on the morning of the 22nd, I called a friend who was a producer at KING-5 television, the NBC affiliate in Seattle. She informed me that the network had just received a news bulletin that President Kennedy had been shot. "Turn on your TV," she said, and we both instantly rang off. I turned to a friend who was with me and said, "Thank God Mrs. Roosevelt isn't here to see this."

Of course, I was stunned and shocked like everyone else. Americans of my generation had never experienced the assassination of a president. That weekend, I attended a memorial Mass where about one thousand people of all faiths were pressed into the church and more were lining the street outside. Television scenes became lasting images in the minds of people throughout the United States and the world: the dramatic and surreal sight of Jacqueline Kennedy in her pink suit climbing on the back of the presidential limousine as the Secret Service agent rushes toward her. And, of course, the solemn riderless horse in the funeral procession.

John Kennedy's presidency offered many lighter moments: his self-deprecating humor when, following Jackie's thunderous welcome in France, he introduced himself, saying, "I am the man who accompanied Jacqueline Kennedy to Paris, and I have enjoyed it."

What is JFK's legacy? Perhaps it was the new focus on outer space or maybe his foreign aid program. But I think rather, most importantly, it was that he inspired several generations of Americans by his call to service: "Ask not what your country can do for you. Ask what you can do for your country." Certainly the Peace Corps is one remarkable legacy, not only for its peaceful involvement with recipient countries, but for providing many mainstream American adults with an in-depth experience and an understanding of world problems and cultures.

✍ Dr. William Bernhard
Surgeon who fought
for thirty hours to save
the life of Patrick
Bouvier Kennedy

*"He was a quick study . . . In my work, there
usually is a lot of family emotion involved.
There was no emotion in this. He was cool, but
concerned. I've never talked about this experience
publicly. It was all too sad."*

THE hyperbaric tank belongs to the Industrial Medicine Department
of the School of Public Health at Harvard, but it was accessible to
Children's Hospital in Boston. And inside was a dreary, grubby room
with a tank at one end, and in front of the tank was a relic rocking chair
with some spokes missing. It also had some cracks in it. I remember
sending a couple of my technicians to talk to the Secret Service agents
and to tell them, "Don't sit in the rocking chair."

So as the afternoon went on, President Kennedy came in. We had
one of our chats (about his newborn son's condition), and immediately afterward, he leaped on to the rocking chair. He was rocking back
and forth and really enjoying it. About the fourth or fifth rock, the
whole thing came apart, and he went head over heels and landed on the
cement floor. The Secret Service agents ran around frantically trying to
pick him up, because he had back problems.

And he got up laughing. He had a good sense of humor. Life was not all grim and gloomy to him.

That story sets the tone for what happened over the next two days.

We were doing research in this facility. I had some ideas that I wanted to increase the oxygenation of these very blue infants with congenital heart disease we were dealing with. If there was some way we could increase their arterial oxygen saturation, they might be a little more stable during anesthesia.

There was a second smaller chamber, a decompression chamber. Everyone who was in there for an hour or so had to go through decompression, so they would not have a nitrogen embolism. That second chamber was only about six or eight feet long. The only time I remember the President came in the decompression chamber was to get some food; he popped in to have a close look at the baby.

Dr. James Drorbaugh was selected to check this baby out in Hyannis. We were doing some research together on another project, and we knew each other quite well. Drorbaugh was the one they brought in, and they did not know what to do with this little kid. The child was obviously dying. He was a three-pound preemie. So the hyperbaric chamber was sort of the last resort.

I was not paying attention to all the commotion outside, the police helicopters. Then I got a late phone call from Dr. Drorbaugh. He said, "Things are not going well. Why don't you come up? Maybe we can do something for this little baby. "

I said, "I'll come over. But I have avoided patients with lung disease in the past. I'm afraid I would damage their lungs with one hundred percent oxygen. I don't like to take any chances."

He said, "Well, we don't have a lot of choices here, so if you're willing to come over, pop over and see him."

So I zipped over. I knew it was the son of the president, but I did not get involved with that. It was just another very sick baby. You can't be star-gazing. I was trying to figure out what I might be able to do. I had never treated anybody like this. The baby didn't have enough lung capacity to boost up his saturation. I listened to him and did not hear a lot of breath sounds, except in his upper chest. I wondered whether he had hypoplastic lungs, lungs that have lot of bronchioles that end up blunted. I didn't know whether he had hyaline membrane disease or hypoplastic lungs.

So we brought the infant down. We pumped the chamber up to three atmospheres absolute. Everything was all right, so we remained at three atmospheres absolute, about equivalent of the depth of sixty-six feet of sea water. Afterwards, we pressurized and checked the baby out. He was a little three-pounder, about as big as a small doll. And his chest was pumping away; his respirations were at least at one hundred. He was trying to stay alive, breathing one hundred percent oxygen.

After about five or ten minutes, Drorbaugh, who was outside the chamber, said, "His EKG looks better!"

The baby's heart was getting a little more oxygen. We checked his saturation, and it had increased from about forty-five to fifty and then almost sixty. So that was a little improvement. Drorbaugh was overjoyed. So we continued at that pace and everything was very stable.

The baby was struggling, breathing about one hundred times per minute, despite a small improvement in oxygen saturation. He was still very short of breath.

So the president came in again and we had a little chat.

I said, "Things look improved on paper, but the baby doesn't appear any better, and I'm concerned we're not going to make out very well here."

The president said, "Yeah, he looks like he's having a really hard time."

I said, "The deal is, he has to have enough energy to keep moving his diaphragm up and down. So he's burning fat."

We were giving him some glucose and water by vein, but we could never make up for the caloric loss he was sustaining by working so hard to breathe.

So I told the president, "He's going to get tired if he keeps this up. And if we have to pick a moment as he gets tired to put an endotracheal tube in, get an anesthesiologist in here, and 'bag' him with one hundred percent oxygen to take over the load of his breathing, the chances of his survival are very, very slim."

So the president left again, and we continued on for a number of hours. I stayed the whole time. I couldn't bear to think of leaving the place, with nobody else knowing anything about it (function of the hyperbaric chamber), and no one there but technicians. There was no way I was going anywhere.

After many more hours, it was sometime during the night, I got the feeling the baby was about ready to stop breathing. I watched the corners of his mouth. He seemed to be using accessory muscles plus his diaphragm.

I said, "Better get ahold of the anesthesia department." They sent a very good anesthesiologist over. He had not seen the baby before. He was pretty impressed that things were not looking very good, so he popped a tube in the trachea, taped it up and "bagged" him (assisted ventilation).

As soon as he "bagged" him, the baby stopped struggling. The baby looked absolutely peaceful because the anesthesiologist's hand was doing the work, rather than this infant.

So we continued on for another number of hours, but things basically did not improve.

Saturation dropped back; his arterial saturation was in the upper fifties. All this time, he had hypertension in his right ventricle, that is, he had fetal circulation. This is the way the baby exists in the uterus. The lungs obviously are deflated—there's no gas exchanged—using the mother's arterial blood to keep the baby alive. The kid was having all these problems because he was receiving unsaturated blood.

There wasn't enough functioning lung to sustain life. And the baby died.

The president had been in three or four hours earlier, but he knew the baby probably wouldn't make it. So it was no shock to him.

I never saw the president again. I had seen him four times over the previous several hours and in some cases we spent a fair amount of time together talking about what we—the doctors—were doing. He had been on the board of overseers at Harvard, and I did not want him to get too depressed about the School of Public Health tank facility. I did not want to say anything that would disturb the university's opinion of this facility used to instruct students.

We talked about a number of subjects. I had been a naval officer about two years after him. We talked quite a bit about the Navy.

I never heard from him or anyone else in the family again. And I've never talked about this experience publicly. It was all too sad.

John Kennedy was an amazing character. He was a diligent, caring parent, but he didn't bleed all over the floor. He kept his emotions to himself, made very intelligent inquiries, and was just the nicest person. He was very engaged. He wanted the best for his child, but he knew from the beginning it (the child's prognosis) was very bad.

On November 22, I was making rounds in the hospital seeing postoperative cardiac patients and the news of the assassination knocked me over. Someone had a radio in a patient's room. I just walked into it and got whacked in the face with this bad news. I remember blessing myself and saying a little prayer about it, because it really didn't fit. I couldn't put the whole thing together. I never gave the whole scenario any thought, that anybody would do anything like that.

He was inexperienced, but he was somebody who could make decisions. He was a typical young naval officer who had to make decisions all the time that could cause his death or the death of other people. When you're in that position, you have to quickly size things up and call some shots. He did that pretty well. The problem with him was that he was not experienced enough to know that other people were snookering him, like the Russians, for instance. They made light of him because he was young, and he was not sophisticated enough to know what they were doing, like loading missiles in Cuba. And the Bay of Pigs was the same thing; he got bad intelligence. Whether he should have been able to figure that out, I don't know.

He was a quick study; just the facts. You gave him the straight stuff, he got it, and that was it. In my work, there usually is a lot of family emotion involved. There was no emotion in this. He was cool, but concerned. Not many people can fall head over heels with a bad back onto a cement floor and come up laughing. I watched this and almost had a heart attack. I saw this man flip into the air, and I could not believe it.

He was a good person. He cared about other people, his family, and his children. He was a straight shooter. He was a good leader, a good man. I say a prayer for him. You should too.

ᘒ Jim Boyd
Medical student working at Parkland Memorial Hospital

"When I arrived home that night I told my wife, 'These socks have Lee Harvey Oswald's blood on them!' My wife replied, 'Do you want me to wash them or frame them?'"

ON November 22, 1963, I was a student at The University of Texas Southwestern Medical School. My wife worked near the medical school, and she came to work early that day so she could take some time off to watch the motorcade in which President John Kennedy would be riding on his visit to Dallas. I recall her saying, "I'll be delighted when he's out of town. The climate for the president in this city is not good."

I was in school that day. But I also had a dental appointment at Baylor Dental School which was across town from the school. When I arrived in the waiting room, I noticed a crowd around a small television on the wall. I recall my friend, the dental student with whom I had an appointment, coming up to me and saying, "The president's been shot. I don't think we'll be doing anything here today."

I left the dental school and drove quickly to the student parking lot at Parkland Memorial Hospital which had not yet been cordoned off. I walked onto the floor that led to the emergency room. The blood bank was on the right and trauma room one, where the president lay, was directly across the hall. Somebody saw me and grabbed me, saying,

"We need your blood. Governor Connally is B-positive and we need your blood." So I lay down on the table and gave a pint of blood.

At about that time, Kennedy was being pronounced dead right across the hall.

The next day, I was wearing my surgical scrubs and went to the surgical area which was on the second floor. I went in through the back stairs since the ER area was secured. In fact, everything was pretty well locked down. There were men in uniform on the roof with submachine guns. I was wearing my white coat, and with some of my fellow medical students, went into the hospital library, where the news people had been sequestered. As soon as we walked in, the reporters descended on my colleagues and me, thinking we were big shots and could offer an update on Governor Connally's condition.

On Sunday morning, the 24th, I was on call with other medical students. We were sitting in the TV room adjacent to the operative suites and were watching as Lee Harvey Oswald was being transferred in the basement of the city jail. We watched Jack Ruby shoot him.

One of our colleagues said to us, "You'd better get up and help the surgery room personnel get ready. There's our next patient."

We ran down there. Because of all the various gases used at that time in ER, we usually put on special shoes. I kicked off my street shoes and went into the surgery room in my stocking feet. A couple of operating room nurses were scrambling to get instruments. It took about fifteen minutes for Oswald to arrive, and by then, four of the surgeons who had tried to save the president's life two days earlier were washing up, ready to go to work. They, too, had been watching television and saw Oswald get shot.

I did a cut down in his ankle to get an IV going as I stood there in my stocking feet. As you can imagine they got a bit bloody. Later that day, I took my socks off before going home. When I arrived home that night I told my wife, "These socks have Lee Harvey Oswald's blood on them!" My wife replied, "Do you want me to wash them or frame them?"

Oswald was shot in the perfect spot to do the most damage. The bullet went into the wall of his abdomen at an angle. It hit his liver, the aorta, and one of his kidneys. It disintegrated a complex series of blood vessels where the small intestine goes into the stomach. All of that was blown out. We pumped thirty units of O-negative blood into him as fast we could go, and it was all coming out of the holes inside him just as fast.

Four excellent trauma surgeons worked on Oswald for half an hour. Later, Dr. Mac Perry, a great surgeon, was stepping back and stripping off his surgical gloves, remarked, "I wish we had had that chance with the president. We had a shot at saving Oswald."

Kennedy's legacy is a family legacy—bright people, charismatic. But flawed and nobody seemed to care. There remains a great deal of fascination with the Kennedys—books, movies. John Kennedy brought youth and a certain energy to our country.

❧ Lillian Brown
Make-up artist for JFK and eight other presidents

"When you touch somebody's face you're getting pretty close to them. And either they were going to invite you back, or they would never invite you again."

I first met John Kennedy as a senator on *Face the Nation*. He did eleven appearances on that program. He would call the producers and say, "Do you want to make some news?" And of course, they could not resist that. He read piles of newspapers every day; they were always scattered around him. And he was fascinated with cameras. He loved cameras and the cameras loved him.

He would ask questions of everybody in the studio. He would go to the lighting man and ask, "How come I get those circles under my eyes?" He would go to the audio man and say, "How do you do this and that?" And he would go to the camera man and say, "How come these monitors don't match?" He would ask dozens of questions, and I'm sure that he was determined to be the first television president, because we were just going from radio into television.

He was fascinated with the media and the media loved him back. No doubt about it.

At one point I suggested he get voice lessons. He had a strong Massachusetts or New England accent. The other thing he did, which I kidded him about, was during the Cuban Missile Crisis, he would pronounce it "Cu-ber." I said, "Jack, you should bring your speaking skills up to the level of some of your other skills. And bring your speaking voice to a more neutral tone." And he did it.

At that time, I was also teaching at Georgetown University. He would kid me and say, "Why is a university professor doing make-up for a politician?" And I said, "Sir, I have three daughters to put through college by myself."

John Kennedy was such a normal person. And yet, he was extraordinarily intelligent, and he would just milk everybody's brains. Everyone who came around him, if he thought they knew something he wanted to know, he would ask questions and try to find out everything he could. He thought that the people in television could guide him to become the kind of television personality he wanted to be. That's one of the reasons he was as successful as he was. And when you realize he made more than fifty appearances on television. And I said to him, "Just make love to the camera." I would say things like that to him because he didn't care.

On television, he was superior as compared to all the other presidents since him and Eisenhower before him. It was because he worked so hard to study for it. He would say, "Do you like this tie? How does this tie look on camera?" And he would ask, "Should I cross my legs?" He would ask all these questions.

And, of course, there were the debates in 1960. The first debate was in Chicago, not Washington. I couldn't go because of my classes, though I gave John Kennedy a compact, and I said, "Before you go on the air, you go in and powder your nose." I did make-up for him before each of his nationally televised addresses. He did an unbelievable amount of advanced preparation. Reams of information. The point is: He always appeared knowledgeable about the subject.

On November 22, 1963, I was at the Washington Golf and Country Club. I had just finished giving a speech and came down, walked across the lobby, and was about to say good-bye to the girl at the front desk. She was white as a sheet. And I said, "What's the matter?" She could hardly speak the words. She was overcome. And I was overcome, too. I couldn't believe it and to this day, I don't know how I got home. I know I drove my car, but the whole time I was overcome with this terrible news.

I was fascinated with this man, and I was, in a sense, a friend of his. Once we realized we worked so well together, he would call me to the White House frequently to prepare him for special appearances.

I stayed home the whole weekend. I did not participate in the funeral, but I sure was impressed with what Jackie did. She was such a cultural person. He was so proud of her. Not just because she was so beautiful, but so brilliant. And when we did the White House tour in 1962 with (television newscaster) Charles Collingwood, the president was proud of her. They had a wonderful relationship.

The desk that he used? She found that in the White House basement where all this stuff was stored. The desk was first used by Rutherford B. Hayes and many other presidents after him, including Franklin Roosevelt. He loved the desk. I always, of course, carried a case with my make-up. And I would never, ever put that case on his desk. He always appreciated that. Other make-up people would set themselves up all over the place and put all this junk on his desk.

He carried a little bit of make-up I gave him in his pocket, and if he was somewhere else and about to go on television, he would use it. I've worked with nine presidents. When you touch somebody's face you're getting pretty close to them. And either they were going to invite you back, or they would never invite you again. Because of the accident with the PT boat, he was in constant pain. Excruciating pain. And when no one was around, he often walked with crutches. He never did it in public or when he thought he was being observed. But I sort of got closer to him than most people. What I would do is help him straighten up, because he would be leaning over in agony. He had that brace in his back. I would pretend to straighten his jacket at the shoulders, and I would push the palm of my hand into the small of his back, and just hold it there until he could straighten up, and look the way he ought to look on camera. Most people did not know the extent of the agony he was in all the time. It was unremitting.

He had numerous advisors and was always asking as nearest as he could get to the truth. It was incredible to walk into the Oval Office when he was by himself at the desk and didn't care how things looked. There would be newspapers everywhere.

His legacy? John Kennedy was not only handsome, well-educated, but he was a president who really cared for his country and really followed his ideals, responded to the needs of the people.

❧ Josiah Bunting III
Military officer, educator,
foundation executive

*"(His administration) may have been on the
verge of committing an overwhelming sin of
intellectual and strategic arrogance with regard
to Vietnam."*

I met President Kennedy approximately one month before graduation from VMI (Virginia Military Institute). It was May of 1963. We were in the middle of a series of centennial Civil War celebrations. The VMI Corps had fought in a battle quite famous at New Market, Virginia. The senior class at VMI typically in the spring went on a two or three-day visit to Washington, visiting various military posts and seeing the sights.

He was wearing a navy blue suit, and of course, he had that famous wide grin. The aide introduced him to our commandant, and then the commandant introduced me to the president. I was what was called the first captain, which is the senior cadet commander. I was very full of myself. The president came right over and stuck out his hand, saying "It is a pleasure to meet you." Then he said in his distinct accent, "Mr. Bunting, I understand you are a Rhodes Scholar."

I replied, "Yes, sir."

And he said, "Well that's wonderful. You have a wonderful time in England and at Oxford."

Then he stood back and said, "Well, it's a pleasure to have all of you here." And then he gave us a talk about the Green Berets, about unconventional warfare, and he mentioned Southeast Asia. At that time we already had advisors there.

When he finished, there was applause; there may have been a question or two. And then I went up to thank him, and I said, "Mr. President, you may not know this, but as our Commander-in-Chief, it is well within your authority to grant unconditional amnesty to all the cadets who are in trouble back at VMI. This is a traditional thing." And he laughed. When I say "in trouble," typically it is what is called "room confinement" or "marching penalty tours" where you march up and down the courtyard with a rifle for an hour because of some relatively minor problem.

He said, "Of course, that should be done."

I can see it still. He waved his hand in the air and made everybody very happy. Then he went back inside and Major General Clifton (JFK's military aide) spoke to us for a moment or two and then we got back on our busses and on to our next appointment.

We just thought this man was remarkable. We wanted to follow him. I don't remember even being conscious of whether he was a Republican or a Democrat. He was a war hero. He was a strong guy. He is what we once had in political leaders. The only thing I can compare it to is that period when we had the Marshall Plan. That was a period comparable in its achievement to and in America's stature in the world. You had the sense that America was still looked at as a fount of goodwill and generosity. In the early days of JFK, really the whole time of JFK, we had that feeling. Idealism and unabashed patriotism. And optimism. The idea, "We'll get it right."

In those days nobody cared about *People* magazine. Nobody cared about owning a house in the Hamptons. Nobody had ever heard of a Lexus. Celebrity was not a big thing. We wanted to be in the Peace Corps. Or the Marine Corps. Or we wanted to be priests. Or get PhDs. This American fixation on running a hedge fund—we didn't care about that. I'm not sure we'll ever recapture that time or that feeling.

On November 22, 1963, I was in the middle of dinner at Christ Church Hall at Oxford. Suddenly, the dean of the college stood up and said, "I must tell you the awful news that the American president has been felled by an assassin at Dallas, in Texas."

I went back to my room to listen to the Armed Forces European Network. I got the news broadcast for the next couple of hours. All of the coverage was on the assassination and of Kennedy.

I still have an achingly vivid memory of it. The cathedral was packed. Oxford is very international and many of the kids there were not American. But the one memory I have which is so vivid is that I was at the back of the cathedral. The pews in front of me were all crowded. And virtually everybody was holding onto each other; rows of people with their arms around each other's waists and shoulders. I can hardly describe the pathos of that moment.

I thought of a famous line of William Wordsworth's, who said of being young during the time of the French Revolution: *"Bliss was it in that dawn to be alive, but to be young was very heaven."* For my generation—people who were eighteen, twenty, or twenty-two years old at that time, the early 1960s—it was heaven.

I was probably not in a completely rational state. The bereavement of others was for the country, or what would happen to the world. I thought of Mrs. Kennedy; I'm not sure why. She was very much a part of JFK.

We have to remind ourselves that his presidency was cut short. It was an unfinished work. I think of the fact that he and Senator (Barry) Goldwater had discussed flying together from city to city in the '64 campaign and debating. Kennedy was someone with whom everything was comfortable: exchanging strategic, political, and intellectual ideas at a time when partisanship did not pollute; a relatively easy, comfortable, and friendly intercourse among members of the two parties.

Most of that generation of people highly placed in politics were veterans of the Second World War. They had that commonality of experience. When someone tells you that George McGovern flew thirty-five missions in a B-24 Liberator over Germany, it's hard to hate him and castigate him as a member of a far out party. Rather, he's an American patriot with whom you might disagree.

I think John Kennedy's presidency was extraordinary and extraordinarily successful. It wasn't perfect. And it may have been on the verge of committing an overwhelming sin of intellectual and strategic arrogance with regard to Vietnam. It's a fairly short distance from the remark in his inaugural address, ". . . . that we shall pay any price, bear any burden. . . . to assure the survival and the success of liberty," to actually implementing a foreign policy which turns out to be based on faulty premises. Again, we just don't know. It was an unfinished presidency.

As a result, I rank his presidency very high, but with the provision that what followed from it was quite ugly. When you look at what people call "the sixties," they're not talking about 1960 to 1964. They're talking about 1967 to 1973. This was a very different time. Young people today have no understanding of the turmoil that occurred.

And JFK lived like what I thought was an American patriot of his time. Now we are losing one thousand members a day of the World War II generation—people in their late eighties and early nineties— and one of the things everybody says about these people is that it's hard to get them to talk. The phrase they use—and you do not hear this much anymore—is that "I was in the service." And they leave it at that. It was something you just did. Kennedy was part of that generation.

Arthur "Andy" Carlson
Army officer who led riderless horse "Black Jack" in funeral

*". . .(T)hat misbehaving horse, knew he was
doing wrong, and I was furious with him. But
I was told that some of the TV commentators
talked about the horse as a symbol
of the deceased president."*

ON November 22, I was doing laundry at a laundromat across the street from the stables at Fort Meyer, Virginia. I saw people clustered around a car, listening intently to the car radio. So I walked over there to see what they were listening to. And when I heard the news, I said to myself, "Well, I'd better get back to the stables. My day off is over."

Since the Army's Third Infantry Regiment, "The Old Guard," is the president's escort, I knew we'd have a very large role in his funeral. We had no idea what arrangements had been—or would be—made, but we knew we'd be involved it.

I had a lot more esteem for the role of accompanying the riderless horse than most did. And I thought it should be done well because it obviously affected the family.

You see, the family is riding right behind the caisson and the horse. They are looking at this horse throughout the funeral procession. It's important to give a good appearance—just in front of the deceased President's family.

I was the first one who started spit-shining the boots in the stirrups. Previously, others would just brush shine them. I thought,

"People are going to be looking at these boots; they ought to have their best appearance."

Black Jack, that misbehaving horse, knew he was doing wrong, and I was furious with him. But I was told that some of the TV commentators talked about the horse as a symbol of the deceased president.

But Black Jack had one bad trait that always bothered me: a runny nose. He would wipe it on my back, or he would blow it on me. And I'd come in from a funeral at the cemetery with horse snot all down my right side. So I started before every funeral to take out my handkerchief and swab out his nostrils. Not during the funeral or out in public, of course, but before the funeral started.

I was mission-oriented; this is my job. I wanted to do it the very best I could. Emotions are for later. On the flyover at the gravesite service, when Air Force One flew over alone, I allowed myself to get choked up then. After that, it was just exhaustion.

The next day, we were back to our regular routine. People were still dying, people needed to be buried.

There were things I would have done differently. I would have asked on the second day if I could put a martingale on him. That's a strap from the bit of the bridle to the girth around the horse's bridle that limits how high a horse can raise its head. Black Jack was raising his head as high as he could. The martingale would have taken a lot of strain off my arm.

I also would have asked if I could ride across the Potomac River in a vehicle on the second day, rather than walk him to save energy. I walked from the Fort Meyer stables to the Capitol, then to the White House, then to St. Matthew's Cathedral, then back across the river to Arlington National Cemetery. At the time, I thought, "I'll walk with him. I'll talk with him. I'll make sure he was settled down and OK."

I learned later the horse's behavior was not a fluke. He was just going back to his early days. I got a call a few years ago from a man who said, as a soldier, he was the first to walk Black Jack. He said when Black Jack got to Fort Myer, where the stables are located, this horse was wild. He said they had to work with the horse for six months before Black Jack could be calm enough to be used in a funeral. And, even then, he would dance around a lot.

At an Old Guard reunion, one gentleman older than me said he had walked Black Jack one time. His instructions were: "The horse knows its job: get behind the caisson, follow the caisson, but don't get too close to the caisson, or he'll eat all the felt off the back." But Tom failed to mind the other end, and Black Jack once kicked in the door of a car.

I received about one hundred cards and letters after the funeral. They were all complimentary. People wrote me about what they thought of my performance and what it did for them. And I received an Army commendation medal for my participation in the president's funeral.

As a nation, we were sad and angry. Most people alive then, if you ask them where they were when they heard the news of Kennedy's assassination, they can tell you. To this day.

It was a traumatic experience for people old enough to understand it. Whether you voted for Kennedy, or you didn't vote for him. Or weren't old enough to vote. The nation was in shock and that misbehaving horse gave them something to focus on. A military funeral is very somber. But Black Jack gave the public some emotional relief.

&~ Robert Dellwo
Attorney and county
Democratic chairman

"Bobby and Ted were 'doers,'. . . and were
expected to take care of their older, prominent
brother . . . 'the boys,' as we called them, were
always busy attending to details."

IN 1960, I was the Democratic Party Chairman for Spokane County, Washington, as well as the county chair for the Kennedy for President Campaign. It was at this time that I first met Jack Kennedy. He came to Spokane to give the keynote speech at the Jefferson-Jackson Day banquet at the Davenport Hotel. He arrived early that day and we spent the day together.

First, he drove with me and members of my committee to Whitworth College, where he spoke in the campus auditorium. It was here that I first realized what an attraction he was. The auditorium was packed and everyone cheering. Then we hastened back to Spokane for an event at Gonzaga University gymnasium. I remember walking up and seeing a line of people waiting to get in.

Of course, that evening was the big speech. The Davenport Hotel ballroom was packed and after his remarks, the reception line was long—about four people wide and stretching for what appeared to be at least one hundred yards. I was bird-dogging it, to make sure everything was going well.

Kennedy started at the head of the line and was greeting and shaking hands with everyone.

After a while, he took me aside and said, "Robert, I've got a problem. I've got to be back in Boston tomorrow morning."

So I took him through the hotel's kitchen and out a rear exit where I had a car parked. We were driven out to the airport and he got into his private plane. We had him there within fifteen or twenty minutes. I almost expected him to toot the horn as he flew over. All those people still in line at the hotel thought they'd be shaking Jack's hand by the time they got to front of the line.

After he was elected president, I made many trips to Washington, both as a representative of the Amateur Athletic Union and as a representative of several Indian tribes. I would often go by the White House, and if he was not available, would just slip a note to his secretary, a note of greetings.

Bobby and Ted were "doers," from my perspective, and were expected to take care of their older, prominent brother. They showed Jack respect and dignity. Jack had a dignity about him, and "the boys," as we called them, were always busy attending to details.

On November 22, 1963, I was driving east of Spokane to a meeting of one of my legal clients—a local water district board. I stopped at a restaurant, which had rooms in the back, where the meeting was to take place. As I was walking through the restaurant, someone, in an insipid, antagonistic voice said, "Did you hear about the death of Jack Kennedy?" And another person replied, "Yes, I heard about it and we're rid of the guy now."

I was shocked and got back into my car immediately and drove to the county courthouse. There were tears in my eyes. I walked into the courtroom of the presiding judge, who happened to be Ralph Foley, the father of the future Speaker of the House Tom Foley. Judge Foley, who had aspirations to be a federal judge, was informing people in his courtroom that the president had been assassinated. He asked everyone to sit side-by-side in a kind of semi-circle and he led a discussion about what people thought would be the impact of the president's death on the nation.

At one point, he called on me. I couldn't speak; I just cried.

✎ Phyllis Elkins
Waitress at Jim's Steak and Spaghetti House, Huntington, West Virginia

"He looked up at me, and he said, 'Do you mind having your picture made with me?' . . . And when I said, 'My pleasure,' he just busted out laughing because we talk kind of South-like here in West Virginia."

IT was in the morning, and it was really good weather. It was a nice day. He came in and sat in my station. There were three of them. Senator Kennedy, Congressman Hechler, and the other gentleman, David Fox, who has passed away. They were having coffee.

He looked up at me, and he said, "Do you mind having your picture made with me?"

I was pouring coffee, and I said, "My pleasure."

And when I said, "My pleasure," he just busted out laughing because we talk kind of South-like here in West Virginia. And that's when they snapped the picture.

He didn't walk around to meet people. He just sat at the table and talked to the other two gentlemen. They only had coffee. And I don't remember if he gave me a tip.

He was such a gentleman. He was wonderful. And good looking! He stayed about an hour. He had a great smile, he really did.

On November 22, I was at work at Jimmie's. Someone ran into the restaurant and told us that President Kennedy had been shot. And I just bawled. I cried and I cried. And I still cry when I think about it.

Jimmie closed the restaurant for the weekend. She had a television for us. And she let us—the employees—stay there. We didn't do anything. We just sat at the counter and watched. The whole weekend. And it broke our hearts. And I'm crying right now. It was horrible.

I will never forget him. I felt close to him. I don't know why. But I did—and I still do. He had a big impact on me.

That picture has been up there—in the restaurant—forever. The customers who come in know that was me in the photo, even though sometimes I was working the grill, not handling tables. I was really good on the grill.

I wish he hadn't been assassinated, because I think he would have really done this country, this world, great. He was the only president I really loved. I really cared about him. He's always been close to my heart. And always will be.

ᘒᕔ Richard Gaudreau
Military pallbearer

"Under my breath, I was saying to the cardinal, 'Come on, just get it over with!' He took the holy water and he said some words in Latin and then he blessed it. Finally, he finished, after six or seven minutes. We, the casket team, all drew from within and said, 'We'll get through this.' And we did."

ON November 22, I was stunned initially to hear over the radio that the president had been shot and possibility killed. Upon notifying the master sergeant, I was instructed to conduct a recall of all USAF Honor Guard personnel. All leaves were cancelled. I later learned the president's body was being flown back to Andrews and was instructed to assemble a team of Air Force pallbearers and to proceed to Andrews and stand by.

At Andrews, I was informed that the Joint Service Casket Team, composed of representatives from all the armed forces, would not handle the President's casket. The Secret Service personnel would do that. I felt that was odd and that we should have taken it from the lift truck. Air Force One arrived at about six o'clock, and I wound up helping place the casket into the ambulance. Like many Americans watching this live on television, the most vivid memory I have is seeing the bloodstains and other matter on Mrs. Kennedy's dress and stockings.

Then I flew with the other members of the casket team by helicopter from Andrews to Bethesda Naval Hospital. There was some confusion regarding the arrival of a hearse at our location only to have it speed away without reason. After some ten or fifteen minutes waiting, the ambulance with Mrs. Kennedy and the president's body arrived. We were instructed at that time that Brigadier General Godfrey McHugh, the president's Air Force aide, would be helping our casket team to carry the casket. I thought, "Why is this?" We could handle this without his help.

Later we were told to proceed to the hospital loading dock to bring in a new casket and place it in the autopsy room and to take the old casket and place on the loading dock. This was done because the first casket was damaged loading it onto Air Force One in Dallas. I later learned the old casket was dumped somewhere in the Atlantic Ocean.

After the autopsy, we placed the president's casket into a hearse, and were directed to the vehicles that would transport us (the casket team) to the White House. Upon arrival at the White House, we formed up and proceeded to carry the casket inside the East Room where it was placed on the catafalque.

Later, the casket team was expanded to eight members because of the weight of the coffin and the ceremony that would have the team carry it up the steps of the Capitol on Sunday. They didn't want it tilted coming down or going up, so we practiced carrying a casket at the Tomb of the Unknown Solider for six or seven hours. We used a "dummy casket" weighing only about four hundred pounds. The president's weighed more than seven hundred pounds. As a result, we had a guard at the Tomb of the Unknown Soldier lie in the casket and carried him.

All of the ceremonies went well except at the end of the service at St. Matthew's Cathedral. Cardinal Cushing wanted to bless the casket. The casket team came down a set of stairs. The flag was raised in front, and we stood at attention holding this very heavy casket. Under my breath, I was saying to the cardinal, "Come on, just get it over with!" He took the holy water and he said some words in Latin and then he blessed it. Finally, he finished, after six or seven minutes. That may not sound like a long time, but it really was. Now we had to carry the president's body to the middle of the street, raise the casket up again, place it onto the horse-drawn caisson. We, the casket team, all drew from within and said, "We'll get through this." And we did. We were physically exhausted.

What is John Kennedy's legacy? That is so hard to put into words. I would have liked to see him finish what he started, that is to complete the four years and be re-elected to a second term. The one big item that stands out in my mind was his commitment to place a man on the moon. It happened six years after his death. It was such an achievement for the United States.

✑ Mike Gefroh
Little Leaguer who caught a
ceremonial first pitch

*"The Kennedys were a catalyst for changing the
American way of life for the next generation."*

IN 1960, I was twelve years old at the opening day of the Riverside
Little League in Portland, Oregon. A huge crowd was present, maybe a
thousand people. The parking lot was jam packed; everybody's family
was there as well as all the media people. Senator John Kennedy was
scheduled to throw out the first pitch.

There was an opening ceremony with a color guard and the
national anthem. I was one of three players chosen to participate—my
role was to catch the first pitch. I'm not sure why I was selected, maybe
because I was a catcher and Catholic. The whole nation—particularly
Catholics—was abuzz with Kennedy's candidacy.

He stood on the mound, threw the pitch, and I caught it. No
one explained to me that when I caught it, I was supposed to walk it
back out to him. So I threw it back to him. He wasn't ready for it, and
the ball flew between him and (the Little League President) as they
were shaking hands. Another player brought the ball back to me, and I
walked it out to Senator Kennedy. He was very cordial, very dignified,
and very well dressed. He said in his Boston accent, "You've got quite
an arm there, young man." He autographed the ball, handed it back to
me, and shook my hand.

On November 22, I was a junior at Central Catholic High School
in Portland. During third period American history class, the principal came on the PA system. He spoke very slowly, trying to remain

composed. He announced that President Kennedy had been shot in Dallas, Texas.

We all said a prayer and later, after lunch, it was announced that he had died. I was sad, of course, and the whole nation, especially the Catholic community, was distraught. School continued that day. The next day, or maybe the day after, there was a special memorial Mass at school. I remember the nuns crying.

Kennedy made me more aware of politics and current events. I remember watching the 1960 Democratic Convention with him running against Lyndon Johnson and Stuart Symington for the nomination. The suspense of the balloting was a terrific initiation into the political process.

What's his legacy? He and his family were kind of like American royalty. I remember watching Jackie Kennedy's tour of the White House on TV and the Hyannis Port crowd playing touch football on Thanksgiving. President Kennedy got us to the moon and started many innovative programs, including the Peace Corps. We went from the post-war recovery days of the fifties to something much more progressive.

The Kennedys were a catalyst for changing the American way of life for the next generation.

❧ Frank Greer
Senate page, media advisor to U.S. Presidents William Jefferson Clinton and Barack Obama

"It's like I was Forrest Gump—a witness to history."

I was born and raised in Alabama, and in 1963, at age fifteen, I went to Washington as a page for Senator John Sparkman. I was able to attend a few social events at the White House and met John Kennedy and his wife. I was in awe of him, and like so many people of that era, I admired and deeply respected him as a political force.

His presidential campaign was a major inspiration in my life. In my ninth grade social studies class at Tuscaloosa High School, we followed the campaign, and as an assignment, had to study and document one of the campaigns. Of course, I was the only one who followed Kennedy. Mine was an all-white school and there was another all-black high school.

As a kid growing up in the segregated South, I admired his courage on civil rights. There were other major figures who were inspiring at that time, such as Dr. Martin Luther King and A. Philip Randolph. John Kennedy also looked outward toward others and toward the world. He wanted America to be respected around the world.

In June of 1963, I heard there was going to be a big confrontation at the University of Alabama, which was three blocks from my house: The university was going to be integrated. And Governor George Wallace was going to "stand in the schoolhouse door" to prevent the integration. So I got on my bicycle, rode down to Foster Auditorium, and crawled under a table. I was ten or fifteen feet away when (Deputy Attorney General) Nicholas Katzenbach arrived to face George Wallace, the little bantam rooster that he was. Then Mr. Katzenbach read a federal court order. The next day, a young black woman, Vivian Malone, was admitted to the University of Alabama. I watched that unfold.

In August of 1963, Senator John Sparkman's office offered me a page appointment. I took the train—the Southern Crescent—to Washington, got off at Union Station, walked out the front door, and looked up and saw the Capitol. I went to the Senator's office and said, "I'm Frank Greer and I'm here to go to work." A few weeks later, I heard there was going to be a civil rights march on Washington. Having gone through the searing experience of the struggle for civil rights in the South, I walked out of my rooming house, and headed down the Mall in Washington. I was astounded to see other white people, including many from labor unions—the United Auto Workers, the steel workers, and the AFL-CIO, who were supporting civil rights.

I had my page identification, this official-looking badge, and I convinced the security people that they should let me up close to the stage. I talked my way up onto the platform and sat down. Later that day, I was ten feet away when the Rev. King gave his famous "I Have a Dream" speech.

It's like I was Forrest Gump—a witness to history.

On November 22, 1963, I was on the floor of the Senate working as a page and was called to the cloakroom. I was handed a note and told to give it to Senator Wayne Morse of Oregon. I ran into the chamber with a note saying, "The president has been shot." Senator Morse then walked over and informed Senator Ted Kennedy, who was presiding over the Senate.

On the following Monday, many of us congressional pages volunteered to assist in the funeral. Several senators and we were bussed to Arlington National Cemetery and watched as the procession crossed the Memorial Bridge and came up the hill. At the gravesite, I stood near Haile Selassie and Charles De Gaulle.

Nineteen sixty-three was a searing year and an amazing experience. The events of that year were fundamental in my commitment to pursue a career in politics and non-profit service. I was, in many ways, a witness to history, and John Kennedy was a major positive force in my life and the life of our nation. He truly inspired a generation of young Americans, including Bill Clinton.

I was inspired by John Kennedy's call to public service, his commitment to make politics an honorable profession, and, of course, his famous line in the inaugural address, "Ask not..." He was an outward-looking, a forward-looking leader, who inspired the nation and the world. Of course, I also admired his book *Profiles in Courage*. Regrettably, today, we have few profiles in courage. In this age of partisanship and selfish parochial politics, John Kennedy was unselfish. He inspired us to think about others, to think beyond our own self-interests. He called us to think about what was best for the nation and the people of the world.

John Kennedy also transformed American politics. He demonstrated the power of television and, since his death, he has taught generations how to inspire with one's words and one's style.

❧ Ron Hall
Artist, art dealer, author, coincidental bystander to assassination

"I said, 'The president's been shot? My goodness, he's right in front of us!'"

ON November 22, 1963, I was eighteen years old, and we (my two friends and I) were sitting on the hood of my car. We were parked right directly below the Texas School Book Depository Building. Earlier we had been stopped by the police. We were not aware that Kennedy was coming downtown. It was just a coincidence—a way of God remaining anonymous. My friends and I were trying to get to TCU (Texas Christian University)—I was a freshman at East Texas State University, and my friends and I had dates with some rich sorority girls at TCU. We were just country boys thinking we were in high cotton because we were going to TCU and had dates for their homecoming. So we were in a hurry to get to TCU.

A policeman stood in front of us as we were going through the downtown on Elm Street and were stopped. Ours was the last car that did not get stopped.

We asked him, "What's the problem?"

The officer said, "The presidential motorcade is getting ready to pass. You'll have to wait until they pass before you can continue on."

I said, "OK, we've got a good seat!"

So we got out of the car and sat on the hood and waited about five minutes. We were facing west on Elm Street, probably twenty-five or thirty feet away from the Book Depository building. While we were waiting, the crowd began to fill in around our car and in the street around us.

All of a sudden, we saw the presidential motorcade coming, and just in front of us, the motorcade had to take a hard left turn. We saw the president. We waved. They waved. Everybody waved. As the president passed in front of us and made the turn, we were not interested in anything else except getting into our car and busting through the crowd as soon as it eased up so we could get on to TCU.

So we jumped into the car to drive away and that's when the crowd started going everywhere. We didn't hear any gunshots, but we had the radio on. At that time, the limousine was probably fifty yards in front of us. The street in front of us was clear, so we drove off.

At this point, the president's limousine was about two hundred yards in front of us, just passed the grassy knoll area. So we were one of the first cars on the road behind the presidential car. At the time, people were running, but we didn't have a clue as to what was going on. So fifteen or thirty seconds later, we were at the grassy knoll, and a radio announcer said the president's been shot.

I said, "The president's been shot? My goodness, he's right in front of us!"

We just kept chasing them. They turned onto the Stemmons Freeway going north, and we followed them as fast as we could to catch up to them. We probably were no more than three hundred or four hundred yards behind. And only one or two police cars were between us. Ours was the first civilian vehicle behind them. We passed the Trade Mart, where he was supposed to be having lunch. The radio was announcing the president's been shot. We kept following and pulled into Parkland Memorial Hospital, into the parking lot.

They had pulled up unto a carport. We did not see them take the president out of the car into the hospital. It was kind of eerie. There were not a lot of people in the parking lot. We stayed in the car, and we were about a hundred feet from the limousine at that time. We knew not to get out because we already were treading on thin ice just being there. We had no agenda; we just happened to end up there. Just to be there was incredible enough. We were listening to the radio and sat there for about thirty minutes, thinking he might come back out, and we would get to see him again.

Finally, a Secret Service-looking guy with dark glasses said, "What are you boys doin'?"

I said, "We were just waiting here, maybe to see the president."

He said, "You all better get on out of here."

We said, "Yes sir."

By the time we got back on the freeway, they were saying (on the radio) that the president was dead.

I thought, "Wow. I just cannot believe he's dead."

We went to TCU, and of course, all the homecoming events were cancelled. I left my friends there—they were going to stay at the dorm—and went to my parents' house and stayed there. It was somber and everybody just watched the television. We were glued to the TV.

On Sunday, as we were going to church, they started saying, "Oswald's been shot." And we thought, "Oh my gosh."

It was a feeling of sadness and heaviness. You didn't know really what was going to happen in the world. I had never seen a funeral for a president or a fallen leader before: the horse-drawn carriage carrying the coffin, the president's widow in black and wearing a black veil, their son saluting the casket. These images are burned on my visual memory.

Whenever I think of Kennedy, of course, I think of the assassination. I don't really think of him having accomplished so much as a president; he wasn't in office that long. He was the president associated with civil rights and integration. I remember the Cuban Missile Crisis and was worried we night have a nuclear war with the Soviets.

I think of him as the assassinated president and me being one of the last of a few hundred people who saw him alive. Within five seconds after I took my eyes off of him, he was dead.

✑ Catharine Hamm
Travel writer and editor,
Catholic who still grieves

"I felt my world tilt. She asked us to observe silence. I don't remember whether she told us to pray. In my case, she didn't have to; I knew what our priests and nuns would have said."

WEEKS before President Kennedy was killed, my father and mother had taken my middle sister and me to a parade honoring the president in downtown Honolulu. Kennedy, it seemed to me, had a sort of aura around him, and that smile was enough to melt even a nine year old's heart.

I might have been predisposed to be enamored of this Irish Catholic president. My grandfather had once likened my mother's countenance to the "map of Ireland." My grandfather died before I was born so I never got to know him, except through her. I knew she adored her father, who was as Irish as Paddy's pig.

And I also knew that being Irish and Catholic wasn't necessarily something one flaunted in those days. There were still people who believed there was some kind of papal conspiracy and that Catholics hid guns in preparation for the overthrow. My mother never denied her roots, but it wasn't until Kennedy was elected that she fully embraced her heritage. He was like a gift from heaven to her and her family, and from then on, she instilled a sense of pride about both Irishness and Catholicism in us, her three daughters.

My dad didn't have quite the same fascination and might actually have voted for Nixon, which would explain why things were a little tense during the campaign. But by 1963, we had moved from Washington, D.C., to Hawaii, a heavily Democratic state. My father, ever the dedicated civil servant, finally acknowledged that a torch had, indeed, passed to a new generation—his. Like Kennedy, he had been "tempered by war." So complicated, so far above my understanding.

As a kid living in Hawaii, life was one giant playground. We worked hard—fourth grade was demanding at Aikahi Elementary School in Kailua—and we played hard. Few days were not play days and many days were beach days. It doesn't get better than that.

That day in November started like many others—leave for school, take off shoes out of mom's sight, walk the rest of the way, and scurry into class, where Mrs. Uehara kept us under control with a firm, but not unkind hand. She returned to the classroom that morning tear-stained and told us the president had been shot and was dead.

I felt my world tilt.

She asked us to observe silence. I don't remember whether she told us to pray. In my case, she didn't have to; I knew what our priests and nuns would have said.

Released from school, we gathered in the corridors. It was quiet, except for an outburst by a kid named Cindy who said she was glad that Kennedy was dead. We shushed her, and in typical elementary school fashion, told her she was stupid and offered to beat her senseless.

When we got home, my mother had the TV on and we watched, as we did for the next three days, the scenes play out over and over. Johnson being sworn in. Jackie Kennedy near him in her bloodstained suit. Lee Harvey Oswald and the improbability of Jack Ruby stepping forward and turning a tragedy into a sickening mystery.

Over and over and over again. We couldn't stop watching.

Our house was quiet for days. It's too simple to say that life was never the same again, even for a kid. Our icon was gone, but his message to us—be proud of who and what you are—has suffused our lives.

&ra; Terri Hazeleur
Led thirty-one girls walking all night to meet the president

*"He asked me how far we had walked. I told him
thirty-five miles. He looked down at my bare feet
and grinned and said, 'Well, next time,
make it fifty.'"*

JOHN Kennedy was very charismatic and youthful. Young people really liked him. My dad was involved in his election campaign. He was a staunch Democrat and chairman of the Democratic Party for Trinity County (California). In fact, he received an invitation to the inaugural ball in 1961, but we didn't have a lot of money. My father was a logger; he worked in the summer, but in the winter he didn't work at all. So, we could never have afforded to go. But it was quite an honor to be invited.

I was fifteen years old and wanted to meet the president (who was coming to dedicate a nearby dam). But I thought the chances were really slim. So, we organized this thirty-five mile hike and thought we would get attention that way to meet him. We started the night before the president's visit; thirty-two girls hiking with flashlights over Buckhorn Mountain. My mom and dad and aunt supervised; they drove their car back and forth and brought us drinks and food. Our flashlights died out in the middle of the night.

We arrived at about five in the morning. President Kennedy arrived around ten. There were a bunch of chairs laid out for the audience, so we plopped ourselves on the chairs. We were tired. The reporters, who were already there, said, "Oh you girls, these chairs are for the dignitaries. You get out of here."

Later as the president was delivering his speech, someone said, "Let all these girls in here." So we were allowed to sit with the dignitaries. After his speech, he started walking down a fenced-off area to meet members of the crowd. All of a sudden, one of the Secret Service agents said, "The President of the United States would like to meet Terri Hodgetts."

My dad said, "That's you!"

They shoved me over the other side of the fenced off area—I caught my britches on the fence and ripped them. So I tied a sweatshirt around my waist and walked up to him. He asked me how far we had walked. I told him thirty-five miles.

He looked down at my bare feet and grinned and said, "Well, next time, make it fifty."

It was the short conversation that lasted a lifetime.

He was shorter than I thought he would be. He smelled really good. He had a beautiful smile. He really made an impression on me, and I think some of the other girls may have met him. The photographer just happened to be there and took the picture that went all around the country.

On November 22, 1963, I was in Spanish class at Hayfork High School. We had about one hundred and sixty in the school and twenty-five in my class. The teacher sent me to the office to get some paper. I got to the office and everyone in there was crying, even the principal. I said, "What's the matter?" They told me what had happened, and I started crying too.

I went back to my class and told the teacher and the teacher said, "That's a terrible joke to play on people, Terri, that's a sick joke."

And I replied, "You know me. I don't play sick jokes."

The teacher realized I was telling the truth. He left the classroom and went to the office. School was let out early.

His death was traumatic. Unbelievable. Back in those days, you really didn't hear about a lot of bad things happening like you do today. I recall the television coverage, especially the drums beating during the funeral.

I always had the impression that John Kennedy wanted the nation to strive to do better. He instilled that in people, like his comment to me, "Next time make it fifty."

He was a compassionate man. He would be finding ways for people to be proud of themselves. Like me. Some little nobody in some little town no one's ever heard of can do something and be successful. It's an encouraging thought.

Father Oscar Huber
Catholic priest who administered the Last Rites

"I will never forget the blank stare in her eyes and the signs of agony on her face."

(ON November 22, 1963) on TV at 11:30 am, I saw his arrival at Love Field and heard the enthusiastic welcome given him. Then I walked down to Lemmon and Reagan Streets, about three blocks from Holy Trinity Church, to await the motorcade that would bring the president along the planned route that would end at the Dallas Trade Mart.

There both sides of the street were lined with people eagerly awaiting the president—there also were the children of Holy Trinity School, their teachers, and lay teachers. Soon the car carrying the members of the presidential party passed by. The President and Mrs. Kennedy were waving and smiling to everyone, and these gestures of goodwill were enthusiastically returned by the happy onlookers along the way. It was a thrilling moment for me as I had never before seen a President of the United States.

I returned to the rectory—ate a brief lunch—and had just finished when Father James N. Thompson, C.M., one of my assistants, who had finished lunch previously and was watching TV—came to the rectory and announced that the president had been shot. We went to the recreation room where we heard, over TV, the president had been taken to Parkland Memorial Hospital. This hospital is within the confines of Holy Trinity parish. Within a short time we were on our way to the hospital. Shortly after we left the rectory, a telephone call came from someone at Parkland Hospital saying Mrs. Kennedy was requesting a priest to administer to the spiritual needs of the president.

Within ten or fifteen minutes we were at the hospital. Father Thompson parked the car while I was escorted by a policeman to an emergency room where I found the fatally wounded president lying on a portable table. He was covered with a sheet that I removed from over his forehead before administering conditionally the Last Rites of the Catholic Church. These Rites are administered conditionally when a priest has no way of knowing the person's mind or whether the soul has yet left the body. In Latin, I said: "I absolve you from your sins in the name of the Father, and of the Son, and of the Holy Ghost. Amen."

During these ceremonies, Mrs. Kennedy was standing beside the president. She and others in the emergency room answered the prayers with which they were familiar. Mrs. Kennedy bent over and seemed to kiss the president. Soon after this, followed by Mrs. Kennedy and the others who were present, I walked from the emergency room into the adjoining corridor. Sorrow and consternation bowed the heads of everyone present. The silence that pervaded the corridor was mute evidence that another President of the United States had died at the hands of an assassin.

During this most trying ordeal, the perfect composure maintained by Mrs. Kennedy was beyond comprehension. I will never forget the blank stare in her eyes and the signs of agony on her face. I extended my heartfelt sympathy and that of my parishioners to her. In a low tone of voice she thanked me graciously and asked me to pray for the president. I assured her I would do so. Shortly after this Father Thompson and I returned to Holy Trinity rectory.

The agonizing countenance of Mrs. Kennedy, her clear answer to the prayers recited, her gentle expression of thanks to me for administering the Last Rites and expressing my sympathy, the difficulty I had in controlling my emotions, the expression of shock written on the faces of the Secret Service men, the anxiety expressed by the people who crowded the corridors of Parkland Hospital waiting for a word of hope about the president's condition, the large attendance at Masses offered for the repose of his soul—all these and many more incidents shall never be erased from my memory.

Credit: DeAndreis-Rosati Memorial Archives, DePaul University Archives, Chicago, Illinois, DePaul University

∝ David W. Knowlton
West Point graduate with a
foreboding premonition

"He spent ten minutes with us. . . . He was
personable and interested in us. It was a
wonderful experience. But I felt such terrible
anxiety, and I think he could tell I was stressed."

I was editor of the yearbook at West Point and went to Washington to present copies of the yearbook to all the top dignitaries—the Secretary of Defense, the Chairman of the Joint Chiefs of Staff, and others. Normally, the president did not receive the yearbook directly; he had his military aide do it.

But John Kennedy always wanted to spend time with the cadets. That's how I ended up in the Oval office. Earlier, we had presented yearbooks to former President Eisenhower and former General of the Army Douglas McArthur. Eisenhower was just a regular guy—like a man on the street. McArthur was a bit of a stuffed shirt; I don't think he even opened the book.

I felt quite comfortable though with those two. But not when I met President Kennedy in the Oval Office.

For the second time in my life, the hackles went up on my neck, and I sensed danger, evil. It had happened to me a year earlier in 1962, when I decided I couldn't get on an airplane that later crashed in Georgia and killed everyone on board. I had terrible anxiety, and was afraid for my life. It cost me seventy-five dollars to change tickets—a lot of money in 1962—and when I arrived at my destination, Los Angeles, I learned that the other plane had crashed.

When I met the president, he could tell I was distressed. He spent ten minutes with us. He said it was the best academy yearbook he'd ever seen, and I thanked him. He was personable and interested in us. It was a wonderful experience. But I felt such terrible anxiety, and I think he could tell I was stressed. I verbalized my feelings to my fellow graduate after we left the White House. I felt such a terrible foreboding.

On November 21, 1963, the night before the assassination, I arrived at my first duty station at Fort Carson, Colorado. On the morning of the 22nd, I was assigned to B Company, Seventh Engineer Battalion. I was the only officer except for the captain, so I was immediately the executive officer, which also meant I was the mess officer. The captain and I went over to the mess to get acquainted. All of a sudden, a soldier burst in and said, "Sir, they've just shot President Kennedy. We're all on alert."

I think John Kennedy was the greatest president we've ever had. But his legacy was unfinished. He was killed before he could have a legacy. I'm an Independent, leading toward conservatism. He had tremendous leadership. I've also admired Truman and Reagan. Of course, we know he was a womanizer. In fact, the White House assistant assigned to show us around Washington was gorgeous. She looked just like Marilyn Monroe. And I don't think she could tell the difference between a telephone and a typewriter.

✌ James Leavelle
Dallas police detective
handcuffed to
Lee Harvey Oswald

"If he'd just followed an old detective's advice one time, we would have had him (Oswald) at the county jail, got him to court, got him tried, got him convicted, got the death penalty on him. . . . But that didn't happen."

ON November 22, 1963, all the officers in the homicide office of the Dallas Police Department had assignments. We had two officers riding in the motorcade. But my partner was on vacation, so Captain (J. W.) Fritz told me to stick around the office and take care of anything that might come in. They furnished a uniformed patrolman to work with me, but he came up in plain clothes, and he and I went out and arrested a man for armed robbery whom I had a warrant for. On the way back from arresting him, we listened to the dispatcher keeping track of where the motorcade was from Love Field.

As we pulled in to the basement where Oswald was later shot, they were approaching Houston Street, where they had turned right for about a half block to get on Elm Street in order to make an exit onto the Stemmons (Freeway). We parked and turned the radio off. We went up the elevator from the basement to the third floor office, and I was told by Lt. Ted Wells that they had shot the president.

And I said, "Oh, yeah, yeah."

Between the time it took me to go from the car to the third floor office, the President was shot. I was not on the grassy knoll with ten thousand other people who told me they were there.

(Later that day) they had Oswald in an interrogation room—just a desk and a couple of chairs. No phone or anything, so there are no distractions. No one was with him. I went in and started talking to him about the shooting of Officer (J. D.) Tippit. At that time, I did not have a clue that he would be a suspect in the presidential shooting. There was nothing to indicate at that time that he was involved in that. He was two or three miles away from that scene (at the Texas School Book Depository Building). He denied shooting Officer Tippit.

He said, "I didn't shoot anybody."

I didn't think too much about it when he told me that, but a day or so later, I got to thinking about that: "I didn't shoot anybody." Because I've worked through other officers' murders, suspects usually deny their involvement by saying, "I didn't shoot the cop," or "I didn't shoot the policemen."

But he didn't say that; he knew we were going to rap him for the president's shooting later, and he's getting his denial in to begin with, that he "didn't shoot anybody."

Captain Fritz came back (to station headquarters) from the Book Depository building. They had found the rifle. They had found the window where he (Oswald) had shot from, and they picked up the empty hulls (shells) from underneath the window. And before he (Captain Fritz) left the building, he asked Mr. (Roy) Truly (warehouse manager) to do a head count on all of his employees. Oswald was the only one missing, and he hadn't had permission to leave. So the captain said to Truly, "Give me that man's address." He got it and he sent people out there, but the address was wrong; Oswald had given Truly a bad address. When the captain walked in (to the Dallas Police headquarters), he started sending five or six detectives in different directions to look for Oswald.

Somebody told him, "Cap, the man Leavelle's talking to has got a name similar to that." So the captain came over, opened the door, and asked me his (Oswald's) name. I said, "Lee Oswald." He looked at Oswald and asked, "Where do you work?" Oswald replied, "The Texas

School Book Depository Building." And the captain said, "You're the man I want to talk to."

So I lost my prisoner and never questioned him again about any of the shootings because Cap had him on the presidential murder.

The first thing I regret is that the president was shot. And even worse that it happened here in my city. We got condolences from many other cities, telling us, "It could have happened just as easily in our city when he was visiting here." I have become good friends with Clint Hill, the Secret Service agent who jumped up on the back of the car. He took it really bad that the president got shot.

I've told him, "Clint, you don't need to feel bad about it because you could have been handcuffed to him and he still could have been shot. I'm a perfect example of that. I handcuffed myself to the prisoner because we had so many threats against him."

The captain and I talked it over, and I said, "I'll handcuff myself so if they take him, they've got to take me. And I'm not going to go peacefully."

And that's how come I was handcuffed to him (Oswald).

If I hadn't had any more information than I had that day, I would not change anything I did (about the transfer of Oswald). But, if I had an inkling something like that might be happening, I would have done what I wanted to do and what I asked the Chief (Dallas Police Chief Jesse Curry) to do about an hour earlier. I asked him to let us take him out on the first floor.

Being it was a Sunday, there was nobody there. During the week the city courts are on that floor, and the elevator stops on that floor. They take the prisoners, drunks, and ne'er-do-wells down to the city court to be sentenced. But being a Sunday, there was no one there. We could have taken him out on that first floor, put him in a car on Main Street, and been at the county jail before anyone knew we had left the city jail with him.

But the chief said, "Leavelle, I have given my word that they (members of the news media) can film the transfer. I want them to know that we didn't abuse him or mistreat him in any way. And the best way for them to know that is to let them film it, so we're going to take him out there (through the basement garage) and they can film it."

That's something else I've thought about years later. If he'd just followed an old detective's advice one time, we would have had him at the county jail, got him to court, got him tried, got him convicted, got the death penalty on him. And who knows? He could still be down there with appeals pending the way courts are handling things nowadays. But that didn't happen.

❧ Priscilla Johnson McMillan
Knew both John Kennedy and Lee Harvey Oswald

"That afternoon, in Harvard Square, someone told me that President Kennedy had been murdered in Dallas. . . . I felt strangled. 'My God,' I said, 'I know that boy!'"

I first met John Kennedy in May, 1953, soon after he was sworn in for his first term in the U.S. Senate. A couple of months earlier I had finished work at Harvard on a Master's degree in Russian Studies and was fairly fluent in Russian. I went to Washington and applied for jobs at the offices of several congressmen and senators.

A friend who worked for a senator on Capitol Hill mentioned that the new senator from Massachusetts was hiring, so I left my resume at his office, too. But when, after a couple of weeks, I had not found anything, I took a job translating Russian political articles for *The Current Digest of the Soviet Press* at Columbia University in New York.

Before the job was due to begin, I received an unexpected call from Senator Kennedy's office. I was told that the senator wanted me to work for him on a short-term project in Washington but wished to meet me first. When I went to see him at his office on the Hill, the first thing I noticed was how thin he was, so thin, in fact, that he looked concave. He apologized for not having a full-time position to offer me, and I said not to worry, I had accepted a job translating Russian, to start in a few weeks.

What Senator Kennedy wanted was for me to do research on a subject he evidently had a special interest in: Should the U.S. pressure France, a country to which we gave financial assistance, to abandon its war in Indochina? I was to work for him for two weeks. I would not be on his office payroll; I was to be paid directly by his father. I would receive seventy-five dollars a week and work out of a small office in the Library of Congress Annex. He wanted his first Senate speech to be on foreign policy, and my research was to serve as its basis. The senator did not tell me why he was interested in Indochina. He did not mention that he had already been there two years before, that he knew quite a bit about the place, and that he held strong views about the French and their colonies. Nor did I ask his views, which I was not to learn for many, many years.

On two successive Friday afternoons in May, I briefed Senator Kennedy on why we should use our clout with the French to make them leave Indochina. After that, my work was done. I went to New York and my new job translating Russian newspapers. Over the next couple of years, I heard from time to time from the senator. He took me out for breakfast once after he had visited his doctor. Another time, after lunch in New York, he said he needed to see his tailor. The tailor's business was just down the street, but he insisted on taking a cab. When he got out of the cab, he quickly stepped into the tailor's shop, and I was left to pay the driver.

I paid my first visit to the Soviet Union during the winter of 1955-56. Two years later, I got a job in Moscow as a rookie reporter for the North American Newspaper Alliance. It was a chance to learn about the country and improve my fluency in the language, and I struggled to extend my visas and stay as long as I could. In November of 1959, a consul at the American embassy in Moscow told me about a twenty-year-old Marine who wanted to defect to the Soviet Union. He was staying at the same hotel I was, the Hotel Metropole, but was angry for some reason and refused to speak with anyone at the embassy. Maybe he would speak to me since I was a woman.

The Marine's name was Lee Harvey Oswald.

A bit to my surprise, he agreed to an interview. That evening we sat in my room for several hours while he told me his story. He seemed lonely and very, very young—lost in a situation he did not understand. I felt sorry for him. A day or so later, I filed a story. Here is an excerpt:

> *With his suit of charcoal gray flannel, dark tie, and tan cashmere sweater, Lee looks, and sounds, like Joe College with a slight Southern drawl. But his life hasn't been that of a typical college boy. . . . Even though Russian officials have warned him Soviet citizenship is not easy to obtain, Lee already refers to the Soviet government as "my government." "But," says Lee, "even if I am not accepted, on no account will I go back to the United States. I shall remain here, if necessary, as a resident alien."*

The article appeared in newspapers back in the U.S., but I did not see Lee Oswald or hear of him again—until November 22, 1963.

That afternoon, in Harvard Square, someone told me that President Kennedy had been murdered in Dallas. Later I ran into a friend and asked whether there was a suspect. "Yes," she said, "Someone named Lee H . . . Harvey something"—she could not remember the name—had been arrested.

I felt strangled. "My God," I said, "I know that boy!"

That evening and the next day, because of my interview with Oswald and my article about him, FBI agents came to question me. I spoke with them, of course, and the following year testified before the Warren Commission. In the summer of 1964, in Texas, I interviewed Lee's widow, Marina, for many, many hours in Russian. My conversations with her and interviews with acquaintances of the Oswalds, along with essays and letters by Lee that were published in the Warren Commission Report, led to my book, *Marina and Lee*, which appeared in 1977.

As for the unfinished story of John Kennedy, I sometimes wonder whether the harsh edges of the Cold War might have been softened earlier, as early as the 1960s, had Kennedy still been President. And there is the question of Vietnam. In 1953, Kennedy hired me to do research on Indochina because he felt that the French should abandon their stake there. A decade later, in 1963 and afterward, would he, as president, have stood up to the pressure from Congress and the generals to raise our stake in that very same Vietnam?

❧ Ann Owens
Inspired by "Ask Not…"
to join the Peace Corps

*"There was a wonderful naiveté about it. The
idea that you could go to another country and
show a side of America
that we really do care. That we really are nice
people. We're here to help you."*

I was in Peace Corps training in the summer of 1962 in Washington, D.C. at Georgetown University. Much to the surprise and delight of all of us, we were invited at the very end of our training to the White House to meet President Kennedy. There were two hundred of us being trained to go to Ethiopia. We were the first group to go to Ethiopia. President Kennedy spoke to us on the South Lawn of the White House on August 8, 1962.

Then he went along the line and shook people's hands. Seeing and hearing him reconfirmed my great passion for him as our president. I was thrilled to be able to meet him. I was one of the people who got to shake his hand. He was very, very special. Very charismatic. Young, good looking. Strong.

I was twenty-four years old. I had taught third grade for two years and lived at home with my mom. It was a good life. I had a nice boyfriend.

But when he gave his inaugural speech, the challenge to Americans, "Ask not what your country can do for you. Ask what you can do for your country," it just really struck a chord with me. It appealed to my sense of service, and he called us to a higher calling to do something outside yourself, outside your country. It resonated with me. I had two years of experience. I was ready to do something different.

There was a wonderful naiveté about it. The idea that you could go to another country and show a side of America that we really do care. That we really are nice people. We're here to help you. Of course, with the Peace Corps, they invite you. You have no link to foreign policy. And it's not like you're going as a missionary.

I was with a group of Peace Corps volunteers teaching English and science and history in Tigray, a province north of the capital, Addis Ababa. On November 22, 1963, a doctor in the Peace Corps came into a house where I was visiting. He had a shortwave radio and was looking very gaunt. And he told us that Kennedy had been shot. And we didn't believe it. He was really ticked. He said, "How can you not believe me? Would I come in and say this if it weren't true?"

Kennedy was a hero in the best sense of the word. I looked up to him. He had fresh, new ideas. A new outlook on the world. That maybe we could get this right this time. We can go to the moon.

We can go to other countries and make a difference. We can help people out. He had new, profound thoughts on how we could get along in the world. The call to something bigger was a great motivator. He was smart. Very clever. A wonderful way with words. There was a cultural aspect to him that I appreciated. That was important to me. To have a president for whom life was not just politics.

⚜ Ruth Paine
Living with Marina Oswald at the time of the assassination

"I have not been able to look in the face the idea that if I led my life differently President Kennedy might be alive. Perhaps most people whose lives touch the matter have a host of 'if only' thoughts. Mine will be with me forever."

I was very impressed with him in office, and of course, Mrs. Kennedy. We felt like we were really being drawn into the activities of the country in a way I hadn't felt before. I feel that the things that happened informed him and made him a stronger president. In April of 1961, there was the invasion of the Bay of Pigs. That was a disaster. And I hoped that Kennedy would listen to his own wisdom more than the advice and counsel of his experts in the CIA. He was almost inoculated by that event to refer to his own understanding and wisdom.

On November 22, I had gotten my children up early to go to the dentist. I turned on the TV set to watch the Kennedys in Fort Worth for a breakfast speech. The Kennedys were a little late for arrival at the breakfast, and the news anchor had to fill time. And he talked about the assassination of President McKinley. There was something in the air and people were worried about his coming.

On that morning, I left with my kids for the dentist with the TV on because I knew Marina would want to see the motorcade and what was happening. But she wasn't up yet. She was feeding the baby in the night, and she slept when she could. When I got back from the dental appointment, she thanked me for having the TV on. She had watched him arrive at Love Field. Then we sat and watched the TV coverage.

Excerpt from Exhibit 460, "Testimony of Ruth Paine," from *The Report of the President's Commission on the Assassination of President Kennedy* (The Warren Commission):

> *We were on the sofa in the living room watching the tel-*
> *evision set when they announced that the president had*
> *been shot. I translated to her that the president had been*
> *wounded in the head. We waited for further word and*
> *the lunch I had prepared sat on the table untouched. I*
> *lit some plain candles. She asked if that was a way of*
> *praying and I told her yes, it was my private way. When*
> *the news came that the president was dead, I told her and*
> *we wept together. She said what a terrible thing it was for*
> *Mrs. Kennedy, how sad for her two children to grow up*
> *without a father.*

I first heard about Oswald being in custody when police arrived at my door and told me so. You have to understand, everybody was terribly upset. The police were. I was. Marina was. We didn't know what was going on. The police asked if Oswald had a gun, and I said, "No." But I translated for Marina, who said, "Yes, he did." She led them into the garage to show them the blanket that she believed the gun was in. It was not there.

And it was at that moment, that I felt, "Oh . . . it could have been Lee! He came out the night before. He could have gotten the gun."

I was feeling like whatever these policemen and the sheriffs want to know, and if there's any way I can help, I'll help. They needed a little bit better practice in terms of what they took and what they told me they took. But I wanted to help in whatever way I could.

They put stuff in the trunk of the car and they said, "We'd better go, you need to make a statement at the police station." My son was asleep. I was trying to think what to do in terms of a babysitter. One of the police thought I was taking too long. He grabbed me by the arm and said, "We've got to get down to the police station right away."

They didn't know who they were dealing with. Another one turned to me and said, "If you don't hurry up we'll just take the children and have them stay with juvenile."

That was a threat. I don't respond well to threats. So I turned to my daughter and said, "Lynn, you may come with us." I was going to be holding her hand the whole time.

I walked over to the home of a babysitter who regularly came to see if they could come and stay with my son while he was still sleeping and they did come. So we all piled into a couple of cars and went down to the police station.

I've had to say, "I could have done things differently. But that doesn't mean that the total outcome of Kennedy's life would have been different."

Excerpt from Exhibit 460, "Testimony of Ruth Paine," from *The Report of the President's Commission on the Assassination of President Kennedy* (The Warren Commission):

> *I have not been able to look in the face the idea that if I led my life differently President Kennedy might be alive. Perhaps most people whose lives touch the matter have a host of "if only" thoughts. Mine will be with me forever.*
>
> *If only I had known that Lee Oswald had hidden a rifle in my garage. If only I had apprised this man as someone able to do such terrible violence. If only the job that I helped him find hadn't put him in a building along the President's route. If only, quite by accident, I had done or not done a dozen things, the country might have been spared the tragedy, and Marina Oswald, whom I love as if she were a sister, would not have turned into an assassin's wife.*

Grief does not go away. That's how grief is. I've been upheld by a sense of the ancestors. There are folks who care who are on the other side of the veil of life and death, who have really helped me.

I was inspired by the grace with which President Kennedy held that office, with his humor, and with his comfort talking to news people. His real interest in international affairs. He represented us so wonderfully. You miss him all the more for knowing how good he was and perhaps could have been in a second term.

✒ Dr. Ira Seiler
Pediatric resident who saved the life of John Kennedy Jr., born not breathing

"I then grabbed the baby back, reinserted the tube, and for about six minutes, breathed air into the lungs of the baby."

I was a young, twenty-nine-year-old, second-year pediatric resident at Georgetown Hospital and had been given the morning off on Thanksgiving, November 25, 1960. I arrived at the hospital at about twelve noon and met Mrs. Kennedy's obstetrician in the hall. He informed me that Mrs. Kennedy was being admitted for an emergency C-section because she had Placentia Previa which causes blockage of the outlet from the uterus. I asked if he wanted me in the delivery room and was informed that he did. I remember thinking that if there was a problem with the delivery or with the baby, I would probably be blamed since I was the low man on the totem pole.

In 1960, we had no neonatologist or intensive care physician to assist in the care of a baby in distress. When JFK Jr. was born, the chief of the anesthesia department held him up by the ankles and slapped his buttocks. After doing this for several minutes, the infant became very cyanotic (blue in color), and I told him the baby needed to be intubated.

He handed the baby to me, and I passed a tube into the trachea of the baby. I then handed the infant back to him to breathe into the baby, since he was the chief of anesthesia. However, he was a bit nervous and knocked the tube out. I then grabbed the baby back, reinserted the tube, and for about six minutes, breathed air into the lungs of the baby. The baby was then transferred to the intensive care nursery, where I cared for him until his discharge on December 9, 1960. The discharge diagnosis was "Respiratory distress syndrome of the newborn." In later years, it has been called "Hyaline Membrane Disease."

After I left the delivery room one of the reporters asked me the sex of the baby, and I replied that I could not give out any information and that he would have to speak to Pierre Salinger, President Kennedy's press secretary. It was later written in the paper that a young doctor came out of the delivery room and did not know the sex of the baby. I laughed.

About a week later I was on the OB floor when President-elect Kennedy was visiting his wife, and I was introduced to him as the doctor who had done the initial resuscitation on the baby. I shook his hand, and he impressed me as being very sincere and a great man. Shortly afterward, on December 9, 1960, I received a letter from him in a plain envelope. He wrote:

> Dear Dr. Seiler:
> I want to take this opportunity to thank you and the other members of your efficient hospital staff for the many kindnesses shown to Mrs. Kennedy during her stay at the hospital. Your wonderful care has contributed greatly for her and my new son to leave the hospital in the very best of health.
> With every good wish.
>
> Sincerely,
> John F. Kennedy

On January 10, 1961, I received a registered letter from the Presidential Inaugural Committee addressed to Dr. and Mrs. Seiler containing a card stating, "President-elect Kennedy has requested the Inaugural Committee to forward to you the enclosed tickets for inaugural events." Enclosed were tickets to the ball at the armory, the governors' reception, the distinguished ladies' reception, the inaugural concert, and first row seats opposite the reviewing stand for the parade.

My wife and I had been sent tickets to all the functions with the exception of the inauguration.

However, three days later on January 13, 1961, I received a special delivery letter from the United State Senate which contained only a card asking me to go to the Old Senate Building to pick up my tickets for the inauguration. When I was given the tickets and was told that we were on the platform, I asked if President-elect Kennedy had actually asked that I be given these tickets. She checked and stated that I was on his private select list and should feel honored, which indeed, I was. We sat on the platform at the Capitol in front of where Kennedy and the dignitaries were assembled.

Several weeks later, I was seeing a newborn at Georgetown Hospital and mentioned to one of the nurses how impressed I was in receiving all the inaugural invitations. She informed me that she had written to the inaugural committee that if I had not been there John Kennedy Jr. would have died.

I wrote (Mrs. Kennedy) a letter after President Kennedy was assassinated and received a reply thanking me for my letter. We had just returned from vacation, and my wife was in the hospital with pneumonia. I had a home office at the time and was very depressed when I learned that he had been assassinated.

His death affected so many people. I thought he would have made a truly great president. His life was cut short; you really don't know how great a president he might have been. That has always bothered me. I considered him a brilliant and honest man. I didn't fully agree with his private life, but that's another story. His legacy is unfinished. He had great potential and made some errors, such as the Bay of Pigs fiasco, but getting the missiles out of Cuba was a great accomplishment. I feel it prevented a possible world war. Recently in the local newspaper, it was mentioned that he had some doubts about the value of the space program since it cost so much to fund. However, the standing of the United States was greatly enhanced as we became the leader in space exploration and science.

❧ Samuel Stern
Staff member of the
Warren Commission

"I think had he lived and had a second term, the world might have been a lot different in many favorable ways.
Particularly I'm thinking of Vietnam. I think he would have found his way through that and dealt with the hawks who were really selling a preposterous notion."

I met John Kennedy several times. The first time was at the Democratic Convention in 1956, when he was competing to be (Adlai) Stevenson's vice presidential running mate. (Senator Estes) Kefauver eventually beat him out for that assignment. I was a runner for the platform committee at the convention. I would sit outside and listen to them debate a plank. And when they had something to be printed, I would rush it down to the print shop in the hotel in Chicago, rush upstairs again, and listen some more.

But, more interestingly, several years after my clerkship with U.S. Supreme Court Chief Justice Earl Warren, in 1961 or '62—or conceivably in early '63—while Kennedy was president, I helped organize a dinner of the Warren clerks for him at the Metropolitan Club here in Washington. One of Warren's clerks, Jon Newman, who is now a Second Circuit judge, was on the White House staff at the time and invited President Kennedy. He was there for the cocktail reception, not the dinner. He was shaking hands with everybody and making small talk and Warren was overjoyed. Warren had been very, very moved by Kennedy and Mrs. Kennedy.

He was certainly charismatic, but I was less than overwhelmed by his presidency and substantially less than overwhelmed by his brother and his appointment of his brother as attorney general. There was the Bay of Pigs and a lot of on-the-job training, catching up to fill the office. So, at the time, I was reasonably critical, despite being a lifelong Democrat. I was much more a Stevenson Democrat than a Kennedy Democrat. In retrospect, considering everything that's come after him, I'm much more inclined to view his presidency favorably.

On November 22, I had just come back from lunch at the Metropolitan Club and got a phone call from a client and friend who was the president of Industrias Kaiser Argentina, the Kaiser subsidiary that manufactured Jeeps and Willys cars in Argentina. He was a devout Catholic and very devoted to Kennedy. He had just heard the news over the radio in Buenos Aires. He called to see what had happened and how serious it was. Initially, the news was that the president had been shot, but not that he had been killed. I remember it vividly—everybody stopped everything.

We were very skeptical of Lyndon Johnson and what that meant to the country. Completely flummoxed by the notion that one insignificant human being took down the most powerful man in the world. It didn't compute.

At the time, it helped motivate me to become actively involved in the civil rights movement, and particularly, in the Lawyers' Committee for Civil Rights Under Law, led by Lloyd Cutler. When Johnson announced the creation of the Warren Commission, I wrote to the chief justice and said, "If I can help, let me know." He passed that letter on to Howard Willens, a good friend who was then liaison between the Justice Department and the commission. I got a call from Willens and was invited to join the commission staff as an assistant counsel.

John Kennedy has become something of a myth. He is larger than life. The most dramatized part of his presidency, aside from the assassination, was the Cuban Missile Crisis. If he did nothing else, that was of gigantic importance to the world, not just the United States. He handled that well. I think had he lived and had a second term, the world might have been a lot different in many favorable ways. Particularly I'm thinking of Vietnam.

I think he would have found his way through that and dealt with the hawks who were really selling a preposterous notion. At the time, I was very opposed to the war. And in retrospect, it becomes even less sensible and supportable. And it skewed this country and the world in major ways. I think he was just catching on how to handle the LeMays (reference to Air Force General Curtis LeMay), and not just the military, but the civilian hawks. His own advisors were very much in favor of going to war and sustaining the war. The seeds of that terrible event were sown in Kennedy's Administration. There was very little in Eisenhower, and it could have been stopped immediately.

Part of the difficulty for Kennedy is the same difficulty that President Obama has had, but in even greater terms. Suddenly you're elevated to this enormously powerful position without much real preparation for it, catching up as it unfolds. You have to respond immediately to huge crises after crises.

His personal life is part of that legacy. His relationship with his wife and all these beautiful things who were around the White House. There's still a sense of recklessness and a sense of being beyond apprehension and consequences. It was part of his psyche. He probably inspired Clinton. And that's too bad. I think when you take that job you have to stop being a sophomore.